# Agnes

A childhood betrayed
and reclaimed

# Agnes

## A childhood betrayed and reclaimed

## Judy King

Published in 2024 by Ginninderra Press,
Melbourne, Australia
www.ginninderrapress.com.au

Copyright © Judy King

A moral right of the author has been asserted

All rights reserved. This book is copyright. Apart from any fair dealing for the purpose of private study, research, criticism or review, as permitted under the Copyright Act, no part of this book may be reproduced by any process without written permission. Inquiries should be addressed to the publisher.

Typesetting and cover design by Workingtype Books

ISBN: 978 1 76109 697 6 (paperback)
ISBN: 978 1 74027 120 2 (ebook)

JUDY KING made her fortune renovating homes in Sydney's Paddington when the working class suburb was on the cusp of gentrification. She led an intrepid life in Asia and Europe, eventually settling in the UK and then Mallorca, Spain, where she has carved out a reputation as a successful sculptor. *Agnes – A childhood betrayed and reclaimed* charts the trials and tribulations of her traumatic early years. Her determination in confronting a repressed past is testament to her enduring strength.

*This book is dedicated to my gifted psychiatrist Luis-Jaime Santaren Castellvi in Palma de Mallorca and to all adult sufferers of child abuse.*

*With special thanks to Frankie Bailey from The Literary Consultancy in London who picked up the manuscript, edited it and nurtured it to its conclusion.*

# CONTENTS

| | | |
|---|---|---|
| **Part One** | | 1 |
| Chapter 1 | Surviving Daniel | 5 |
| Chapter 2 | Sydney, Mother, And Aunt Marnie | 24 |
| Chapter 3 | Woolloomooloo Wharf | 44 |
| Chapter 4 | Rosemont | 51 |
| Chapter 5 | The North Shore | 63 |
| **Part Two** | | 75 |
| Chapter 6 | Chatswood | 79 |
| Chapter 7 | Penicillin | 90 |
| Chapter 8 | The Farm | 95 |
| Chapter 9 | Roseville Baths | 107 |
| Chapter 10 | David Jones | 116 |
| Chapter 11 | The Dressmaker | 129 |
| **Part Three** | | 145 |
| Chapter 12 | Mother Miriam | 149 |
| Chapter 13 | Truths and Lies | 162 |
| Chapter 14 | The Inquisition at Rosemont | 180 |
| Chapter 15 | Maroubra | 195 |

| Chapter 16 | Coogee | 203 |
| Chapter 17 | Acting The Part | 209 |
| Chapter 18 | Rosary Villa | 225 |
| Chapter 19 | Charles Burgess | 229 |
| **Part Four** | | 237 |
| Chapter 20 | A Child for God | 241 |
| Chapter 21 | Rebecca Lea | 254 |
| Chapter 22 | The Homecoming | 265 |
| **Part Five** | | 275 |
| Chapter 23 | Aunt Marnie Revisited | 279 |
| Chapter 24 | The Reunion at Rosemont | 288 |
| Chapter 25 | Her Brother Bert | 296 |
| Chapter 26 | Her Brother Jim | 306 |
| Chapter 27 | Madge at Home | 312 |
| Chapter 28 | Uncle Ben and the Open Road | 325 |
| Chapter 29 | Filial Extortion and New Discoveries | 346 |

# Part One

It is an age-old observation that in every human group there is a predestined victim; one who inspires contempt, whom all mock, about whom stupid malignant gossip grows, upon whom by some mysterious agreement, all unload their bad tempers and their desire to hurt.
—*If This Is a Man* by Primo Levi

A slave is a person who cannot speak his thoughts.
—Euripides

# CHAPTER 1

# SURVIVING DANIEL

She is dreading the arrival. Since boarding the plane in London, like a dog pulling against a leash, she has felt she is going the wrong way—sucked back into a past she thought she had escaped forever. Freedom isn't the price of a plane ticket, she thinks, as we take ourselves wherever we go. Her apprehension has no effect on the big Boeing that, landing with a thud, sways from side to side in a series of kangaroo hops before the mighty brakes tether the beast and bring it to heel. A spontaneous uproar of cheers and clapping explodes in the cabin as the sensation of rolling smoothly on terra firma signals that the turbulent flight is at an end. The uproar is tempered when passengers are advised to remain in their seats. Two burly Bermuda-shorted men are enacting the Australian ritual of disinfecting the plane by moving through the aisles to spray the cabin from high-held aerosol cans. When the red-headed one pauses near her aisle seat, his freckly lower arms seem familiar. But, she realises, it is the odour of hair oil, fermented with alcohol-impregnated upper-body sweat, that is resurrecting her long-dead father. The father who holds her from the grave. Who traps her in troubled, hard, blue eyes—before vanishing.

A deep foreboding amplifies the resistance she is experiencing. All is then quickly swept into the noisy hubbub of movement and chatter that follows the signal to disembark. She is delayed by the act of searching under the seat for a book called *Families and How to Survive Them*. She has scoured it for clues during the long flight, in preparation for returning to the place where she was born and grew up.

The delay means that when she finally gets to the overhead locker across the aisle, she sees a red-gloved hand at the end of a crane-like arm snatch her stashed duty-free bag and dash away with it through the cabin. She is left with a blurred image of a tall woman with curly auburn hair, merging like a film fade into the avalanche of disembarking passengers. The woman might have been wearing a grey tracksuit, but she cannot be sure. The red glove, however, sticks in her mind. She imagines herself screaming 'THIEF! THIEF!' as she has seen in the movies but, instead, simply stands there in disbelief, opening and closing her mouth like a fish.

Conditioned from childhood not to make a fuss when it comes to anything untoward, she doesn't react like other people. Subterfuge and evasion are old friends. Like a lizard changing colour, she feels safe blending into the background. She never screams. Not that she can remember anyway. Perhaps the potential was killed off in her before it got started. Once or twice, she has contemplated buying a battery-operated 'Screamer Alarm' for her handbag but, because so rarely conscious of her safety, the idea would waft away from her when the threat that provoked it simply abated.

All the carefully chosen presents during the stopover in Singapore gone! What can she do? The evidence is flimsy: tall woman, a mass of curly hair that could well be a wig, and an easily removed red glove. Even if she apprehends the thief, it would be no use as, by the time she spots her, the stolen goods would have been transferred and the plastic bag discarded in a convenient bin.

Agnes bites her lip. Tears sting the back of her eyes, then slither like sluggish raindrops down her cheeks. She is struggling to get a grip. After *all* you've been through in recent years this is a *minor* blip, she tells herself. For God's sake just put it out of your mind. It's not the end of the world.

A popular quote, attributed to Albert Einstein, and read in a magazine she browsed on the plane, sticks in her mind: 'Insanity is doing the same thing over and over and expecting different results.' Her two marriages, and most of her romantic liaisons, had ended in similar fashion. On her knees, and seriously out of pocket. If the Einstein quote was accurate, it was a definite confirmation of her insanity. But *what* is she repeating, over and over? *What* is it that she cannot see?

Agnes closes stinging eyes and sinks back into the padded comfort of the aeroplane seat to take stock. The plane is almost empty of passengers. She is catapulted straight into an all-too-familiar fugue state. This can manifest out of the blue. Someone may be speaking directly to her, but it is as if they are contacting her from a great distance. In books, when a character has something to say, there are useful little speech-marks to signpost the way. Conveniently placed to assist the reader. These days, there are no such useful little clues popping up in Agnes's head. All is undefined. All is simply one big blur.

*Can I help you Madam?*

She looks up into the beautiful face of a Singapore Airlines hostess. Not the girl who served her during the flight, but one she is seeing for the first time. Petite and impeccably groomed, her soft touch on Agnes's arm, her radiant smile, seem like visitations from an angel. All the SA hostesses wear differently coloured patterned sarongs, and this woman's version is a vibrant aqua shot through with turquoise, like the Mediterranean Sea close to the shore on a perfect sunny day. Her shiny jet hair is scooped into a neat bun that shouts—"rescue". Agnes melts under her gaze and starts describing what has happened, a life of loss impregnating the tale. Her speech is clumsy—the more she babbles, the more she ends up in knots. She feels she is floating outside her body—unable to find her way back. The hostess gently interrupts her endless ramble.

*Report it at our office in the airport, Madam.*

The hostess accompanies Agnes with professional care through the cabin. She then bids her farewell with a heartbreaking smile that propels Agnes forward to float through the corridors ahead like an astronaut bouncing in space. But the sweet reprieve is short-lived. With the view of Passport Control looming, her apprehension returns. *Get over it,* she mumbles to herself, as she burrows in an overstuffed handbag to locate her passport.

She replies awkwardly to the Passport Officer's curt questions. What did she expect from an official she has never laid eyes on before? A rowdy welcome? Her eyes fill with tears yet again. She jams her glasses in front of her eyes with such force, she bruises her nose. The emotional waterworks keep coming like a leaking tap and she surreptitiously dabs at them with a bit of shirt sleeve hanging out of the arm of her mink coat. She is drowning in an overwhelming sense of failure. Now, at 64, when those of her generation are retiring, she is getting started—yet again—and for the umpteenth time. Here she is, after 30 years, still marooned in the dark. *Why* do those she trusts exploit her? How is it possible she doesn't see what is so *obvious* to everyone else?

The memory of that summer morning spent at the notary's office in Mallorca forces its way back, along with the dread she had felt as she dug her fingers into the leather seat, closed her eyes and held her breath as she waited for Daniel to sign the separation agreement. The lawyer, Francisca, looked frazzled with impatience. Agnes had wished she had chosen someone to represent her at this signing who was less irritable. Someone with more patience than Francisca, who had prompted Daniel through gritted teeth:

*'Por los buenos' means 'for the good'. Whatever you bring to the marriage you take away from it.*

Francisca had spelled this out as if addressing a dim child, pausing between each word in heavily accented English, her dark eyes smouldering. Agnes's own frustration was certainly reasonable too, given she had translated the legal term *'por los buenos'* into English for Daniel dozens of times before. This was the second attempt at an official signing and Agnes had felt compelled to speak:

*It couldn't be fairer, Daniel. Right up your alley. I know you wouldn't settle for anything less.*

She had enjoyed repeating this latter phrase—one he had once tacked on to the revelation he alleged he had received back in early 1994:

*Agnes, my darling, I can't settle for anything less.*

He had insisted that he had heard a voice in his ear whilst captivated by the glorious hues of an evening sunset as he drove home, a soothing Chopin nocturne on the car radio. The voice had apparently urged: 'You must marry this woman.'

At the time it had swept her away. The declaration being divinely inspired. A prompting from the heavens to marry her. And, to her eternal shame, her naïve schoolgirl heart had led her to a fairytale Catholic church wedding with a reception in a picturesque ancient monastery in Mallorca.

Eight years later, in the notary's office, she had gambled on beating Daniel at his own game by invoking this pompous phrase, this false invention of himself as an upright, moral Englishman. A ploy to coax him into signing the agreement. She knew this well-worn performance by heart. The theatrical upper-class Englishness that permeated everything he did. Indeed, it was doubtful there was anything much else to him. She had met him at a party in London. It was hard not to notice him as he waved his arms around and raised his voice above the hubbub with unabashed confidence. He made people laugh. Made them notice him. Agnes always felt awkward at parties. The only part she really enjoyed was getting dressed to go.

Daniel's next comment clangs in her head as she waits for the passport stamp:

*My wife is insisting that we do this today.*

Agnes had said nothing. She had fixed her eyes on an enlarged map of the area on the wall behind him and steeled herself for the fray.

Nearly a year had gone by since, upon seeing a corporate tenant safely installed in their London duplex, she had subjugated herself to final odious sex with Daniel in a nearby flat. A flat he had bought with *her* money for his now deceased mother. When Daniel had gone out the following morning, she had phoned her son who dutifully arrived with the suitcase she had secretly packed. He had driven her to the airport where she had caught a flight to Mallorca and, upon arrival, called Daniel to say she wouldn't be coming back. It was cowardly, but what can a tree do when it is being sucked dry by a parasite?

The separation hadn't altered the way he went on addressing her as 'My Darling Wife'. The cloying salutation peppered the lengthy pompous letters he wrote to her from Rome, whence he had subsequently disappeared to rent an apartment. Given her acceptance of his cultural superiority perhaps he had thought all this overblown erudition would win her back, but instead it reminded her of the way he had constantly humiliated her, quoting Suetonius, Tacitus and other Roman historians as a means to exclude her from conversations. During her time with him she had lost the connection—if she had ever firmly had a grip on it—that knowledge was attained through learning, settling into the notion that some people were *chosen* to know, and she wasn't one of *them*. But, in the notary's office, fighting to survive, her ignorance of Tacitus and Suetonius no longer had any relevance. She had known Daniel for precisely what he was—a mere parrot. Empty of substance. A man with no profound grasp of anything more than how to bring her down.

Although she never replied, the letters just kept coming, along with postcards also addressed to 'My Darling Wife' or 'Dearest Beloved Wife', and all with accompanying hugs and kisses. It made Agnes wonder if others had also seen Daniel as ridiculous. A phony.

Even the London real estate agent had seemed to see through him. She knew the agent admired the way she had singlehandedly organised the rental of the London duplex. Talking about Daniel with him, she had felt as she imagined a prisoner must feel stepping into the light from solitary confinement. No need for discretion now she had left this ridiculous man.

But Daniel's attempts at contact had persisted. The local florist had managed to locate the flat she rented in the Port of Soller to deliver red roses from him on Valentine's Day; but no bouquets could compensate for the way he had cheated and defamed her after she had extended him a generous helping hand. A fact he would probably never acknowledge.

The tension had been palpable on that day in the notary's office but, eventually, Daniel had signed the form. Childishly petulant, his lips quivering, with a dramatic flurry of the pen he had scrawled his signature in the square marked X. Agnes's long-standing Spanish residency would save her from a messy and costly English divorce.

Now, as she waits for clearance at the passport desk, the shock of the night before her wedding to Daniel seeps back into her consciousness. The discovery that he had grossly overcharged her on the purchase of a 50% share in the upper two floors of his house in Notting Hill has never failed to revolt her. She had done the deal as a favour because he needed her investment to provide the full funds to enable him to buy a flat for his mother, Daniel having claimed he couldn't live with the vexatious woman one moment longer.

But it had all been achieved far too quickly, and she had come to the realisation she might be well and truly stuck with a bad bargain. Why, then, marry someone she patently couldn't trust? Oh God! She had felt the noose tighten around her neck. How could she possibly cancel at this late stage? So many of their friends, some from far afield, had been invited!

Her heart had raced like a trapped bird, fighting to get out. Her renewal of faith. Her baptism and confirmation certificates sent from Sydney. The endless paperwork. The dresses for the bridesmaids who were all to wear, like her, white lace-up wedge espadrilles simply because Daniel found them sexy. And then there was the vintage Daimler that an English friend had kindly spruced up to drive the newly married couple from the church to the reception.

That awful day before the wedding, reeling in shock and

overwhelmed with conflict, she had paced up and down in bare feet on the tiled floor of the bedroom. Watching her intently with a fixed expression was Daniel. She had tried not to look at him. The persistent voice in her head kept cautioning her against going ahead. To walk away. But she had already moved in with him with her possessions. Her antique chests of drawers already shared bedroom space with his William and Mary on stand. Her books were arranged in bookshelves alongside his high-minded literature in serried rows. He had even purchased a new mattress for the antique double bed she had sent over from her place in Mallorca. She had personally paid out a fortune for the reception. This had to be the worst mess her compulsion to problem-solve had ever landed her in! She was going mad! She wanted to die. She was 52 and had believed she would at last be loved and cherished. That she would be supported and no longer be forced to battle on alone in the world.

And then Daniel, sprawled on the bed, had spoken, his tone calm:

*My Darling-Wife-To-Be. Don't fret. Believe me, I love you. Here. Take this cheque.*

And he had torn the offering out of the cheque book on his lap. £10,000. It was the lifeline she was looking for and she clutched it with relief. At least it was *something* to offset her own vast expenditure. It was a credit to Daniel's carefully crafted machinations that Agnes still has no memory of exactly how, let alone why, she had bought that fateful 50% share in the two floors of the Notting Hill house. Especially after the financial losses that had followed her first marriage, when she had made a solemn vow never to mix love and money again.

As she is finally waved through Passport Control, chunks of her life with Daniel start to organise themselves in her brain, like the pieces of a challenging puzzle she would far prefer to throw straight out of a convenient window. It had been agreed between them that after the outlay of funds to buy his mother a flat to facilitate her ejection from her longstanding home, Daniel would use a portion of what was left of Agnes's purchase money to finance the merger of his, and his mother's, separate living quarters into a luxury four-bedroom residence which he and Agnes would then sell on at a profit. Then, they would buy a small flat for the two of them and Agnes would be reimbursed. No ambiguity. It could not be clearer.

Alongside the conveyance, wills were drawn up leaving their respective half shares to each other. And here lay the rub. The sudden heavy paperwork did not include their verbal agreement. When Agnes suggested that it should be clearly stated, along with an independent valuation, her beloved had argued persuasively about 'trust'. If there was no *trust*, then where was the *love*? How could she sully the beauty of their forthcoming marriage with yet more ugly legality?

Agnes's insistence had smouldered, smoked for a bit, before being extinguished under layers of gift-wrapping: satin knickers, naughty nighties, drop earrings, and the lovely gold wedding band (By Appointment To) they chose together. She had gulped it all down like a starving child. What remained of good sense had been drowned in a whirlwind of music after midnight and the flicker of candles reflected on the glossy walls of fancy restaurants.

Daniel had a kind of eccentricity that went comfortably hand-in-hand with his pedigree Englishness: public school, beneficiary of a personal batman during National Service in Scotland, Trinity College Oxford (sent down after six months—yet never mentioned) world traveller, fantastic mimic, fluent in several languages, splendid cook, wine connoisseur, rubber of shoulders with the rich and famous and a dedicated collector of art and antiques.

But what Agnes had not twigged at the time was the importance of the background setting for his presentation. The Notting Hill house was his stage and integral to his performance. He was the house—and the house was him. He would be naked without it.

Recently diagnosed with a chronic illness, Daniel's mother wasn't expected to live long. Yet, despite illness, she had successfully appointed herself as unofficial receptionist for her son's custom-made upholstered chairs and sofas—a business which was run from his upstairs kitchen. Mother and son lived their separate lives in their respective halves of the property. By the time Agnes was being secretly courted on the top floor, Daniel had grown old waiting for his parent's early demise and was joking about pushing her down the stairs. A sense of his thwarted plan was evidenced by the way he would check the share portfolio he would inherit, as though he had already done the evil deed. Agnes still remembers the amounts, the banks, the list of company names. Chatting about who would get what was common between Daniel and his younger sister, Carmen, who was willingly instructed about the ins and outs of it all by her impressive big brother.

'Mother', too, revelled in talk of her estate. She used it as a form of control. Gillian Holloway was a dramatic, domineering and remarkably handsome woman. Slim, smartly dressed, and brimming with energy, it didn't look to Agnes as if Gillian would be leaving the spacious first floor—with its lovely Georgian windows and gracious plaster wall mouldings—for anywhere more important than the supermarket. Although never having been an actress, she was as theatrical as a grand Duchess in a panto. Simply a hard-working woman at the side of her husband in a small seaside department store, she had nonetheless managed to send her children to private schools. The woman was, in fact, quite a *force majeure*.

But Daniel's wedding announcement had left Gillian Holloway and her close admirers and fellow church goers flummoxed in disbelief. Seated around a tea tray in her pink lounge one afternoon, the group conversation had combusted. From her landing vantage point, Agnes had overheard Gillian shrieking in astonishment amid the general consternation:

*How can he be marrying? He doesn't know anyone!*

It was as if Agnes's own presence in the house was completely invisible. As Gillian didn't attend the wedding—which Agnes had changed from a quick, registry office 'Yes I do' in London, to a grand spectacle in Mallorca—the woman had obviously decided to deny the nuptials had ever happened, choosing to completely ignore her new daughter-in-law's existence.

Henceforth, Agnes would watch Gillian in action like an episode in a TV soap, the emotional highs and sulky lows unfolding before her. But it was the announcement that she would be moving out that had evoked Gillian's undiluted hysteria:

*I won't be evicted from my beautiful home!*

Her tantrums and outrage—stoically borne by a son entrusted with her affairs—only strengthened his cause for eviction. The coterie of Gillian's pals from the church were in and out. Even the bishop was summoned. Her doctor hid in a broom cupboard when she forced entry into his surgery. Gillian became a human storm.

It was all settled when her youngest daughter, as instructed by big brother Daniel, flew in from New York. She had, Agnes noted, her mother's luminous almond eyes. A late arrival to the family, she had grown up weaving a spell, like a ballet dancer on a music box, rigidly performing to please.

Although the new one-bedroom flat intended for Gillian was only a few streets away, and one of the church retirees lived in the same block, it was barely half the size of what she always referred to as 'My Beautiful Home'. Agnes had thought warily at the time that Daniel might later come to regret economising on this purchase. To dampen down her misgivings, she had let the natural designer in her take over, throwing her energy into contemplating the reconversion of the house with its wonderful wide-open staircase, big airy rooms, high ceilings and beautiful roof terrace. Situated on a corner in fashionable inner London, it would be an easy job, with a quick sale assured—after which she and Daniel would create a life together on equal terms.

'Prediction is difficult as it involves the future', said Niels Bohr. Agnes could never have foreseen what would happen next. Daniel kept delaying getting started on the project. Meetings with architect and builder were continually cancelled. She found herself gradually ground down. Days of being thwarted spun into weeks, months and then years. She became desperate, any pleas for action being twisted into personal attacks against her. Daniel would rant at her, leaving her dazed, confused, and often sobbing on the floor:

*You're so greedy! It wouldn't matter how much money you had— it would never be enough. They all said you were a hard-headed businesswoman and how much softer you are since you met me. You should thank me for saving you from yourself! You know what you're like!*

This pronouncement of his became a daily rebuke that she accepted in confusion like a wimp. Nothing was what it was originally intended to be, and Agnes had started to doubt if the agreement they made had ever happened. The capital she had worked so hard to rebuild since the nervous breakdown that followed her first marriage was starting to resemble a dowry—a 'payment received' for Daniel agreeing to marry her.

The travelling had been an upside at first. She had enjoyed the short trips they made to various European cities to celebrate their birthdays: Paris, Rome, Prague, Florence. And then there was the annual long-haul jaunt to New York to visit his sister and brother-in-law to celebrate their wedding anniversary. And, when Daniel ran out of the personal, there was the public. Christmas, New Year, Valentine's Day, Burn's Night, Easter, St Georges Day, and so it went on. He relentlessly orchestrated their calendar like a cowboy pulling a steer on a rope, dragging her from one event to the next—a terrified animal dazzled by a bright light.

It was in Mexico when she realized she was in serious danger. Her health run down by the torturous existence at home, she had picked up a bug that forced her to stay in bed. For several days she ran a fever that turned the giant cactuses outside the window into distorted spike-headed demons capable of attack. But it was what she had overheard outside the bedroom door that frightened her more:

*She's definitely a hypochondriac. Something not right going on in her head.*

Sister and brother-in-law had apparently joined Daniel in a rear-guard action. Haunting voices devoid of sympathy. She was an interloper in enemy territory. Her Valentine-loving husband's effusive concern for 'My Darling Wife' had run out of steam.

Back in London, still weak, she envisaged herself exiting the upper floors in a body bag. After all, with his mother rehoused, she was now the only impediment to his complete ownership.

As Daniel gained more and more control over her, he liked to show off as Lord of the Manor by throwing lavish dinner parties. After the meal he would lounge back at the head of the table and hold court. Listening to these same old stories repeatedly had become unbearable to her. Blatant overtures to other women made Agnes realise she might well be on the list for replacement. He had recently flirted outrageously with a friend of hers who visited briefly from Australia, and she had no words to excuse his behaviour. It seemed her fifty per cent share on the house deed meant nothing. Daniel still retained the bulk of her financial investment and there was no way of forcing him to do the renovation work, or of achieving a sale without the work done, or of getting him out of the house. Her plaintive insistences to get started on the renovations now barely elicited a response. She could weep, cajole, shout. All to no avail. He had metamorphosed into a monster.

A monster masquerading as an English gentleman.

He managed to stop her buying a car and insisted upon driving her everywhere. To escape him, she joined a health club and swam furiously up and down the pool till the contortion in her neck temporarily released. At the exercise classes she met busy working women and lusted after becoming one of them again. She would sit in a cloud of steam in the sauna and feed on the talk around her. It was a way of orientating herself back into a half-normal world.

When she finally had to admit to herself that Daniel had no intention of doing up the house and selling it, she stopped spending any more of the small savings she had left and quietly invested them in the purchase of a studio flat, situated within walking distance of where they lived. Then she rented it out. But she should have kept its existence secret. That was a foolish oversight. Daniel, as always sticking his controlling nose in anything she did, insisted she cede him a small share in the purchase. And, although she knew it was more than unwise, she found herself unable to refuse.

She thought of getting a job but felt incapable of managing even a checkout counter in a supermarket. She did, however, manage to supplement her income one summer by advertising holiday lets in a local magazine for the primitive, but liveable, house she still owned in Mallorca. The house that, one day, she planned to turn into a small hotel.

It was a complete myth that Daniel was supporting her, as he liked to pretend. She had long started to wonder whether the furniture business she saw floundering from month to month had ever been worth the £30,000 a year he claimed. Yes, he paid the bills on the house and their food, or at least a proportion of it, but it had never crossed her mind to think what he had really done with the thousands left over after the relatively small amount expended on his mother's flat. Then it dawned on her—he was enjoying healthy 1990s rates of interest secured on *her* money! She, in contrast, had become the impoverished one—buying her clothes at charity shops.

Events had suddenly swung in her favour when Gillian Holloway died. She had held out well into her eighties. When she became enfeebled, she had received help from the local authorities, but the lack of a second bedroom in the small flat had meant there was nowhere for a carer to stay overnight. And she had become even more isolated when the old friend who lived in the same block died. Even the little gang from the church had gradually fallen away.

The search for a retirement home became inevitable. Indeed, Gillian's splashy entrance into a select care home on the coast, shortly followed by a showy ride down the stairlift in a veiled red hat with matching heels, belied a weariness of heart that made Agnes think of the iconic line in *Sunset Boulevard*—'I'm ready for my close-up, Mr DeMille'. She sensed Gillian was nearing a final performance. Therefore, it didn't surprise her to hear that, before her mother-in-law had a chance to make any lasting impression at the seaside home, she fell ill. Within days she was rushed with a stomach infection to Brighton hospital, where she gradually went downhill. Agnes remembers how she and Daniel had set off in the car on an icy evening, the hospital having contacted them to say they didn't think Gillian would last the night.

Like snapshots in an album, to this day, Agnes retains only a few blurred images of Gillian's funeral—a quick service with a handful of platitudes to a small congregation. After a certain age, few are left behind to mourn. Daniel and his two sisters had seemed as disinterested as the rest.

Gillian's coffin had rolled towards the furnace smoothly, as if indifferent to its fate. Agnes had pictured the ferocious jaws of a devouring dragon-mouth snapping suddenly shut and swallowing— along with Daniel's mother—a multitude of Holloway family secrets Agnes would never know. There were no tears. In fact, Gillian's departure had a strengthening effect upon Agnes, jolting her into scheming about how to regain control of her life. It was so very easy to spot the bad guys in the movies. Then why such resistance to counteracting the less-than-subtle bad guy under her very nose?

Concurrent with Gillian's demise, the furniture orders dried up and the upholsterers announced their retirement. Regardless, Daniel was flushed with the success of everything he had planned and now he had his mother's little flat at his full disposal. Agnes knew her moment to strike back had finally arrived. Clasping her shaking hands together behind her back, she had calmly suggested modernising her old house in Mallorca for them to retire to. Why not now finally renovate the Notting Hill house as planned and then rent it out? They could live like kings in sunny Spain on a healthy income derived from it and Gillian's flat could serve as Daniel's pied-à-terre in London!

All this, admittedly, would be at her own expense and, as a business proposition it was in fact a disastrous idea for her to convert the big rambling Mallorca house into a single luxury residence. But a prisoner does whatever she can to escape. So, with this alluring carrot dangled in front of Daniel, the long-protracted London renovation, although much scaled down, finally went ahead. Agnes quickly had plans drawn up with an architect for the retirement house in Mallorca and, as Daniel refused to let her borrow on the Notting Hill house, she took out a mortgage on her studio flat and got started. A future goal in mind, she no longer cared about Daniel stinting on the work.

Miraculously, after months of high drama, the London works were finally completed and it was no surprise on completion to overhear Daniel indirectly claim credit for her efforts, whilst pointing out the concealed hall ceiling light:

*My wife had the idea for this small detail.*

Implying, naturally, that this was the sum-total of her contribution.

The day they packed up their stuff and put it into storage, Agnes felt as if she was walking on air. A relocation agent had rented their two floors in Notting Hill for the summer to an acting couple who would be shooting a film in London. Agnes went ahead to Mallorca and Daniel stayed behind to prepare for the tenants. After sending out a printed relocation notice to the old crowd, he joined her in early summer in a house she had rented, as their supposed 'retirement home' remained a construction in progress.

If she still harboured any doubts about leaving Daniel, they completely evaporated when he joined her adversaries to scoff at her when the local authorities shut down her building work. Because of a building infraction, the site was now cordoned off with a barrier of black and yellow striped tape.

How he had sneered at her misfortune:

*You crash around without knowing what you're doing. Everyone knows what you're like!*

Overcome with disgust and fury, she had punched him on the arm as hard as she could. She had initially aimed for a spot he would never forget but changed her trajectory upwards at the last minute. A cowardly retreat followed, then his return from the bathroom to dangle the bruised limb under her noise, whining like a whimpering girl:

*They all say you Australians are a rough bunch!*

She had suddenly seen red:

*I'll show you how rough we can get Daniel if you don't get out of my sight!*

But this unfamiliar fighting spirit had quickly ebbed away. With so much at stake Agnes soon regretted the outburst. Nonetheless, it had changed matters. After the 'stop work' order, a hardened distance developed between them. Ever gregarious, Daniel had quickly fallen in with the frivolous good-time crowd who descended every summer upon the resort, strolling along the seaside promenade and thronging the waterfront cafés and restaurants. Knowing she had only ever been a means to an end, she had figured he wouldn't miss her—especially with so much more interesting company on offer—and so she locked herself in another room and went to bed when he left for the night's carousing. It was the heavenly life he had longed for: poolside parties in gardens, soothing guitars, scantily clad women, and lots of booze.

She would rise early—when he was going to bed—and take off into the mountains to wander through the olive tree-lined paths she knew so well. Struggling with crippling anxiety, these early-morning adventures spent walking ahead of the August sun probably saved her life.

When the afternoon temperatures climbed, and the garden floated in a heat haze, and the stone path outside burned the soles of bare feet, she turned on the air-conditioning in her solitary space and ironed clothes, losing herself in smoothing crumpled cloth. Her pent-up angst would burst forth with the first flow of steam and the fresh, crisp smell lifted her spirit. She hoped the pile of clean ironed clothes on his bed would smother any suspicion Daniel might have about her behaviour. It was what a woman did, after all. There was no indication to the contrary. He remained confident he had her securely on a leash.

And then, suddenly, the long-planned moment arrived. With Daniel immersed in the holiday gaiety in Mallorca, she went to the airport and flew to London the day after the three-month tenants moved out. Alone for the first time in a house where she had been held hostage for nearly seven years, she had to act swiftly. Like an unexpected blessing, a neighbour she met in the street offered her £8000 to rent the place for a month while he did up his kitchen. She instantly accepted and went to live the month out in Gillian's empty flat. An additional bonus followed for, whilst in residence at the house, the same neighbour agreed to allow the agents to show potential long-term renters around and, when one prospect phoned to make an offer on behalf of an American corporate tenant, Agnes was able to use the £8000 to pay for the new carpets and wardrobes required to clinch the deal.

It was during those months alone in London that Agnes had realised the only human kindness she now experienced was out on the street. There was the encounter with the lady from the spiritual centre who had lost her daughter in a car accident—and owned two brown and white Jack Russell terriers. And then there was the pleasant single black mother in the rooming house next door, who regularly took her young daughter in a pushchair to a nursery on her way to work. There were also the busy professional women she met at the regular exercise class at the gym.

At this point, Agnes accepted as 'normal' the way Daniel singularly claimed the success of finding the new corporate tenants. It was completely in keeping with the way he had taken over her past and her present as if they were his own. To assert further control, he faxed endless, unnecessary changes to the lease. But at this stage, what did she care?

Potential liberation was on the horizon. Daniel would arrive back in London at the end of September to sign the lease with an 'option to renew' for a second year. And so, the day finally arrived when Corporate America, would change Agnes's life.

But the option to renew the tenancy would never be taken up. The terrorist attack on the World Trade Centre in New York on 11th September 2001 sent most of Corporate America rushing home from overseas locations—their own London tenants included.

*Mejor sola que mal acompañada*—Better alone than in the wrong company. Agnes would often repeat this mantra to herself as she struggled with the complicated building project that, under normal circumstances, she would never have contemplated.

## CHAPTER 2

# SYDNEY, MOTHER, AND AUNT MARNIE

As she watches the effusive family reunions in the airport, she admonishes herself: forget the marshmallow nostalgia—it got you nowhere. Along with birthdays, Valentine's, Christmas, anniversaries, and all the rest of it: *mejor sola que mal acompañada*. Better alone than in the wrong company. The mantra comes to her rescue and enfolds her like a security blanket.

A call from her youngest brother in Queensland had started the pull back to Australia. He and his wife were in financial difficulties, living out their retirement dream of breeding horses on a Brisbane farm. Mysteriously, shortly after, a gift-wrapped parcel had arrived from her mother. After thirty years of not even a card in the post—an astonishing revelation. The sight of a nightdress with baby smocking and bows in her mother's favourite pink and yellow, a matching dressing gown and fluffy peep-toe slippers with feathers and satin piping—stuff she would never dream of wearing—made her wonder if her mother wasn't suffering from a form of Alzheimer's that caused her to muddle her daughter with herself.

She had rung Tammy Hailstone, a near neighbour, for a long-winded explanation:

*Oh, Agnes, your mother is in her element! When it was clear she needed domestic help, I contacted the local council. They didn't just send one girl, but three or four. I can see a couple of them across the road right now—tripping over themselves to look after her. She's a real favourite. They take her shopping, to the hairdresser's, the doctor's, clean the house and organise the food from meals on wheels. She's particularly fond of the English girls—the ones on a working holiday. She gives them orders like a headmistress, but none of them mind. She never stops talking about her clever daughter overseas. She recruits them for parcel duty—to help lure you back here. There are more treats in store. You know how effusive and convincing she is!*

More likely, old Madge was showing the carers she cares, Agnes had thought—irritated that Tammy had presumed she shared her sentiments. But Tammy's call had explained the youthful handwriting on the flowery gift card inside the beautifully wrapped parcel, ending with *love you, miss you, longing to see you, come home soon*. A carer had obliged! She, yet again, felt like a helpless target of conspiracy. The last time she had spoken to Madge, she had been ordered never to ring again—a ruling she had not found difficult to obey.

Struggling for stability after finally escaping Daniel, she had flown back to London from Mallorca to seek help at a three-day personal development program, run by the Landmark Forum. Based in a grubby part of Euston, it had taken place in a huge bare-walled room which resembled an aircraft hangar—more like a rescue shelter after a disaster than a pathway to higher understanding. Shelving misgivings, she had settled into one of the hard, uncomfortable chairs. The high stage had seemed like a strange cavernous mirage. It dwarfed those assembled below. To her surprise, she had found herself unexpectedly swept into the mass dynamic. A featureless speaker, who was like a cross between a marketing manager and hellfire preacher, was rousing the group to action:

*It's time to open your minds to heal past rifts! Go back! Revisit the past! Heal all resentment and estrangement! Now is the moment for reconciliation and closure!*

Buoyed up by the messages vibrating through the hall, yet without being aware of making a tangible decision, Agnes had found herself in a phone box, contacting her mother:

*It's me, Agnes. I'm ringing to ask you what went wrong between us and open a new dialogue.*

*Are you completely crazy!?*

*We need to heal the past.*

*What past?! It's the early hours of the morning, Agnes, and you're getting me all churned up!*

Click—and the phone had gone dead.

The monitors on the Landmark course had encouraged persistence, so Agnes had tried again. But hardly had she stated her name before the embargo fell like a guillotine:

*NEVER RING AGAIN!*

Listening to some of the 150 other attendees' joyous accounts of reconciliation on a distorted microphone, Agnes had realised that not only were her memories of the past frayed and shrouded in mist, but there were complete blanks in her existence—with no attached memory at all. Her problem with her mother was clearly beyond the boundaries of a few days' self-improvement in an uncomfortable echo chamber.

Back in Mallorca, she followed the Landmark experience with different kinds of healing therapy: massage, reflexology, guided imagery, crystals to balance chakras. She abandoned herself to crooning jargon-filled practitioners with enigmatic smiles who inhabited soft-lit rooms clouded with incense and bedecked with Eastern religious statues. Traversing the landscape of healing had become as challenging as the problem.

Once, a demented woman in a small mountain village had tapped the muscles around her neck and shoulders with her knuckles and thanked her absent mother for 'spiriting in' to listen to the complaints against her. Then there was the mystical specialist in the back room of a health food shop, dressed in an Indian print, painted with heavy black eye make-up, who had gasped at the sight of Agnes's tongue.

With the hypnotic sound of a sitar in the background, Agnes had been treated to a glimpse of the specialist's own heathy pink tongue as an example of what to aim for. The ransom for this assessment was embedded in the extra mandatory purchase of a pile of vitamins and healing potions that had cost the earth.

On yet another occasion, she had mistaken Reiki therapy for Reiki massage as she lay, bemused, in a dark, silent room, her eyes closed, waiting for the masseuse's hands to whirl into action. When she eventually opened her eyes to enquire what was wrong, she saw the white-clad practitioner with arms outstretched, hovering her palms over her chest like Jesus's prelude to the loaves and fishes. The girl had spoken in honeyed tones:

*Your father is inside you.*

As Agnes had been focusing on her mother's ruinous behaviour during her childhood, her father's appearance—out of the blue—had come as somewhat of a surprise. But she had taken no notice, paid what she considered an inflated fee, and never went back. With the sole exception of a straightforward relaxing massage, alternative healing had felt as practical as a damp squib. She decided that exploitation of the vulnerable was equivalent to an unregulated licence to print money.

Her next adventure clearly bore this resolution out in spades. She had confided how bad she was feeling to an eccentric woman she had come to know as they both regularly emerged at the same time from an early morning swim. A scientific approach was recommended as they towelled themselves dry on a deserted Mallorcan beach, and Agnes was subsequently put in touch with a middle-aged English psychologist. This expat—a woman—lived in a dark, run-down stone terrace in an obscure rural village. On the wall by the front door was a brass plaque, like something one would see in Harley Street, stating the practitioner's profession, her membership of the British Psychological Society, and trailing a line of abbreviated degrees. This paragon managed to make such an accurate diagnosis that Agnes ended up doing her shopping, taking her to London for the treatment of some mysterious infirmity, and supporting her financially down to her underpants. Agnes had never been in any doubt that she was a suitable case for treatment, but the protracted relationship only turned out to be yet another descent into hell.

But solutions can often appear in the oddest of places and, lo and behold, a casual comment from one of the girls who worked in the local branch of her bank led her to the psychiatrist she had been searching for all her life. He didn't speak English and she certainly wasn't confident of her grasp of Spanish—but then she had never really been confident about anything. He had advised her candidly:

*The chances of being able to change reduce with age but, if you like, we can try and see how the transference goes.*

Working with this man in a different language, and with an uncertain outcome, paled into insignificance beside the task of extricating herself from the charlatan psychologist. Facing the loss of generous twice-weekly payments, and easy access to loans, the woman with the formal brass plaque upped the pressure. Agnes attempted to ignore the stream of letters and emails that followed her dismissal note—sent by registered post. She would quiver like a tiny bird hiding from a cat as she listened to the phone ringing, once managing to go without answering it for over a week, during which time she would continually watch a DVD of *The Servant* – Pinter's 60s masterpiece about a manipulative reversal of roles which, on some level, she knew without doubt reflected her toxic relationship with the succubus psychologist.

But it wasn't until Agnes's new psychiatrist gently explained that she was suffering from a chronic level of fear that she finally understood. It explained her pathological fear of Daniel, her fear of the domineering psychologist and, yes, of so many others. She had finally found a safe harbour with a consummate professional. Agnes would enter psychotherapy whole-heartedly, coming to greatly admire the 'father of analysis'—Sigmund Freud. Long accustomed to listening to the problems of others, she had always grappled to find a voice to express her own. She was 'neurotic'—a pejorative word she had heard so often used as a complaint, but usually without the user understanding its true and indelible meaning. Her therapist had reassured her:

*You are here for yourself. This time is for you.*

Initially, Agnes did not feel there *was* a self. She could *speak* of herself all right, running on and on, but who she *truly* was behind the words remained a mystery. When the specified fifty minutes of her session was up, and the expectation was to be quiet, she gradually managed to train herself to stop talking. At first, she had found this imposed discipline offensive, but came to cherish the containment. Additionally, her analyst's extensive knowledge of five-thousand-plus years of civilisation stimulated her to enjoy an education that her pervasive early anxiety had denied her.

After each session, as she left him, she would repeat her mantra:

*Mejor sola que mal acompañada. Better alone than in the wrong company.*

And he would nod in affirmation.

A middle-aged Australian woman in analysis, in Spanish, with a Catalan psychiatrist. She had treasured all those precious sessions and had never disclosed her relationship with him to anyone.

Hardly had she put down the phone to Tammy than parcels from her mother had arrived at her door with accelerated zeal. Frills had been replaced by gifts that grew exponentially in size. Following in the wake of a silver lipstick-holder, matching compact, soft handbag, small drawings of Federation houses in Hill End, came huge coffee table books that weighed a ton and must have cost a bomb to send: *Australia Today, Australia Then and Now, Sydney Waterfronts, Australian Bushrangers, Australian Islands and Coastlines.* All showed up at regular intervals over the months ahead. It was after struggling home from the Post Office with the *Complete Works of Banjo Paterson* that Agnes had decided to call her mother and put a stop to it. But the railroading had commenced:

*Did you get the parcels, Agnes? Why didn't you ring sooner? When are you coming home, darling? I need to see you! You'll be sorry when I die if you don't come!*

As Agnes put the phone down, Al Pacino's lament in *The Godfather* vibrated in her ear:

*Just when I thought I was out THEY PULL ME BACK IN.*

This outreach from Madge was clearly suspicious. However, the therapy sessions seemed to have prompted a growing desire in Agnes to investigate her past and had, eventually, propelled her to book a flight to Sydney. She and her youngest brother were to hire a car and drive to see their mother in the town where she lived—an hour from Sydney. This would then be followed by a trip into the country to visit the small country hamlet where her father was born and grew up. As brother Jim had a photographic memory, Agnes hoped he could help her reclaim lost childhood memories. Not just the odd memory; whole chunks of total amnesia.

Outside the airport now, as she joins a fast-moving queue at a taxi rank, she can smell the sea from nearby Botany Bay. 'Captain Cook chased a chook all around my library book!' – the kids used to chant at school. The late afternoon sun is blinding and so she is glad when a taxi door opens, and she can tumble in with her stuff.

Speeding below, the rhythmic sound of tyres over a smooth surface, punctuated by bumps to slow the traffic, is soothing. She is on the Eastern Distributor—a brightly lit, but unfamiliar, two-lane highway which transports her in and out of a series of tunnels. She feels as if she is in a homogenised bubble that could be anywhere in the world. Then the taxi suddenly rises above ground, and her heart leaps at the sight of Moore Park Golf Course and the roads around it, which she knows so well.

The cheery voice of the solid-necked driver breaks into her reverie:

*Sit back and relax, love. Next stop Potts Point.*

He is wearing a leather cap, and she notices a tattoo on the muscular arm below his short sleeve. It depicts Popeye the Sailor Man, captured just after he downs a can of spinach. The tattoo bobs up and down in animated motion as he turns the wheel through the heavy traffic in Darlinghurst. She sinks into the soft upholstery in the back seat, as instructed, and feels the tension of the arrival leave her. *It's not madness,* she whispers to herself. *It's the anxiety that trips you up.* She prompts herself that part of being in analysis is learning to train her mind to reflect on her reactions.

The car pulls up at Number 1 Grantham Street, off Macleay Street. She had been to the area many times in the past, yet today, shrouded by the veil of absent years, it looks mysterious.

The driver jumps out and opens the boot with a thud. In awe, she watches from the back of the taxi as, in one continuous muscular movement, he manages to settle her suitcases at the entrance door of the apartment block; his provocative swagger demands attention:

*Keep the change!*

She is grateful to him for the smooth ride and the attention to her cases. He tips the front of his cap like a professional chauffeur, before driving off.

She reflects on the small vignettes in life that unexpectedly lift one up. The on-board 'Singapore Girl' and the cheerful driver have already filled her with more warmth than any family member she can think of. She resolves to give more importance to moments such as these that come, unsolicited, like surprise gifts.

The entrance door to the serviced apartments is under a low awning which is masked by the thick branch of a silver gum tree. The main trunk is so gigantic she reckons it could have been present years before the first settlement. A gust of wind blows a pile of leaves in with her through the door and her arrival interrupts a heated discussion at the reception desk. The confrontation is between a girl with streaked fair hair and a woman in a maid's uniform with Slavic features, who is built like a wrestler. The latter puts two fingers up to the former before storming off.

The receptionist's young cheeks are flushed with fury as she busies herself with the booking sheet under the counter. As Agnes leans on the desk, she can smell the girl's lavender perfume. She exudes freshness as if she is not long out of the shower. Perhaps she has just started her shift. Her eyelids are painted green, and she has pencilled a perfect dark line which extends out beyond thick lashes. It makes her look like a blonde Cleopatra.

Agnes sees that the girl's hands are shaking with pent-up emotion. She feels sorry for her. She would like to comfort her. She takes stock. Aware of the need to curb a reckless tendency to empathy, she stands appropriately silent. In the long pause that follows, the green eyelids remind her of a line from a $7^{th}$ century Chinese poem she has heard somewhere: 'Eyebrows painted green are a fine sight in young moonlight'. She speaks to the girl:

*Agnes Keen. I booked a one-bedroom serviced apartment for eight weeks. Front of the building with a sofa bed in the living room. My brother will be joining me during my stay for a night or two.*

She glances at a drinks dispenser behind the girl and thinks it lowers the tone of an otherwise discreet decor. The receptionist bites her lip as she concentrates on locating Agnes's name on the bookings list. As Agnes waits, fatigue starts to distort her surroundings and she struggles to fill in the squares on the registration form with a biro that only works intermittently. The sleeping pill she had taken after the on-board meal out of Singapore has had no effect—until now. Her vision is swimming, and she starts to panic when the blonde Cleopatra asks for her passport and she can't find it in her overstuffed handbag. It is jammed with so many sundry items it could be a lucky dip. But there it is! Hiding in the pocket of her coat.

The lift stops on the sixth floor. Any residual angst falls away when she opens the door and sees the view. She has arrived in Paradise.

Unfamiliar skyscrapers, like giant guards in shiny new uniforms, fill old gaps in the Sydney skyline across the water. It is as if they are protecting the carpet of green that is the Botanical Gardens, which rolls down to the harbour's edge. She can see the back of the art gallery: a classical building that echoes Greece and Rome. For years, the grandest building she knew. Behind is The Domain—hidden under a canopy of enormous Moreton Bay fig trees. It is the Australian equivalent of Speaker's Corner in London, and where anyone can stand on a soap box and declaim to anyone else who is prepared to listen.

The white sails of the Opera House are shimmering in all their pristine purity to the right of the balcony. She is old enough to have seen it being built, and she recalls now joining in the street protest in support of the architect, Jørn Utzon, when he was dismissed by local government. The harbour bridge far behind, which joins the northern suburbs to the city, has always been in her life.

Once, long ago, she had wandered across it with the intention of jumping off but, for want of finding a place to launch herself, walked on.

But this isn't the right time to think of that event. Or is it? She drops everything on the floor, closes the curtain, sheds her coat, and staggers into the bedroom, where she flings herself onto the freshly made bed and falls asleep.

\* \* \*

She wakes with a start, her heart pounding and her arms clutching a pillow as if it is the side of a life raft. She is full of anguish. The surge upwards, from the depth of the sea to the surface, is over. She made it. She didn't drown. She's in a bedroom in Sydney and can see a thin beam of sunlight through the closed curtains.

She grapples to make sense of the rest of a disturbing dream about her mother and her Aunt Marnie. Wearing sun hats and summer frocks, the two women were sitting together on the edge of Elizabeth Bay Wharf—a harbour marina within walking distance of where she is now staying. She seemed to recognise the big-brimmed straw hat with its black band that her mother would wear when Agnes was in her early teens. In the years before her mother's hair was cut and permed. In the dream, dishevelled, long strands of hair, the shade of shiny crow's feathers, fell to her mother's shoulders. Agnes had loved the colour of that hair and wished she had inherited it instead of her own ginger mop that makes her feel like she belongs to an alien tribe. The rosy-hued dried flowers around the brim of Marnie's hat had also seemed familiar. Younger than her mother and married to her brother, Parry, Marnie is her mother's only ally in a large feuding family.

In this early waking state, Agnes isn't sure of the style and colour of the frocks. The shapes and shades of the material curl away like a stream of smoke as she wrestles to hold on to the images. Probably Marnie was in blue and her mother in pink or yellow, for they are the colours Agnes associates with them. The sunglasses both women were wearing denied her a glimpse of the expression in their eyes. From a distance, they were a snapshot of languid serenity, framed by rows of anchored sailing boats nudging each other gently in a soft breeze. Up close, their mouths were contorted, and Agnes now knows they were absorbed in the gossip she hates. They were naming and shaming trollops, harlots and hussies. Brazen, saucy, wanton females who steal good women's husbands.

The scathing damnation of Marnie and her mother was not only reserved for women of questionable morals, but all single women until safely married. It had caused Agnes to equate the single state before marriage with the stain of original sin on the soul before baptism. Their talk must surely have been exaggerated but, as her mother would swerve between extremes, it was hard to gauge. Indeed, it seems to Agnes, even now, that her mother's only true motivation in life back then was to dress in expensive clothes and to air her outdoor personality when hobnobbing with the socially superior. Who was she? And who is she now?

A glimpse of memory surfaces. She is around ten. Her mother sinks into a bubble bath—her face as expressionless as the full moon as she reminisces over the eggshell-blue underskirt which once shimmered like fragments of sky through the fine silk of Marnie's wedding dress. Just a smattering of blue to lift the white, her mother recalls. Agnes listens in rapt attention. Her mother is in love with that dress, for she has always pined after a big fancy wedding, her own having been a hurried affair before Agnes's father went off to war. Her mother imagines her young daughter one day wearing the same gown when she floats down the aisle. At least that is what she tells Agnes. But this is no ordinary mother. She has a contradictory nature. Her marriageable daughter wearing a touch of blue is easily cancelled out by:

*You'll never get a man with a face full of freckles like that!*

The unexpected morning dream continues to unsettle Agnes. In it, she was rowing a small boat up and down in front of the two women who intermittently dipped bare feet in the cool water as they talked. The metal fixings that held the oars squeaked whenever Agnes exerted pressure on them, and she had tried to row smoothly, so as not to disturb the two women. Her mother was smoking a Capstan cigarette, intermittently picking bits of tobacco off her tongue. Agnes can suddenly picture the red cigarette pack on her mother's dressing table in time long ago. The self-same red she painted her nails.

What had woken her in a panic is that, in the dream, she drowned. Or disappeared. She's uncertain now, in the light of day. It's hard to fathom. She was—and wasn't—drowned at the same time. She was simply not there anymore. The boat was empty. And the horror of it was that neither her mother nor Aunt Marnie appeared to notice. They were blind to the empty vessel bobbing adrift inches from their feet. Blind to the fact she had evaporated.

At home, when Agnes was growing up, she had claimed an old art book as her own because no one else ever looked at it. Pictures in the book now drift into her mind. The dream seems to have connected her with 'The Fall of Icarus'. In the mythical story that inspired the painting, Icarus fell to earth after his wax wings melted. He had flown too close to the sun. Bruegel painted his Icarus as he slips into the sea with a tiny splash, unnoticed by either a farmer or the crew of a nearby ship.

What does the dream mean? Her mother would have blamed her for hallucinating—'seeing ghosts' as she used to complain. This maternal influence is so potent in her life it can still make Agnes doubt what she sees with her own, wide-open, eyes.

Thirst drives her back into the here and now. Drops like tiny diamonds are covering her forehead. The mirror on the bedroom wall shows curvy lines from the pillowcase stamped on the side of her cheek. The skirt and stockings she slept in are clinging to her like a second skin. She has experienced four seasons in a week. Leaving Mallorca on a hot spring day to land in a freezing cold snap in London. On a whim. There is no one to tell her not to. She had bought a mink coat from a stall in the Portobello Road. A nuisance to lug around in tropical Singapore on the layover, but why not? And here she now is—in glorious, warm, autumn Sydney sunshine.

This really is a raging thirst. Drinks stored in the ugly dispensing machine at the reception desk come to mind. Then she remembers the half bottle of water she salvaged from the plane. Gulping it fast brings on a fit of coughing. She jogs on the spot to make it go down.

Then, sliding through the thick, grey pile carpet in stockinged feet, she discovers, to her delight, a mini kitchen in the living room: an electric kettle on a tray with teabags, powdered chocolate, coffee sachets and brown and white granulated sugars. On a granite countertop: a hotplate, microwave, cupboards with crockery and cutlery and a small fridge with milk and a minibar. How wonderful to be in a place of her own and not be staying with friends or relatives!

The water pressure is fabulous. She revels in a delicious long shower. Sitting out on the balcony afterwards, scenting the early morning air, she feels revived. She sips a hot mug of tea and is wearing a crisp new blue patterned cotton kimono—purchased in Singapore and safely hidden in the suitcase out of reach of the thieving red-gloved hand. The croissant and biscuits taste all the better for being squirrelled off the aeroplane trays. The fabulous view is ever fascinating. Fitting the new into the familiar absorbs her like a jigsaw puzzle and helps pacify the feeling of being a stranger in the land of her birth.

'*Aurora Australis*'. She identifies the icebreaker through a pair of binoculars. It seems it has only just docked on the wharf below. The ship is generating a mass of movement on the street in front. Then she spots Harry's Café de Wheels—the hamburger joint she remembers from her youth. It must be over fifty years old. Groups of sailors from the ship are heading there in droves. Its reputation as rough and sleazy, where the uncouth hang out and refined women don't venture, looks to be intact. Over sixty years old as she is, she can now go exactly where she pleases. She's anonymous. No one will notice her. No waterside worker is going to whistle and make a spectacle of her. Gripped with a sudden desire for a meat pie, she decides to stroll down there.

She unpacks her clothes. She has chosen outfits which she hopes will impress her aunts. Insane as it seems, after decades, she still yearns for their acceptance as an equal. She knows she is stuck in a time warp. But it is not only her. She will subsequently recognise that the aunts also have not moved on. She puts on a crushed black linen dress under a black and white striped jacket. Crushed linen is a fashion statement and, conveniently, there is no need to iron.

She slips her feet into a pair of black leather thongs and does up the strap behind the heel. They are identical copies of sandals worn by her Aunt Charlotte back in the late fifties when she left on an ocean liner for a honeymoon in Europe. Head-girl Charlotte. University Honours graduate Charlotte. Her grandmother's favourite daughter who married a wealthy grazier—which was the icing on the family cake, apparently. Amazing how, when so much else is forgotten, the sight of those prim, neat feet in sandals lives on in Agnes's mind.

The recognition from the aunts that she longs for conflicts with loyalty to her mother who hates the lot of them and has always expected her daughter to follow suit. Hatred is such a strong word, but no other could adequately express the churning anxiety in Agnes's aging body. It is a sensation that never goes off the boil. Her hope, after all these years, is that the aunts may have transcended the notion that 'daughter is like mother' and are open-minded enough to see her for what she truly is—her mother's complete opposite.

Aunt Charlotte's fairytale romance with her country grazier was the desirable prototype—the route to happiness her sister Madge believed should have been her own rite of passage to matrimony—many years earlier. As a young woman, Madge O'Connor had tried hard to put herself in the way of it by working as a nanny in the homestead of a grand property in the hills of the Great Dividing Range of New South Wales. It was the era before synthetic fabrics, when fortunes were shorn off a sheep's back. Her boss's husband was one of four brothers, their names forever synonymous with Australian polo. They soared to fame not only in their own country, but also attained great heights on the international circuit.

As a boy, Agnes's father—a second-generation son of Irish immigrants—started work at the brothers' stables and, by the age of 18, was invited to travel abroad with the ponies as one of the grooms. Eric Keen had grown up in the saddle. Rode to school. Rode to the shops. Rode to collect firewood. Rode to his work at the polo stables. He and his father, the overseer of the grand property, rode the boundaries of the vast acreage together. Eric knew every tree and dam. He was as comfortable in the saddle as a city kid on a bike. His talent as a horseman being recognised by the polo brothers, they taught him how to refine his seat in the saddle and, via their instruction and his own pin-sharp observation, he mastered the game until he was good enough to fill in at Sunday practice matches on the homestead field. He not only learned to play polo, but all the techniques the brothers used to train a novice horse. This would be a skill he would later adopt independently, along with the brothers' lucrative practice of selling trained ponies after a tournament, to cover the vast expenses.

Madge Anne O'Connor would speak of her own former employers with adoration. As a child, Agnes imagined them like royalty. The enticing, vivid description of their fabulous house and garden become part of her imaginary world. Relaxing in a hot bath, Madge's mind inevitably drifted to musing on her halcyon times at 'Pink Dale'. Black and white photos attested to her youthfully intoxicating black-eyed beauty. Adding to her glamour was a grandiose 'Presentation' dripping with every conceivable upper-class flourish. How could the young groom, just back from tending the brothers' ponies at a tournament with a maharajah in India, not believe that the vivacious and well-dressed new employee was anything less than an heiress, working as a nanny to the owner's children for some character-building pocket money?

As for Madge, there can be only one outcome to the first sighting of Eric Keen—the well-built blue-eyed man with the film-star looks. Watching him in his tight white jodhpurs and high leather boots as he cantered across the field at a Sunday practice match. Admiring the flawless under-the-neck cross shot which scored a perfect goal. And if there was any doubt about the electricity between them when their eyes met on the side-line, a further encounter under a pergola dripping with blue wisteria flowers in the famous garden would seal the promise of eternal love. Transported by the power of youthful attraction in the perfumed moonlight, it was easy for the two young people to envisage that earthly manna would flow from the wonder of it all, along with countless other blessings to sanctify their union.

The stark reality after their wedding in Sydney—that neither bride nor groom had struck gold—took some time, if ever, to assimilate. This realisation, and one that neither of them seemed to arrive at, was hampered by the fact that the pursuit of the truth was never a priority for either of them.

Agnes's father's expectations were further blighted when he found out he was designated as illegitimate. A bastard. There was no way around the damning euphemism printed in black and white on the birth certificate he needed for the wedding. **Father: not known.** It also answered the mysterious disappearance of his 'sister' at 16 to work as a dressmaker in Sydney. He would never forgive his grandparents for passing him off as their son. How could he continue to face the small country town where he grew up? They all knew what he didn't. Without a backward glance, he cut the betrayers out of his life and adopted his soon-to-be wife's family with alacrity.

His burgeoning talent on the polo field, which once led to the plausible expectation of becoming part of an international team, ended abruptly when, after the invasion of Poland, Australia followed Britain in declaring war on Germany. He joined the Australian Air Force and was married in uniform.

Things could not have turned out worse for Madge. Hard on the heels of the bombshell of a lost fortune came the Japanese attack on the Pearl Harbour US Naval Base in the Pacific on 7$^{th}$ December 1941, with no warning.

Early the following year, when she was heavily pregnant with her only daughter and her husband had been posted to New Guinea, US defence units started arriving in Sydney. Within months, the town was crawling with American servicemen with disposable incomes, nylon stockings, cigarettes and free access to every fashionable article ever manufactured. It was a further unforgivable climbdown for Madge who, after boasting of socialising with wealthy graziers at the magnificent property in the Great Dividing Range, now had to live with her own mother in an overcrowded flat with her five sisters. Women of her age were dating generous Yankee boyfriends. Even Madge's own oldest sister, Sill, was constantly dolling herself up to be whisked out the door by yet another American suitor.

But what inflamed Madge almost beyond endurance was spotting, one crushing day in Ocean Avenue, her oldest sister's best friend, Patricia Murphy, flaunting the spoils of the Australian/American alliance. When Patricia's American Sergeant returned to the States, he sent her a Schiaparelli black and shocking-pink tight-waisted suit with embroidered arrows, along with a rosy pillbox hat and, to top it off, a pair of black wedge sandals by Lotus. What was more, Patricia was, according to Madge, permanently soaked in enough Chanel No. 5 to send the neighbours rushing for a gas mask.

Agnes's father was already decoding enemy messages in Darwin. He needed no degree in counter espionage to understand the confetti of printed messages ejected from Japanese planes that fluttered around him in the jungle. They informed the enlisted men in New Guinea that the Yanks in Australia were getting off with their women. If knowledge of the influx of male flesh bearing cigarettes and nylons made him feel insecure, he had no need to be. His only daughter was doggedly at her post, pushing out his wife's belly to keep suitors away.

The unhappy wife could have committed mass murder. The doe-eyed wonder of the romance under the wisteria in the fabulous garden was under threat. Madge was raging. Her schoolgirl heart—formerly the absolute property of country graziers with double-barrelled names and quadruple-figure acreages—had betrayed the home-grown for the imported. She yearned to have her own Yank, like her sister and Patricia Murphy. Yet all she could do was to imagine what she was missing out on. A bad habit that became the norm.

The arrival of the only redhead in the family elicited no fanfare of trumpets. Agnes was christened Helen Agnes. However, not long after the ceremony at the local Catholic church, her mother, holding a baby daughter who looked like a visiting fairy in a flowing white robe, will change her name. It will happen after the hated Patricia Murphy, bosom pal of eldest sister Sill, all dolled up in American imports, has the temerity—bloody slut that she is—to stand by the cot and call Agnes 'Little Hell'. Madge can never forget a slight. *She* could call her daughter whatever she liked, but *anyone else* did so at their peril. No longer Helen, Agnes becomes Agnes Helen Keen, which she remains. The new name legally registered, mother and daughter will move to live out the war alongside other Royal Australian Air Force wives in houses the government allocated near the Air Force Base in Dubbo. When the Yanks disappear, Agnes's mother's only recourse is to return to the idealisation of the double-barrelled names on the quadruple-figure acreages.

After such an unwelcoming arrival into the world, Agnes will soon figure out that leaving home was only sensible. Why stay where you're not wanted? She has no memory of her first three-year-old effort to run away, but the desire to escape which started as a toddler has continued for what now seems forever. Madge has never tired of recounting how a famous Aboriginal tracker had found her tear-stained little daughter asleep on the banks of the mighty Macquarie River that runs through Dubbo. The photo on the front page of the local newspaper of Agnes, cradled in the arms of her native rescuer, immortalised the event. The safety of permanent walkabout obviously held an early appeal. Agnes's mother, when recounting the anecdote, would complain about having to drag her small red-headed daughter from the smiling tracker's comforting arms. The inference being inescapable, Agnes is in no doubt where the reluctance to be returned to Madge originated.

Agnes's first *actual* memory is of her mother running away from *her*. Just four years old, she is propped up in a bed on the veranda of a Dubbo hospital. She is feeling sick and confused. Later she will learn she is in isolation because she is suffering from infectious scarlet fever. In time, she will become familiar with the irritable expression on her mother's face when she looks up at her lonely child from the paddock below. Little Agnes wants to run to her, or wave at her, but she can't move.

Madge will turn swiftly, without acknowledging her, and Agnes will watch the back of her mother's lovely silky jet hair—tucked in a neat Victory Roll. She will observe the wobbling heads of tall grass and wildflowers brush the hem of her mother's tweed skirt as she gets smaller and smaller before disappearing into the distance. And the bereft child will be plunged into a deep sadness. A sadness that, to this day, still seems to be lodged permanently inside her.

## CHAPTER 3
# WOOLLOOMOOLOO WHARF

The reception area at the Grantham Apartments is deserted when Agnes sets off for Harry's Café to satisfy her meat pie craving. She finds her way to Embarkation Park with its moving commemoration of the soldiers who once passed through the gate of Woolloomooloo wharf to go off to the Great War. When she looks down the steep flight of stairs that lead to the wharf, she regrets not wearing jeans. She is decked out in one of the outfits bought simply to impress the aunts. The pencil skirt restricts her movement. The Aunt Charlotte sandals are not ideal either. She clutches the side of the rail and lowers herself from one high stone tread to the next. A vertigo sufferer, she tries not to look down. When she arrives at the bottom, the sun is directly overhead. It burns into the top of her head like a knife slicing through butter. She wishes she had worn a hat. Freckly redheads should never go out in the midday sun without a hat.

The glare is blinding. She is standing in the middle of a wide grey street. Wide enough to be an airport runway. She is at the intersection with Cowper's Wharf. Cars whizz around her. She is disoriented. She tries to figure out which side of the grey expanse to gravitate to, as neither offers shade. She opts for the wharf side, where she clings to a flimsy strip of shadow which survives under an overhang on the fence of the naval base. The crowd of sailors she saw earlier from the icebreaker have disappeared—presumably now back with their families, sharing adventures of their voyage in the snow-capped Antarctic. Their rosy-red painted ship is thawing out in the sunshine. The colour looks joyous, and Agnes imagines it glowing like red cheeks on white skin against the snowfields. She looks up to see a helicopter, painted the same rosy colour, as it lands on the helipad at the back of the ship with a flurry and churn of blades. It is like an enormous bee discovering the right flower.

She pauses outside Harry's Café, but the heat is relentless and so she decides to forego the pie. Her sight blurs in the haze as she tries to orient herself. She catches sight of an old-style pub on the corner of Bourke Street. Alone on an otherwise deserted patch, it looks as if it is marooned in the past. She finds herself approaching the two-storey red-brick structure with a morbid curiosity. A set of swing doors are set in the brown tiled wall. Three listless palm trees, taller than the building, stand on the pavement. Opposite is a new luxury wharf conversion hotel which she has never seen before. A nearby sign advertises the inclusion of expensive floating apartments. She has read about them. One had sold to a famous Australian actor. 'Foster's Lager' appears in big letters under the pub awning and through the open door she can see 'Toohey's Old' and 'Toohey's New' labelling the beer taps on the counter of the bar. She cannot count the number of times she has sat outside pubs that looked like this as a child—waiting in the back seat of the car for her father to emerge. He would suddenly pull the Holden into the curb with an air of urgency and splutter: 'I'll be right back.' Then hours would tick by with no sign of him.

Now, in this minute, she recalls one particular afternoon. She was waiting with her brothers, in silence, outside the Royal Exchange in Gresham Street near Circular Quay. For three long hours. In addition to the tedious waiting, she had disliked the strange way her father had looked at her when he finally approached the car. It was how he often became when inebriated. A glazed-eyed, gormless stare would dominate his face—like a dog about to smell another dog's backside.

The sight of the downbeat pub brings back to Agnes the sweltering summer when she used to visit a similar place in a derelict part of Newtown. She would go there with Uncle Parry—Aunt Marnie's husband. She had just turned 16 when her parents suddenly upped sticks and moved to the country. Without her. Made completely welcome in a friend's home for the summer, she had never understood why her Uncle Parry had dragged her out of this sanctuary and forced her to live with him and his wife—a house in an area where she knew no one and was decidedly *not* welcome.

How strange to have dreamed about her mother and Aunt Marnie last night and to now have these old memories of her father and Uncle Parry suddenly resurface outside this rank old pub. She tries to recall more and yet knows that much of the unwelcome time with her aunt and uncle resists resurrection.

But events that refuse to deny memory return. The painful, lonely tram rides from Parry and Marnie's house in Maroubra to the city and back. The feeling of being desperately cold and hungry. The walk across the bridge to finally end it all—her heart a cornered bat fluttering around in her chest and attaching itself to time. A gap. And then the following morning when she had woken up in a boarding house for old people with no idea how she got there. And hovering above it all, out of reach, like a deep red sunset on a mountain top, the fire in the Maroubra house. A fire she has always felt responsible for. A fire her aunt and uncle said didn't happen, and yet a fire that goes on burning inside her.

Agnes crosses Bourke Street to get a better look at the full side façade of the old pub. The sight of a shiny metal barrel leaning against the brown tiled wall makes her shudder. Her stomach turns over. She's dizzy now and feels like throwing up. Worse is the constriction in her throat. It must be the sun on her head without a hat. She can't stay there.

She rushes through the metallic haze of traffic as if carried on wings, back up the street towards Cowper Wharf, a rush of adrenaline sweeping her up the steep stone staircase to Victoria Street. As she climbs, she rips the back of her skirt. It's open halfway up her leg but she doesn't care. Amazing how much less effort it takes to get to the top, compared to the quivering, tentative struggle down.

Desperate to outstep the inner turmoil, she strides through King's Cross willy-nilly and then runs down William Street and up again in a mad panic. Traffic whizzes by. This is the main artery into the city from the Eastern Suburbs and it pulses with motorbikes, cars, buses and trucks day and night. She rounds the corner into Darlinghurst Road and sees the sign on the side of the Crescent Hotel—'Ginseng Korean Bathhouse'. On impulse, she dashes up the beige carpet stairs.

The hypnotic melody of an Eastern string instrument, floating mesmerically through the sound of waves washing to shore, is quite compelling. The receptionist wears a gold satin Chong Sam and has seashells nestling in the folds of the long shiny black hair curled up on her head. She thinks of the soothing air hostess and muses on the manner of Asian women in general, for whom service is an art form. She gazes into the fathomless eyes and splutters:

*I just tore my skirt...*

The woman advises her with a gentle smile:

*Turn it around waist to side and it look like fashion.*

Agnes struggles with the waistband. The woman smiles again:

*You like massage?*

Agnes floats down a low-lit carpeted corridor under dangling chimes and enters a dressing room, where she slips out of the Aunt Charlotte sandals, undresses, and puts her clothes into the designated locker. She washes and dries her dusty feet in the shower room and slips them into dainty white slippers. Her body nestles into the white towelling robe provided and she follows the signs to the massage rooms with her overstuffed handbag under her arm.

The masseuse is a short, fine-featured, auburn-haired Croatian woman who, Agnes will shortly discover, has fled the war in her county over a decade ago and settled in Sydney with her daughter.

It is during the second part of the treatment, when the masseuse is running oiled hands firmly down Agnes's thighs to her toes, that her mother's odd obsession pops into her head:

*You've got your grandmother's legs!*

Madge would use this rebuke as if the sight of her daughter's teenaged calves in nylon stockings was equivalent to the discovery of stolen goods. As if Agnes had wilfully misappropriated, a generation down the line, that which was meant for her. In fact, her mother was so permanently peeved by this that, years later, when the surgeon amputated Agnes's grandmother's right leg below the knee to stop the advance of bone cancer, it provoked in her small brain a reconnection with the old resentment. There and then, outside Grandma's room, on the ground floor of St Vincent's Private Hospital in Darlinghurst Sydney, where the patient lay in bed surrounded by flowers and with a tent over her stump, complaining of pain in toes she no longer had, Madge had returned to familiar territory:

*You've got her legs, Agnes, you'll see. Enough said. This might be you one day!*

This direct frontal assault on a day of terrible loss for Grandma had caught Agnes entirely unprepared. In fact, she had never learned to prepare for—or anticipate—Madge, because she was always responding to a mother she had invented.

Now prone on the masseuse's table, Agnes remembers everything with precision. Standing in the hospital corridor. An adult. Earning her own living, and yet effortlessly pulled back into childhood, where she was stranded. Defenceless. There had been no mistaking the glee in her mother's eyes. Unjustly attacked, Agnes recalls now how she had dissolved into pathetic tears. Madge could get to her every time. You might even say she played her like a musical instrument. A handkerchief had been thrust at her in annoyance at her tears. Triumph had given way to intolerance—her daughter's huge emotional response obviously being more than Madge had bargained for. The ensuing sobbing then drove Madge to further cruelty:

*Stop your blubbering! Stop your blubbering at once!*
The hissed sneer had slid through clenched teeth. Agnes recalls being grateful they were in a public place. If it had happened at home when she was a teenager, her mother would have knocked her head against the dining-room wall, where most of her brains had already joined the plaster.

After the operation, Grandma had all the courage in the world. She learned to walk with an artificial leg and to drive an automatic car. The leg squeaked, which was particularly embarrassing when she hobbled up the stairs to the dress circle where she liked to sit for her evenings at the ballet. Agnes would organise these outings to cheer her up. A few drops of oil or a mechanical adjustment might have helped, but no one ever made such practical suggestions to Grandma. She offered up her leg to God. Agnes always imagined it clad in a sensible, well-made shoe winging its way to heaven.

The rest of Grandma followed her leg a few years later. News of her death arrived when Agnes was in Bruges, having just sent her a white tablecloth adorned with delicate patterned hand-made lace. It was what you bought in that part of Belgium. In an effort to prove her worth, Agnes had regularly sent Grandma quality souvenirs from all over Europe. She had always craved her recognition just as she craved that of the aunts. She wanted to join what she imagined was their exclusive club. She had hoped that lavishing money and gifts on Grandma would bring her the love she sought: a touch, a smile, just one little word would have meant everything. But it had been pointless. Praise, encouragement, even gratitude, might give a girl a big head. Anyway, Agnes's substantial financial gains in her twenties, in Grandma's opinion, would have been better invested in financing the university studies of her intelligent male cousins.

As for Agnes's own academic achievements, she had never been able to defend her consistent failure at school, or her mysterious inability to concentrate on the written word. Not only did she not belong but, on occasion, she used to ponder whether her mother might have been given the wrong baby. She figured not belonging was equivalent to feeling you had arrived with the wrongly allocated sex. But she had never had a problem feeling like a girl, even though Grandma shamelessly favoured the men in the family over the women.

She stares at the ceiling of the treatment room. *Why* didn't she belong? *Was* she abnormal, as they constantly inferred? She would do it. She would consult Uncle Ben as part of her planned family investigation. Uncle Parry had joined Grandma in heaven long ago, but Aunt Jean, who had offered to help, advised her in a letter that Parry's widow, Marnie, was willing to see her.

Now, lying prone in the Ginseng Korean Bathhouse, she has decided that she has always felt not only alienated from family, but from the world.

# CHAPTER 4

# ROSEMONT

Back at the Grantham Apartments, the blonde receptionist with the green eyeshadow hands her a note. It reads:

*Darling Agnes,*
*Sorry to have missed you. Hope you've recovered from jet lag. Marnie can see you on Friday afternoon at 3.30. You have the address and know she had a stroke. She got her speech back but still slurs her words. She's in a wheelchair but manages remarkably well. I didn't have to persuade her as she was keen to see you again. If you can't make it ring and let her know. I told her if she didn't hear, to expect you.*

*Longing to see you. Come and eat with me at Rosemont on Saturday night at 7.30. I'm still settling in but will push the boxes aside and make space for the two of us at the dining table. Look forward to hearing how you get on with Marnie when we meet on Saturday.*
*Love*
*Jean*

The note gives welcome structure. She'll see Marnie on Friday and Jean on Saturday night. Younger than her mother and around ten years older than 'Super Aunt Charlotte' Jean seems to have taken an interest in Agnes's effort to recover the past. Jean has recently purchased the family apartment from her widowed oldest sister who, in her late eighties, no longer wishes to travel to Sydney from Melbourne—where she has lived half her life.

Back on the balcony, as Agnes munches a piece of spicy cooked chicken from the local deli and sips a glass of red wine, she is blessed with a magnificent sunset—gold, pink and violet hues are expanding in streamers to fill the evening sky. The city appears to stand still as twilight mutes the range of colours into pale smoky lines above it. Light from the skyscrapers reflects rivers of rainbow pastels on the surface of the harbour. As she suspects it would, Harry's Café emerges in glimmering neon, like a huge psychedelic glow-worm. Below the safety lights of the cranes on the wharf, the hamburger joint is pulsing like a spaceship about to lift off. The warm night air gradually fills with the sound of revellers.

She finds herself repeating the name 'Rosemont' like the line of a song. During her growing up, all decisions about their lives were made there by her maternal grandmother. 'Rosemont.' She enjoys rolling the letters around her tongue. She sees the name as it once shimmered in pale amber letters on a glass panel above the entrance door of the red-brick apartment block. When a child, she was in awe of this building—especially the red carpet and honey mahogany panelling that lined the vestibule. But it was the lift next to the staircase that really enthralled her. That spoke to her of European cities where famous composers and writers lived and died tragically, where Impressionism was born, and scientific discoveries made. She loved the Bakelite lift indicator numbers, too, set as they were in a brass panel inside the wire metal doors. And there was something so tantalising about the way the rope mechanism clanged upwards that always excited her. She would envisage herself in one of the luxury apartments she had seen in fifties American films, where lift doors were a symphony of movement, opening directly into spacious apartments. She would picture herself sitting at a piano next to George Gershwin who would be singing 'The One and Only You'.

But such a song would have been considered an aberration at 'Rosemont', where children were never special and were certainly no novelty. The tribe of offspring fought for a teaspoon of attention. Staunch Catholic Grandma gave birth to 13 of them, of which eleven survived. By the time grandchild Agnes came along, the boys were long gone, and 'Rosemont' was an all-female establishment comprising Grandma, her eldest daughter Sill, and her three younger sisters: the fabulous Aunt Charlotte, Aunt Carol (the kind one in the middle) and Aunt Tina who was only three years old when Agnes was born.

Aunt Sill acted as surrogate mother to her younger sisters whenever they were home on holiday from a convent boarding school. She administered decrees on taste, manners, skincare, and the dark art of thought control. In exactly the way the Inquisition pasted over texts in astrological works deemed blasphemous to Catholic doctrine, she banned any talk not in keeping with the tableware. In fact, when Agnes, aged seven, visited 'Rosemont', 'Pass the butter, please' was the start and end of what she was allowed to say. Aunt Sill monitored the past and kept it firmly under lock and key. In fact, keeping up appearances in the family was everything. Family wheels were oiled on proverbs:

*Don't wash your dirty linen in public.*
*Cleanliness is next to godliness.*
*Children should be seen and not heard.*
*You can't have your cake and eat it too.*
*Blood is thicker than water.*
*Beggars can't be choosers.*
*The one that pays the piper calls the tune.*

It all boiled down to sticking with the family, changing your underpants every day (in case you had an accident), and whatever was in your head, *keep* it there, especially at the dining table. Meals were beautifully presented on lovely serving plates. Aunt Sill was addressed formally as Miss O'Connor and her mother as Mrs O'Connor. Nobody would ever dream of violating the established order.

On a summer's day, from the roomy apartment's front windows, you could see the sun sparkling like thousands of diamonds on the sea in Sydney Harbour. Apart from learning how to eat a peach with a knife and fork, the only other thing Agnes can recall is 'Aunt Carol the Kind' who, safely away from the others, would let her look through binoculars to see the tiny tugboats welcome the big ships inside the Heads, guiding them through the deep waters of the harbour to safe moorings at Darling Harbour and Circular Quay. As the flotilla had slowly disappeared out of sight of the windows, Carol had once whispered in her ear:

*You see, Agnes? You can be small and strong like a tugboat.*

Then she had kissed her.

Carol would never speak in that talking-down-to-children way, like the others did. There was a painting in the family art book that Agnes had claimed as her own, entitled 'The Fighting Temeraire'. It was by Turner, and it depicted a grand warship that stood in the front line at the Battle of Trafalgar. In the painting, the once-mighty ship is being towed by a small feisty tug to the wreckers' yard, and the moving imagery has forever reminded Agnes of that rare and magical moment, at the window with Carol the Kind.

Grandma's intimate contract with the Almighty was all-consuming, and all the family offspring were turned by her into devout Catholics. For Agnes, as her first-born grandchild, being part of the divine plan to propel Grandma safely into the arms of her maker was a good deal more noble than being blamed for a mother's thwarted expectations and so she always felt safe with Grandma. As Grandma's disinterest was devoid of conflict, this deeply religious woman was, by default, trustworthy. She secretly wanted to be Grandma's child and live at 'Rosemont' with her three young aunts. She had embraced Grandma's belief in sacrifice and would do God's work in a leper colony when she grew up. Any lost fingers, toes, and thumbs from contact with the disease would be offered up to God—like Grandma's amputated leg. The little seven-year-old was ready to be spiked with swords, eaten by lions, stoned, flayed alive, beheaded, or burnt at the stake, like the early Christian martyrs.

Agnes will later wonder if, along with Grandma's legs, she has inherited Grandma's madness as, according to her mother (never a reliable witness) a few years before her first grandchild's birth, Grandma once spent time in the padded cell of a psychiatric hospital. Whilst residing in the country, one beloved teenage daughter had apparently died of a ruptured appendix, and it seemed that Grandma had sincerely believed God had taken her as a punishment for her sinful use of contraception. Her psychotic episode had been attributed to grief. Grandma had even lamented to little Agnes in a rare intimate moment:

*He took my Bess, my angel, the kindest, sweetest most helpful child!*

Perhaps constant childbearing had continued to affect Grandma's mental health, for it appeared that, one morning, Aunt Sill's eyes had been prised from the printed word by the sound of frantic chirping. She had run to release what she thought was a trapped, winged creature in a closed room but instead had found her mother, clothed in a white nightdress, balanced on the ledge of an open window, preparing to fly down to the branches of a Moreton Bay fig tree below. Aunt Sill's nursing training had not prepared her for a case of metamorphosis. But miraculous powers often arrive in a crisis. Just the week before, a newspaper had reported that a country-dwelling mother had lifted a tractor off a son who was pinned underneath, and that same superhuman strength was gifted to Aunt Sill in the critical moment. She had hauled her mother from the window back to safety, locked it, and phoned for help.

Perhaps also in sympathy, or because she also secretly wanted to escape, Aunt Sill will develop a bird-like twittering stutter that remains with her for life. Her speech becomes hesitant and clipped, giving the impression that, as soon as the words are out, she wants them back. With her emaciated parent valuing the laugh of a kookaburra over the spoken word, Sill—the young bookworm—will dutifully take on her mother's responsibilities alongside her father, and the remaining children will be farmed out to various institutions. It is at this precise moment in the history of the family that Madge O'Connor would take up her position in the grand property homestead in the Great Dividing Range of New South Wales, in a Herculean effort to better herself.

News that her husband was dying of cancer would jolt Grandma back to sanity. Her husband, an extraordinary man famous for pioneering cars and aeroplanes, would die two years and seven months before Agnes is born and his emboldened wife will take control of the profitable cotton factory he had established in Sydney when the Depression had forced the family to leave a farm in the country. Taking the place of her deceased spouse would give Grandma the right to rule. It was an established norm that a woman could only govern by default, unlike on the dancefloor when a girl must always let the man lead. Thus, Grandma would elect to replace insanity with rigid conventionality. Presumably sons were valued over daughters because Eve gave the apple to Adam. Sons would work in the family business, while those daughters who didn't become nuns (none did) were encouraged to join the caring professions: nursing, physiotherapy, speech therapy or social work, while they waited to find husbands. Sill was the exception, working as her mother's secretary.

Grandma deferred to nobody. Her one and only absolute Master, to whom she prostrated herself entirely, was God the Father. His location was never clear: here, there and everywhere, but you always looked up to find him. His fingers were the rays of light that exploded through the clouds with the sun.

The anguish of struggling against a backward evolutionary slide had pushed Grandma prematurely to old age, where she remained suspended like a specimen in formaldehyde. Nothing, however, decreased the strength of her presence. The widow who now ruled the clan was a Prometheus, a Pygmalion, a Caesar, and was as infallible as the Pope. Extraordinary tales abounded of her brave feats in the country before the Depression: how she nailed a black snake's tail to the floorboards, blasted the heads off several others with a shotgun, and chased a thieving pet kangaroo—who stole the bread out of the wood oven—all around the garden.

Little Agnes wrapped the stories about Grandma around her and made them her own. She caught on to another family tale at this time—that the predominance of raven hair and dark eyes in the family was an inheritance from a distant relative on the father's side: an Englishman who married a Tahitian princess while captaining a ship in the South Pacific. She, of course, was not a beneficiary of this desirably exotic magic.

Elizabeth Arden night cream and day moisturiser kept Grandma's skin soft. Cheeks and nose were dabbed with a powder puff as light as a clump of fairy floss. Red lipstick was worn on the mornings she attended the boardroom at the factory. Little Agnes mirrored her lip movement as Grandma applied the colour roughly, like a dash through a word, as a careful Cupid's bow would be too frivolous. For the devil could lure even the most vigilantly faithful into vanity.

The sombre grey skirts and white blouses Grandma favoured made her look like a nun. But the nun had definitely departed the convent once she pulled nylon stockings onto those famous, fabulous, shapely legs and slipped her feet into a pair of expensive English medium-heel court shoes that always looked new. The saggy flesh on her underarms would wobble like creased tissue paper in a breeze as she moved, and she would squint with concentration while securing a three-stranded set of pearls around her wrinkled neck. The acquisition of a set of cultured pearls was a prescriptive rite of passage for all O'Connor girls.

On a good morning, a red felt hunting-style hat, full of jaunty feathers, was fixed above the bun on Grandma's head with a hatpin. A black snakeskin handbag, with a clip that snapped shut like a rat trap, was normally chosen to accompany the hat. Grandma's image flickered like a triptych painting in the three mirrors of her mahogany dressing table as she paused to dab 4711 eau de Cologne behind her ears and wrists, wiping off the excess with a delicate embroidered handkerchief. Grandma's belief in always buying 'quality' was almost as intense as her devotion to God. Clothes, handbags, shoes, cars, carpets, furniture were unfailingly discreet, subtle and expensive.

Little Agnes always cherished a rare sense of belonging whenever she was allowed to accompany Grandma in the Humber. A Saint Christopher medal on the shiny wood dashboard kept them safe from accidents, and a Black Watch tartan cashmere travel rug sat on the burgundy leather upholstery as a promise of warmth.

When the world said goodbye to the war, it will explode into the Keen family house behind a high wall on New South Head Road, Rose Bay. Henceforth, it will travel with them wherever they go. Eric, the returning Air Force man, will have no more intention of settling down with his wife and children than his wife has of making a home for her family. His desire to return to playing polo will find a willing ear with his mother-in-law who is at her wits end fending off her eldest son Mack's demands to take over the cotton factory: a threat that is having a bad effect on Ben and Parry, his two younger brothers.

The plan to unite all three sons in a polo team, with her son-in-law as Captain, will arrive like a gift from the Almighty. Polo will end the bickering. Polo will re-establish family prestige after the fall inflicted by the Depression. Her daughters' future husbands can also make up a team. A family dynasty of players passing the baton from father to son will surely follow. Eric, the Saviour, shall be rewarded with an automatic job in the cotton factory. No qualifications, or assessments are necessary—just being a Catholic male, married to an O'Connor girl, with an understanding of the standard plot of a romance novel, is reference enough. Protestants need not apply.

Mack and his brother-in-law Eric are around the same age. From the outset, an edgy discord exists between the two men. Mack resents the attention lavished on the handsome ex-serviceman, and especially by his straitlaced mother who turns into a fluttering butterfly whenever Eric enters the room. For the new polo team, whose good fortune depends completely on the Grand Matriarch, work is about to take a decided back seat to play. However, the saga of work financing play will continue over the decades until the balance severely nosedives firmly in favour of *play* on Ben's watch—and the cotton factory is no more.

For now, ponies are carefully chosen and purchased, and Eric employs the training techniques he has learned from the brothers on the grand property in the Great Dividing Range. He will ride the ponies patiently for hours up and down a fence till they respond automatically to the lightest pull on the reins and cease flinching when a polo stick swirls alongside their flanks. Thus, the feuding O'Connor brothers will declare a truce, uniting behind Eric as Captain to form a team. By the time they ride out onto the field together, there will be enough new members of a revived post-war polo club near Mascot Airport to challenge them to high-level weekend practice matches.

The gene from the Tahitian princess that apparently fashions the O'Connor women into classical beauties is overcooked on the male side to produce men with faces like burnt toast. All share a full-faced five o'clock shadow that appears within hours of shaving. Excessive body hair and a rough demeanour makes them look more like mafia gangsters than middle-class gentlemen. But Mack and Ben's swarthiness doesn't appear in the stubble on Parry's chin, for he has inherited his mother's pale complexion and feathery brown hair.

Eldest sister, Sill O'Connor, minister of taste and keeper of family secrets, could, by consulting her book on etiquette, have provided the wherewithal to smooth out her brothers' rough edges, but they are beyond her jurisdiction. One could also be forgiven in thinking that Grandma, the Grand Matriarch, may have considered courtesy and politeness unmanly. All the brothers are afflicted with septum trouble, further complicated by excessive nasal hair. And, as if nature's assault on male O'Connor noses isn't enough, Parry has received a blow that leaves a bump in the middle of his that resembles a tiny crater. Surviving an accident-prone childhood, Parry has arrived at adulthood also having lost half a finger in a mysterious accident. It isn't just his fairer complexion and misshapen nose that make him different. He is quietly spoken and sympathetic, establishing himself as the reliable one to turn to for help in a family crisis. Eric depends on him as the peacemaker in the team when tempers between the other two hotheads flare out of control.

But broken noses, five o'clock shadows and missing fingers do not diminish the transformative effect of a man dressed for polo. For what man does not look handsome sporting a pair of white jodhpurs, long polished leather boots, a smart team shirt on his back and a helmet crowning his head? By the end of the first official polo season after the war, the new team's names will be engraved on major New South Wales and interstate trophies. The international circuit within their grasp, Eric can tap into contacts in India, England, and America. He knows how to manage polo ponies on board ship. The predicted profit from selling the trained steeds after a tournament will convince the Grand Matriarch she is making a lucrative investment. Although Mack still holds a grudge against the golden boy, he defuses the bile in his belly with an extra beer, or shot of whisky, and will bide his time.

If being surrounded by sumptuously draped elephants and wined and dined at banquets in a Maharajah's palace weren't dazzling enough experiences, then the treatment the team receives in California will have them floating on air. After winning matches, they will be elevated on a podium in the manner of Olympic medallists. The glittering gala champagne dinners will go on for days. Rising above the ephemeral, the short-lived and the transient are the solid, weighty, *huge* sale prices for the ponies to high-profile buyers: Spencer Tracey, Walt Disney, David Selznick. The prices paid by these luminaries even outshine those paid by the Maharajah of Jaipur.

The wonder of it all will come to a shockingly abrupt end. A dramatic spiral downhill, like the crash to earth from a punctured air balloon. Eldest son Mack—still nursing that huge chip on his shoulder—will run off with all the money, his shocked teammates left stranded. The brazen thief flies into Sydney Airport and sets about investing his ill-gotten gains into establishing a cotton factory in competition with that of his mother.

Parry O'Connor's reverse-charge call from America leaves the Grand Matriarch in a state of complete shock. But, with characteristic stoicism, she offers it up to God and sets about making arrangements to get the three stranded players home.

Eric Keen's dreams of becoming an international polo player are cruelly shattered, destiny having dealt him a hard blow. An additional jolt to the already besieged O'Connor sense of dignity comes when errant eldest son, Mack, manages to lose the ill-gotten gains from the fabulous pony sale in California. The cotton factory he sets up goes broke, and he will suffer the humiliation of being bought out by his mother.

Madge will rave on with increasingly exaggerated versions of her husband's apparent affair with an American film actress, repeating herself like a demented parrot. To shut her up, the inhabitants of 'Rosemont' will step in to soothe the beleaguered wife with a shopping trip to David Jones. Herewith, a new practice is implemented that will become the norm. Opposite Hyde Park, the famous department store becomes the appointed dynasty store of choice. In the years ahead, any O'Connor (or née O'Connor) wife displaying signs of insurrection will be coaxed back to their matrimonial duties with an expensive, good quality outfit, plus shoes and handbag, which Miss

Sill O'Connor, in her role as public relations officer and minister of good taste, will help select.

At the time of the generous family gesture to appease Madge O'Connor, neither the Grand Matriarch, nor her first in command at 'Rosemont', could ever have imagined that an account casually opened for a deeply thwarted wife as a temporary appeasement would become the source of regular and brazen exploitation.

## CHAPTER 5

# THE NORTH SHORE

Friday has dawned and with it comes Agnes's appointment to visit Aunt Marnie. The air is cool and the sky full of fast-moving clouds. She falls in with the quick pace of people rushing to work along Victoria Street to King's Cross railway station. Peak-hour commuters dash in all directions. She squeezes into a packed Eastern Suburbs train into the city, forced in the squash to stand next to a tall man in blue overalls with a hooked nose who reeks of body odour. To avoid further unpleasant peak-hour crushes, she decides to alight at Circular Quay and catch a ferry across the harbour and then board the North Shore train at Milsons Point.

As she is so early for her afternoon appointment with Marnie, she decides to get off the train at Gordon and find Lennox Street. It had already crossed her mind to go there but, for some reason, she had resisted giving the idea the weight of a plan. The family had moved there after her brother Jim, then a toddler, miraculously survived a fall off a high wall onto a grassy stretch in front of their house in Rose Bay. This narrow escape of one of her 'souls for heaven' had caused Grandma to step in to help Agnes's parents find a safer place to live. What Grandma didn't know, however, was that nowhere was safe with a mother whose preferred occupation was staring into space, and an absent father to whom the children were invisible. For, after the catastrophic end of his international polo exploits, Eric had been promoted to sales manager of the cotton factory, which meant he had to constantly travel interstate to visit branch offices and see clients.

As Agnes's train moves further up the North Shore line, houses and gardens expand and clusters of trees thicken beside the tracks. Agnes and her school friend, Maria, once rode their bikes through the sleepy streets outside the train window, freewheeling down hills and peddling like crazy up the other side. She now recalls the thrill of discovering deciduous trees—the wonder of the autumn colours and the sight of bare-bone branches. Henceforth, as she knew no other area with deciduous trees, she has associated falling leaves with money and luxury, along with flowering shrubs and trees like camellias, rhododendrons, magnolias, and azaleas, which proliferated in the suburbs of the Upper North Shore.

Gordon Station hasn't changed. It is still the leafy backwater she remembers. She heads for the left-hand exit and consults a map in the Gregory's Street Directory she had bought at King's Cross. Poor concentration makes her a bad map reader. She wishes she wasn't so muddled. She starts to feel like a spy, prying into a past that doesn't feel fully her own.

Lennox Street is the second parallel street after Glenview Street. She stops to photograph the sign from different angles as if it is an important monument. Which, for Agnes, it undoubtedly is. A fanfare screech of cicadas greets her entrance. She is pulled forward by unseen hands, drawn to the mottled light pattern on the ground, imprinted there by the tall trees interrupting the sun. The kaleidoscopic patterns hold a deep resonance. The early morning clouds have disappeared. The sky is now a roof of cobalt blue.

She had never lingered in the Lennox Street house. She would jump out of bed early in the morning and eat a bowl of rice bubbles, which she drowned in milk and sugar. She liked them every way—even dry straight out of the packet. She would slurp down the mix in a hurry, eager to get to the tree house in the bush and see if there was a message for her in the bark post box, before rushing back to get dressed to catch the bus to school. She would skip down the street singing the advertising jingle: *snap crackle pop, snap crackle pop, snap crackle pop.*

She observes that the native wattles, dense clumps of gums and banksias trees, and the former maze of paths winding through them, have been pushed back behind new roads. She wonders if the tree house is still there. She doesn't have the right clothes to go and look, as she has worn stockings and high heels and a striped cotton dress under a white jacket in preparation to see Aunt Marnie. She decides to come back, more suitably dressed, on another occasion.

As she turns back up the street, she sees a horizontal flash of yellow and red that must have been a rosella or parrot, for she recognises the familiar squawking. The atmosphere pulses as the midday heat intensifies and the cicadas up their pitch. She can hear the calls of faraway currawongs above the treetops and wonders if the little finches and willy wagtails still chirp and bob amongst the low-lying scrub in the early morning in their search for seeds.

The street is deserted. The parked cars look as if they have been asleep forever. She knows it instantly, although the number on the caramel brick bungalow has changed from 13 to 11A and a huge L. J. Hooker sign, with 'SOLD' plastered over it, smothers the façade. Along with the other dwellings in the street, the house is built well back into the block. The wide, flat grassy strip between the low brick garden wall and the kerb of the street is still there—once the no-man's land where she played with the other kids in the street. She can see through the smeared glass of the bare windows that the house is empty. The dusty rooms are covered in piles of old newspapers.

She spreads a handkerchief on the step leading up to the balcony entrance so as not to dirty her clothes and sits down. She is suddenly unsure what to do next.

An elderly lady with heavy frown lines and a big fleshy nose appears on the other side of the low wall. She is accompanied by an old, droopy-eyed golden Labrador on a tattered brown lead. The woman shouts. Her voice is a little shaky, yet strong:

*Are you the new owner?*

*No. No I'm not!*

When the woman cups her hand around her ear, Agnes stands up and moves towards her:

*I used to live in this house when I was a child.*

*Well, my goodness me. I probably knew you! I've been in No 23 for 66 years. Name's Beryl. I moved in when I was 19. As a young bride. Now I'm the last of the original owners.*

One side of the woman's face is slightly fixed. It appears numb, giving her speech a laboured impediment. Agnes wonders if Aunt Marnie might look like that. The woman seems expectant, as if requiring more elaborate information, and so she mumbles a response:

*We were only here for a few years. As kids. It was a glorious time and then we left.*

She realises she is struggling to remember. The woman regards her quizzically:

*Were you here when Paul Rushford had that terrible accident?*

*No. We weren't here then.*

Agnes has replied rather too abruptly, for she cannot bear to admit the fact of the matter. That they had left this house only *because* of the accident. Paul's name coming right at her from the long-distant past has really startled her. But Beryl, apparently, is on a roll:

*It happened after a terrible storm in late January. Sydney had been sweltering in a heatwave. Bush fires were raging in the Blue Mountains. The nights were stifling, dogs were panting, and cats disappeared under the houses. Steam poured out of car radiators. A section of track buckled, stopping the trains. And there was so much dust! Tar on the road melted like gravy boiling in a saucepan!*

She is sounding like an Old Testament prophet as she continues to paint the scene in melodramatic tones:

*Late in the afternoon, everything went still. It was how you would imagine the Last Judgement. I had a presentiment that something awful was going to happen. Thunder exploded like the stamping foot of an angry beast. Lightning cut jagged lines in the dark sky. Then waves of torrential rain. Cyclonic downpours raged throughout Sydney and East Gordon all night, and the next day, the street was covered in fallen debris. A black overhead power line had come down. It was dangling from the roof of your old house like a giant snake. Right here. Fell onto the grassy stretch exactly where I am standing.*

Agnes is aware of a familiar horrible sensation, like ants crawling over her skin. Her ears are ringing. She feels she might be going to be sick. But the grim tale isn't over yet:

*We all loved Paul. Kids in the street followed him like he was the Pied Piper. He was going to be a scientist—like his father. He must have thought the overhead cable was safe to pick up. He was in bare feet. He lit up like a firecracker. They put him in an iron lung, but the shock was too severe. He died the next day in the Royal North Shore Hospital.*

Agnes recalls it all. It has hit her like a sledgehammer. It has emerged from a dark place. Like so much past horror, it has never left her. Denial has rendered it inert. Memories now come tumbling like stones crashing down a ravine. Her stomach contorts. She had been holding Paul's hand when he picked up the cable—but was saved because she let go. She can't listen to this any longer. An old woman, probably lonely, who is subjecting her to these histrionics.

As if reading her mind, Beryl pauses. It makes Agnes wonder if the woman has worked out that she is being deliberately evasive. However, the coup de grace was on its way:

*There was a silly woman living in your house who they all blamed for not reporting the live cable to the authorities. Paul's family left the area after he died. Then the next lot in your house changed the number from unlucky 13 to 11A. Must have been before your time.*

Yes. Must have been.

She thanks Beryl rapidly, managing to collect herself. She is aware she has responded in a dismissive way, but she is desperate to distance herself and establish some form of inner equilibrium. In a last-ditch effort to be polite, she bends down to stroke the dog:

*Well, lovely to meet you both. Goodbye.*

Agnes slowly plods down the street with heavy feet. She wants to describe to someone the internal tearing apart she is feeling. If she had been back home, in Mallorca, she would have rung her psychiatrist and made a special appointment. It would be superfluous, unethical, to ring him from Sydney. But his last words to her now come back like a gift:

*You're no longer a child, Agnes. Assimilating knowledge of the past can only make you stronger.*

Everything has changed. A relentless sadness infuses the clear sunny day with a strange haziness. She must cancel Aunt Marnie. She cannot possibly force herself to be nice to her today. She would need all her energies to face this cruel bitch of a woman whom she hasn't seen for thirty years. Strange that she has never before thought of her aunt's behaviour as cruel. Probably, as always, she has accepted she deserved the punishment, even though she has never known what she was supposed to have done.

She dials the number of the care home on the mobile she hired at the airport. What luck! Marnie was having a bath and couldn't come to the phone. The nurse is very understanding and would give her aunt the message. And, yes, Agnes would be in touch to arrange another visit, so goodbye for now.

She slumps onto a wooden bench at Gordon railway station and watches vacantly as trains come and go. She can't remember ever cancelling a meeting at the last minute, especially because she felt she could not cope. But she is positive she would have blundered on mindlessly and made a complete fool of herself. It is, without doubt, the right decision. As she stares fixedly ahead of her a buried memory emerges.

I am so excited when I find Paul's note under the bark in the tree house telling me to come to his house that day. Boys of 13 usually shun nine-year-old girls like me, but Paul isn't like the others. When I appear at the door, he pulls me through the house with the rest of the kids. He goes barefoot like Robinson Crusoe, and Lennox Street is his island. His Jewish parents came to Australia from Berlin to escape the Nazis. They love each other like the songs on the radio. The laboratory at the back of their house, where Paul and his father do scientific experiments, has a small sink, a Bunsen burner, Petri dishes and lines of glass retorts scattered along what looks like a wide kitchen bench. They have lots of books in their house: on shelves, on tables, on chairs and even in the toilet.

The day the storm ends, my mother shouts at me. Paul is on the ground. There is a bald man with a garden rake trying to get the cable out of his hand. My mother brings out rubber mats from under her washing-up tray. I don't know what to do. I feel so terrible that I climb up the tall tree opposite and stay there, hidden behind the foliage. They put Paul in the back of the ambulance on a stretcher and speed off with the siren screeching. I wish I could go with him. It is nearly dark when I come down from the tree.

There is a lot of running around and shouting in Lennox Street after that. Angry-faced people bang on our front door with heavy fists, yelling, their teeth bared like growling dogs. They say bad things about my mother, but I don't understand what they mean. Two men come in a police car. It has a light on top and a siren that isn't turned on. A tall man wearing a suit sits in the back. He asks things and writes in a notebook. He can't talk to my mother because she isn't there. She went on a flying boat with her mother to New Zealand. My little brother and I shake all the time. Nobody ever comes to our house, so it feels like we are living somewhere else. I can't see the neighbours' faces. I don't recognise anyone. I keep seeing my hand pulling away from Paul's hand, and his body lighting up in a purple haze. A blue glow hovers around his lips. I don't understand how it all happened and why he didn't get up. But I know my mother has blamed me. My father too.

Perhaps I should go and find Dora. Dora taught me all about shadow-plays.

*When I first got to know her, she told me that in England, where she grew up, she would have been called eccentric, which was okay for women of a certain age. People feel uncomfortable when they can't slot others into boxes, Dora says. She once told me people see her like anything from a bag lady to a criminal in hiding. But she doesn't care what they think. I don't understand a lot of what she says, but I get the same good feeling with her as when I have my hair cut, and how I imagine a cat feels inside when it purrs.*

*I am the only one in the street to get inside Dora Chadwick's gate. I help her load sacks of clay and white powders, Japanese paintbrushes, a basket of shopping and garden tools—all piled into a wheelbarrow parked on the brick path that leads to her front door. Her house is hidden behind a row of pine trees.*

*Dora has books in her house like Paul's parents but, unlike their place, all the walls are covered in colourful paintings. The hallway through the middle of the house leads to a double studio room at the back. There are glass doors looking onto a stone-paved terrace which is overhung by a giant jacaranda tree. Clay pots are dotted everywhere; honeycomb shapes, and pregnant-bellied shapes, trailing ferns and variegated leaves and tropical flowers sprout out of them. Birds splash and shake their feathers on the edge of a clay bird bath. It is the most beautiful garden I have ever seen. When I turn back to the front of the house, I notice the whole inside wall of the studio is covered in posters of Australian wildflowers.*

*Dora says: You must have seen these flowers in the bush?*

*I've seen the bottlebrush and waratah, I reply shyly. Naming things isn't my strong point. With most adults I get anxious and remember nothing. But I shall never forget what Dora has told me. She says I've fallen in love with the wildflowers. She says she supposes if you've grown up with a thing, it's not quite the same as travelling the seas to discover it. I don't know how to reply, so I shrug my shoulders and try hard to look at her with the good intentions I feel. She shows me how she distils her drawings of wildflowers into a few fluid lines that she uses to decorate big vases and the inside of ceramic bowls. She works the clay in a room with a sink off the back studio and fires the pots in a brick kiln in a garden shed. Those she is satisfied with are sold through a gallery somewhere.*

*Dora asks: Would you like to see some tricks with light?*

*I have hardly nodded 'Yes' before curtains are pulled, a screen comes down, and the lights are off. Dora fixes the beam on a stand and picks up a cut-out shape on a thin stick: one of a bird, then of a cat, and then a butterfly. She holds them between the source of light and the screen so that the form intercepts the light and beams the shadow onto the white screen behind. What I'm making artificially is what you see happen naturally on the ground as the trees interrupt the sun, Dora says. Then she splays her big hands in front of the light to make the shape of a bat in flight. Next, she opens her fingers to make a huge spider. A pointed fist creates the head of an ostrich, and a cupped hand with two open fingers a snail with antennae. The closer the shape to the light, the bigger the image and the further away, the smaller it becomes. I am transfixed.*

*I feel strange here, in the company of a woman others view with suspicion, but Dora ignores my reticence and persists in encouraging me to experiment with the shapes for myself. Once I start, I become engrossed and forget everything.*

*Dora exclaims with a smile—Look at all the shapes you're making! Now look at these wonders!*

*She pulls out papier-mâché figures she has collected on her travels in South-East Asia. There are kings and queens in gold-trimmed robes, warriors on horseback wielding swords, dancing girls with legs and arms that can be moved like puppets. She works them below the screen in front of the light, changing her voice accordingly for the different characters.*

*They dance, they fight, and they sing. All are calling my name. It sounds like gibberish to me, as the voices are in a foreign language, but it is thrilling all the same.*

*Before leaving the following day to join her sister in England, Dora Chadwick gives me a book: Wildflowers of Australia by Thistle Y. Harris, which I keep for years – that is until it disappears, along with everything I own, when I am 16.*

*Inside the cover is written:*
*To Dear Agnes,*
*Well done. Go on being yourself.*
*To see the world in a grain of sand*
*And heaven in a wildflower.*
*William Blake, 'Songs of Innocence'*
*Love Dora Chadwick.*

\* \* \*

Shadows are starting to appear when Agnes rouses herself from where she has been sitting. She has barely moved for hours, seated quietly on a bench at Gordon train station. Remembering. And remembering. Now she no longer has the station to herself. The handful of passengers coming and going during the afternoon has swelled to a crowd because the first commuters are arriving home from work.

She jumps up suddenly, and hops on the next train bound for Wynyard. As soon as she gets back to the Grantham Apartments, Agnes phones Jean to tell her she has had to cancel Marnie because of a stomach bug. And, for the same reason, would have to cancel dinner on Saturday night. She knows instantly that she has spoken to Jean in a tone far too terse. She is still holding back a dangerous urge to unburden herself. There is a short pause before Jean speaks:

*Well, I'll be in contact when I get back and we'll choose a date for a get-together with the others.*

Jean sounds suddenly formal and is obviously wounded by Agnes's sharp rebuff. The call ends.

The Lennox Street visit has left Agnes exhausted and disillusioned with the whole O'Connor clan. She looks at the clothes in the wardrobe she had carefully chosen to impress the aunts and wonders why she bothered. She cannot now imagine sitting at a table and making polite conversation with any of them.

Deciding to take a swim in the pool, she puts on a towelling robe she has found behind the bathroom door over her costume. She rides the lift to the lower ground floor. Guests in the apartments will be getting ready to go out for dinner and Agnes is hoping to have the pool to herself.

She is in luck. The pool is at her complete disposal. The over-chlorinated water makes her skin itch, but the view of the harbour lifts her spirits. She swims up and down in a mesmerising rhythm trying to tranquillise the earthquake that has taken place inside her. The temperature is caressingly warm and soothing, but it is not enough to calm her churning thoughts.

She towels herself off and settles on a lounger under a light, knowing she is slowly being taken over by a past she has, till now, assiduously resisted. It doesn't have to do with her willpower, her wanting, or not wanting. She simply feels a profound unease, as if she is a ship moving into uncharted waters. It is like waking from a dream into an empty space—a space that is hers, alone, to fill. *Yes. You are alone*, she tells herself. As the old saying goes, you are born alone, and you die alone.

She had retained no memory of Paul when she had arrived in Lennox Street earlier that day, yet everything has flooded back. His smile. His parents. His home. The accident. Indeed, she realises now, in these quiet moments by the pool, that his death explains the irrational fear she has always had of electricity. Something inside her shut down a long time ago on that day. The day she let go of his hand. And survived.

Agnes resolves to stay alone in the apartment and write what she can now remember of the years that followed Paul's death.

It will be a beginning.

# Part Two

'My dream stands in front of me, still warm, and although awake I am still full of its anguish: and then I remember that it is not a haphazard dream, but that I have dreamed it not once but many times since I arrived here. Why is the pain of every day translated so constantly into our dreams, in the ever-repeated scene of the un-listened-to story?'
—*If This Is a Man* by Primo Levi

## CHAPTER 6

# CHATSWOOD

The Keen family reassemble in a single-storey timber house three train stops closer to Sydney on the North Shore—far enough away to be safe from enemy fire in Lennox Street. Surrounded by dark-brick bungalows, their white-painted timber house is situated on a corner at the top of a hill and looks like a lighthouse in a sea of baked brown. An art nouveau-style glass panel of red, blue and yellow lilies above the front door suggests it dates from Federation at the turn of the century.

In her schoolbooks, Agnes writes: *Agnes Keen, The Corner of Rose and Edmond Street, Chatswood.* The address sounds posh, like living in a double-barrelled name. And, as if to compensate for the lost bushland paradise, the surrounding streets are named after flowers: Rose, Daisy, Iris, Tulip, Zinnia and Violet Street all run off the busy artery of Archer Street that cuts the suburb in two.

With a lane running parallel to Rose Street, the block would be an island but for two small brick semi-detached houses facing Archer Street at the end of the back garden. Dirty-faced children spill out of the doors and windows of the semi nearest the lane. Squawks and clouds of feathers, followed by Mrs Cleary's anguished cries, can be heard as her unruly brood persecute chickens in the galvanised iron-roofed shed that abuts the Keen back fence. Plump, with strands of wet hair over her red face, Mrs Cleary is worn ragged with housework and changing nappies. Her kids are too young for Agnes and her brothers, and the parents deemed far too working class for Agnes's mother and father.

A thick wisteria vine in full bloom smothers the roof of a four-posted construction adjacent to the Cleary chook shed. It is where Eric Keen parks his car. Agnes feels sure her parents' choice of house must have been influenced by the sight of those trailing blue flowers under which their love was first kindled in that famous garden on the property in the Great Dividing Range. The purchase of the house, in the normal way of things, has probably been financed by Grandma.

From the front door in Edmond Street, a hall cuts the interior of Agnes's home in two. There are three bedrooms off to the left, on the right is a den, and a living room that no one ever goes into. Agnes's parents sleep in a set of shiny wood single beds in the big front bedroom and Agnes sleeps in the small bedroom next door. Jim resides in what is left of the third small bedroom after the construction of full-length luxury wardrobes to house the adults' clothes.

A step down at the end of the hall and there is the dining room. The kitchen is off to the right and on the left a narrow hallway leads to Bert's spacious bedroom and a dilapidated bathroom. A solemn mahogany sideboard sits strategically against the left-hand dining room wall camouflaging plaster holes. Displayed on its top are polo trophies from India—and from the California debacle. The lath and plaster walls are so fragile that every time the back door in the corner of the long exterior wall is slammed, it triggers a fall of plaster snowflakes. This is exacerbated by the children's habit of dashing out as quickly as possible to avoid a confrontation with their mother. Deterioration of the walls, along with the ugly green and yellow patterned lino on the timber floor—an obstacle course for bare feet—will evidence the family's precarious existence over the next seven years. Lip service is paid to Grandma's vision of re-forming the crumbling interior into a modern home, but after the installation of her parents' wardrobes, followed by the execution of a set of architect's plans for the renovation, all progress has stopped.

Unable to make the leap from word to action, Madge has, from year to year, reiterated to their few visitors (and without the least embarrassment) that the builder will be 'starting next week'. This pronouncement always precedes the ritual of displaying the architect's plans, which live in the top drawer of the sideboard. She would unfurl the detailed drawings, spreading them out on the dining room table by way of explaining the transitory nature of her family's shabby existence. Books would be used to hold down the sides of the tracing paper: *Art Treasures of the World* traps one side, and *Lust for Life*, a biography of Vincent van Gogh that had arrived in the mail with the *Reader's Digest* subscription, anchors the other. The books add gravitas to a ceremony no one escapes.

Having attended the showing of the plans and carrying the two books down the hall from the den so frequently, Agnes has eventually become so familiar with the design that she is called upon, much to her chagrin, to explain the finer details of a construction that will never be realised. In this way, the family live like supporting actors in backstage dressing rooms, preparing for the outdoor theatre where they are obliged to perform their prima donna mother's half-baked script to the world.

Agnes's survival is no easy matter as only the impossible, it seems, will satisfy her mother. She still trades with God to stay alive, but since their arrival in the new house, the very sight of her is an irritant to her deranged parent. If not literal death, she is certainly in danger of being maimed for life. She has unofficially claimed the den as her private space and often sneaks in via the glass doors off the front veranda. This avoids the exposure of direct hall access and a chance encounter with her mother. Sequestered in the den, she peruses a selection of Van Gogh paintings in what has become known in the family as 'The Art Book', for her favourite occupation is to endlessly flick through its pages. She also examines the contents of her mother's orange floral knitting bag—parked on the inside doorknob during the move and long forgotten. What she learns of world events comes from its contents. Entwined amidst a tangle of wool are *Sydney Morning Herald* front pages recording the Bombing of Pearl Harbour, The Allied D-Day Invasion, the Liberation of Paris, Peace Celebrations in Europe, the dropping of the atomic bomb on Hiroshima, and the Coronation of Queen Elizabeth.

Further down in the depths of the bag she has also discovered *Women's Weekly* photos of the polo people her mother loves and admires as they pose at tournaments and picnic races. There are also a few American dollars—presumably left over from her father's ill-fated trip to the Riviera Club—and Madge's flying boat ticket to Auckland.

Agnes's eyes fall heavy with tiredness; she stretches out on the floor to doze. Because of a recurrent nightmare involving a courtroom judge, she now wakes in terror at the very moment the chief judge is about to announce her execution. Her body is always as cold as ice—and she is utterly unable to move.

She has started dreading going to bed. This suffering coincides with an increase in her mother's lethargy—a lassitude so chronic that Madge now screams out to Agnes to bring the cigarettes and gold lighter that live in a cut-glass ashtray on the dressing table only a few steps from the bed in which she reclines. Madge will usually be wearing nothing but a string of cultured pearls, for Agnes's mother believes contact with the skin increases the pearls' lustre, and the process, for some extraordinary reason, is more effective when horizontal rather than vertical.

One evening, overwhelmed by the horror of the relentless nightmare and desperate for help, instead of keeping her usual distance, Agnes hangs around her mother. But, upon broaching the problem, her mother interrupts her and packs her off to do the ironing. It is after being summoned to bring Madge a cup of tea in the bath that Agnes will determine once again to talk to her mother about the nightly torture of nightmares. But before she has a chance to speak, her mother starts raving about one of the aunts:

*That simpering, conniving bitch!*

This is the vitriolic response to news that Aunt Sill has taken Uncle Ben's new wife, Beth, on a trip to David Jones and bought her a sinuous, black Balenciaga tunic dress, weighted at the top with a black fox collar over the shoulders. And, on top of that, the greedy wimp has apparently managed to wangle herself a veiled flowerpot hat. There are shoes and a handbag too, but no descriptive details as yet. Madge is screeching like a banshee and rolling from side to side like a porpoise in a tank:

*She'd suck up to the devil to get what she wants!*

Uncle Ben and Uncle Parry's new wives, Marnie and Beth, were already friends when they met the brothers. It is probably Marnie who has, in all innocence, told Madge about Beth's bonanza shopping trip. But, before long, Marnie's own grievances against the family she married into will provoke her to abandon her gentle-natured friend in favour of the acerbic and feisty Madge.

Madge's mind is jumping wildly now. She swerves from the Balenciaga tunic and unknown shoes and handbag to musing on memories of the ice-blue petticoat under Marnie's wedding dress. The one she still imagines Agnes wearing when she gets married. The tirade culminates in the customary admonishment:

*Agnes—you'll never get a man with a face full of freckles!*

Madge's current obsession with the shopping trip denies Agnes a chance to speak of her nightly suffering. 'Rosemont's' enchantment with Ben's new wife Beth has branded her, in Madge's eyes, as a villainous interloper to be undermined at all costs. It is never clear to Agnes which of the two her mother hates more—her brother Ben, or Beth. Agnes is expected to hate in solidarity with her mother. Any attempt to defend Beth will get her a clip across the ear, so she remains silent.

It is not only Beth who has been indulged by 'Rosemont' largesse. Ben, it seems, has been given the latest model Holden Sedan, while Eric—who drives hundreds of miles in his position as Sales Manager—must still make do with an old Ford. On top of all that,

Aunt Sill's old friend, Patricia Murphy, has divorced her Yank. She is back in Sydney and about to marry a wealthy newspaper man. Plans for a Spring wedding are apparently all over the *Women's Weekly*. The rotating wheel inside her mother's demented head eventually lands on the Hollywood actress who 'kidnapped' Eric all those years ago:

*And the nerve of that sly bit of work in America who got her hooks into your father!*

Agnes is constantly baffled by the way in which her mother regurgitates the past, triggered by the indignation of some recent event. What is it that causes her to care about lives that have nothing to do with her own?

Mercifully, the hot bathwater starts to soothe Madge's agitation. Indoctrinated in the strictest modesty by Grandma and the nuns at school, Agnes always grapples for fixed points in the bathroom when she attends her mother's bath-side so she can avoid looking at her body. Below the maternal chin lies mortal sin. Agnes must be careful to keep her soul clean in case she dies before making a last confession. It helps that the narrow space between wall and tub obliges her to sit in the foetal position with her knees almost in her mouth and her head stretched back. Focusing on the peeling paintwork on the ceiling, she keeps very still so as not to irritate her mother, until a maternal shriek over a past resentment triggers a fresh snowstorm of plaster. At such times, Agnes assiduously leaps up to catch the flakes before they hit the water, aware that she can rely on her mother ignoring anything that requires the instigation of a repair.

Although she detests it, Agnes feels, in a strange way, privileged to be her mother's confidante and will henceforth equate listening to other people's problems as being allotted a special place in their hearts. What she already knows, at nine years old, is that tragedy, for her mother, does not mean premature death, war, fatal disease, accident, loss, betrayal, or hunger as in the great works of fiction, but is the redirection—the veering off unexpectedly in another direction—of money, property, or gifts she expects to come her way.

Still burning to talk of her recurrent nightmare, Agnes hooks her eyes onto the streaky flames that run along the metal plate below the gas heater, which are constantly reigniting to keep My Lady's water hot. A daddy-long-legs struggles in a spider's web in the corner of the small frosted-glass window positioned high up near the ceiling. Her mother's neck is perilous territory, like a lighthouse warning a ship off its course. The devil is tempting. The prospect of boiling in oil in hell is ever-present. Agnes, though desperate to unburden herself, knows she really should choose another moment. She hears her mother chide:

*Look at me when I'm talking to you, for Christ's sake!*

Agnes's last refuge from the devil is to fix her eyes on the rusty drip marks scarred into the enamel under the taps. It is where her mother's feet surface to reveal the ten crimson stop lights on her toenails. She can't confront the whole, but dislikes the body under the water in bits, starting with the feet. Drowsy from the steam and trying not to listen, her willpower deserts her, and she confronts a vision of the floating breasts. After a brief investigation, there is some consolation derived by concluding that breasts couldn't really be a sin because there is a picture in 'The Art Book' by Jean Forquet (French School) of the Virgin Mary holding baby Jesus with one whole breast falling out of her bodice. But, unlike the Blessed Virgin, her mother is a freak, devoid of maternal instincts, which makes her body tainted and, somehow, perverse. Regardless, what *must* be a mortal sin is the black hairy fox, now being soaped with abandon under the water as Agnes struggles to avert her eyes.

Unwanted confidences continue to be heaped upon her as she awaits her chance to speak, her mother has come full circle and has returned to the subject of Beth and the Balenciaga dress:

*That grasping, heartless bitch! She's completely fooled Sill! On pain of death, Agnes, close your eyes and hope to die if you ever repeat a WORD I tell you!*

The mounting pressure of the unspoken is killing Agnes. In utter frustration, she hears herself scream at her mother:

*It's you who are the heartless bitch! You're a wicked mother who only thinks of herself!*

Madge rises out of the bath like Lazarus back from the dead. She hits her small daughter across the face, before falling backwards in astonishment to create a resultant flood over the bathroom floor.

Agnes is already apologising. She kneels in the swirling pool of water as if the bathtub is a sacred shrine. She no longer cares about the nudity. She holds the towel out for her mother. But she must—*must*—spill out the nightmare and beg her to stop it for her sanity's sake.

She tells all. Tells of the way the judge and jury always shake their heads and proclaim her guilty. Of how she is always struck dumb. Always unable to defend herself. She begs her to make everything better. She promises she will do *anything* her mother asks, if only she will help her stop the nightly horror.

Her mother appears to listen, but then Agnes makes the fatal mistake of mentioning the visions that often accompany the nightmare. Visions of the electrocution. The mere mention of Paul's name pitches Madge into a deep fury:

*If you don't shut up about that boy, I'm going to give you a clout that you'll remember for the rest of your life! He was a troublemaker! His father was a madman, and the wife wasn't much better. They should have kept him in check. They let him do whatever he wanted. Budding scientist?! Little genius?! He should have known better than to pick the cable up!*

*But I feel terrible when the judge says, 'Guilty as charged' and my voice won't come out!*

*You shouldn't feel like that!*

*But I DO feel like that!*

*Well, STOP feeling like that, or I'll give you such a hiding you won't be able to sit down for a week!*

*I'm going to tell Daddy! He'll understand and want to help me. He might make it go away! Someone HAS to do SOMETHING, because I can't bear it!*

Of course, Agnes never speaks to her father. As an adult she can vaguely remember how, straight after the electrocution, he bizarrely accused her outright of not looking after her mother! But she is driven to such despair by her nightly terrors she has, in the heat of the moment, decided to bypass the usual agent of contact with him—Madge—and go direct. Perhaps he really *could* help her?

But Agnes is wrong about Daddy. It's unusual for him to be home early from work as, normally, he gets home after the children are in bed. As he walks into the house, she runs to him and clings to his knees. It is a chilly evening in early spring. The back door is open, and the jasmine in bloom on the paling fence is filling the room with perfume.

Eric Keen looks down in annoyance at his small daughter's hands as they clutch at the front of his treasured camel hair coat. Agnes pleads with him:

*Stop the nightmare, Daddy! They say I'm guilty! My voice won't come!*

*What's going on? Get up, Agnes, and don't be so silly.*

He tries to push her aside as he calls out to tell her mother that he's just seen Alex McLeod at the Royal Automobile Club. An encounter with anyone from the polo crowd is a cause for celebration, especially a sacrosanct character like Alex McLeod.

Agnes is so crushed by her father's casual indifference that she drops to her knees, covering his shoes in hot tears. She can smell the boot polish on the leather. Eric Keen always keeps his clothes spotless and footwear shining. When Madge spins out of the kitchen, excited to hear about Alex McLeod, the sight of Agnes's supplication infuriates her. She rushes at Agnes and screams:

*Let go of him! Let go of him, this instant!*

When Agnes persists in clinging onto her father's coat, Madge hits her fingers with a rubber egg flip from the kitchen. Agnes looks up at her father imploringly. His swimming-pool-blue eyes are bloodshot and swirl uncertainly. He is irritated at having the conversation piece he brought home to his wife side-tracked by this vexing child's interference. Agnes is still holding on like grim death as Madge slaps her hard across the face. Agnes feels as if she's been hit by a truck. A high-pitched ringing swamps her hearing. Looking up from the floor, she sees her mother hook her piercing eyes into those of her husband:

*Smack her, Eric! She's telling lies. Going on about nightmares and that brat of a boy in Gordon who caused us all that trouble. She's driving me crazy. I told her to shut up a million times, yet the same rubbish keeps pouring out of her! For Christ's sake, smack some sense into her!*

Eric Keen looks bewildered, standing just inside the back door with his briefcase still in his hand as his wife goads him with a diabolical chant:

*Smack her! Smack her! She's too strong-willed for her own good. She never stops moaning about her feelings. What right's she got to talk about feelings?! She's got no right to complain! She's lucky to have a roof over her head! Beat some sense into her, Eric! NOW!*

The briefcase falls out of Eric's hands onto the cracked lino floor. Suddenly, without looking down at his daughter, he pulls the belt out of the waist of his pants and cuts Agnes hard around the legs. Agnes runs into her bedroom and shuts the door, leaning against it with all her might as there is no key. Her father follows, hot on her tail. He almost squashes her arm as she struggles to keep the door shut. He bangs on it with his fist:

*Open this bloody door immediately!*

She can hear the thwack of the belt striking the back of the door, imagining the pain in her legs intensifying. He temporarily hesitates. But, within seconds, she hears her mother behind him, shrieking:

*Punish her! Do what I tell you!*

The bedroom door is flung open with her parents' combined might. Agnes manages to scramble out past their feet and bolts for the back door:

## CHAPTER 6  CHATSWOOD

*Catch her before she gets away!*

Agnes is leaping over the step down into the dining room and, with a moment of undiluted joy, sees that the back door is open—her father's brown leather briefcase is leaning against it and has prevented it from closing. But he tackles her like a rugby player. She comes down with a thud and feels a terrible rain of blows around her legs as his belt descends with violent force. Madge's anger has jumped into her husband, the way a bush fire jumps a road, instantly igniting the brush on the other side. His swimming-pool eyes are fixed on his wife, as he mercilessly cuts into Agnes's flesh with the belt. His carelessness leaves Agnes dumbstruck. Tangled up in their great love, she is invisible.

She knows she is in serious danger. Scurrying like a crab towards the back door, in agony, she screams for help through the gap. Her mother interrupts her escape trajectory to the street by slamming the door shut and so Agnes has no choice but to beg her for mercy:

*Stop, stop, please stop! I'll never say anything again! I'll never talk about it again!*

Blood is running down her legs. She is spreadeagled on the floor. The last thing she sees as she stares up, before she passes out, is her tabby cat, Ness, out on the veranda. Balanced on top of the canary cage, the cat is peering down at the tiny yellow bird imprisoned beneath.

The little bird could just as easily be herself, towered over and entrapped by these two enraged, unreasonable, adults.

## CHAPTER 7

# PENICILLIN

Agnes wonders if she has died like the Little Match Girl in the Hans Christian Anderson fairytale, who, after freezing to death on earth, finds a warm fire in heaven. She doesn't want to be in the house on the corner of Rose and Edmond Street, so she keeps her eyes shut. She feels peaceful, and is not alone, for she has her picture-show in her head. Cloud-formed balloon men, wearing black and white striped pants, somersault across the screen of her mind. They bounce around on pogo sticks. They juggle bright objects. They leap on one another's shoulders and then they are gone. Her mind-screen goes black like an intermission at the pictures. Then in comes a pod of dolphins, swivelling balls on their noses, clapping flippers and leaping through golden loops before floating off. Agnes wants them back but knows her willpower can only bring exploding ink spots and darkness. She cannot influence what arrives on the screen. Performances don't end, but merge into others. But, even in a blackout, Agnes knows new figures, animals, shapes, colours will arrive—if she waits patiently.

She is deeply immersed in a jungle landscape when she detects a smell like toothpaste and hears a male voice she doesn't recognise:

*My pretty? Is there any one home in there?*

Gentle words float down from a peppermint tongue like a shower of stars from a magic wand. She is gazing into the kindly grey eyes of a bald, portly man with several double chins. When she tries to sit up, she falls back. The big face distorts like a reflection in the

Hall of Mirrors. She surrenders the struggle and closes her eyes. A soft, fleshy hand gently brushes strands of hair off her wet forehead. A sucking sound indicates a peppermint imprisoned behind teeth:

*I'm Doctor Finnegan. How are you feeling?*

Blubbering about feelings has ended her up in the present predicament. The doctor's interest in her astonishes her, but she hesitates before replying in case her mother is listening. She tries to lift her head to see if Madge is there, but flops back on the pillow. She feels limp and dizzy and her throat hurts when she speaks:

*My cat was on top of the canary cage. I have two cats, Ginger and Ness. Ness, the tabby one, insists on sleeping there. I call him Ness, like the end of my name, Agnes. When I lift him off the cage he always comes back. Please believe me. I'm not guilty. I don't know what I did. They never say. They point fingers and say, 'Guilty as charged,' and then pass a sentence I don't hear. I can't get my voice out.*

*You're not guilty of anything, my pretty. You're an innocent child. We almost lost you. We're rejoicing with the angels that you're back with us. Don't fret yourself now.*

*She's not talking that nonsense again is she, doctor?*

The sudden harsh interruption makes Agnes shudder. She closes her eyes as her mother's cautionary hand tightens on her wrist. From far away she hears the doctor's warm and friendly tone change. Amazingly, he is scolding her mother:

*Severe throat infection... raging fever... mouth ulcers... care... nourishment... this child is in poor physical health...*

Days and nights merge. Her picture-show goes fuzzy. Black spiders crawl over her. Snakes slither in the folds of the sheets. One minute she is on fire and the next so cold she turns to ice. She waits for the smell of peppermint and the touch of the cool pudgy hand. When the doctor does return, she hears her mother attempt to take him on:

*She's very self-willed, doctor. We can't control her.*

*Mrs O'Connor, your child is still chronically run-down and very seriously ill… and you still haven't told me how on earth she got those deep cuts on her legs…*

Aware the doctor favours her over her mother makes Agnes fears Madge's vengeance. So, when she feels a little stronger, she praises Madge's cooking to him. Informs him that her mother carries her meals into her on a tray. She doesn't have to make this up, for Madge is a good cook, and the curried eggs on toast and the kidneys and bacon in brown sauce on toast are the best flavours Agnes has ever tasted. She is ravenously hungry now she is recovering. Bowls of strawberries and ice cream are gradually replacing visions of the gnarled face of the judge in the courtroom. But what Agnes doesn't share with the doctor is the unfettered joy of eating in peace, without her mother constantly hovering behind to grab each dirty plate.

Penicillin saves her life and iron injections cure the anaemia. And, today, the physician is banging hard on the front door as if he suspects he may not be let in. When Madge rushes inside the bedroom to check the state of her daughter's sheets, Agnes sees that her face is already set in the silly, false sympathetic expression she puts on for these medical visits. Wearing a red-and-white chequered, freshly ironed gingham apron with a frill around the bib over her dress, her mother looks like a magazine model advertising a cleaning product. It's amazing to Agnes to see her mother's outdoor personality, for once, enacted indoors. Ever since the doctor has emphasised a continuance of strict hygiene, Madge vacuums his daily visit trajectory up the hall from the front door to the same worn green carpet around Agnes's bed.

She hears her mother dash down the hall to open the front door to Doctor Finnegan, who has come to take the stitches out of Agnes's forehead:

*Close to the hairline, my pretty, so your beauty is secure. With that face full of lovely sun kisses, nobody will notice it.*

Not only do the dreaded freckles receive an upgrade, but a hairdresser in the shopping centre in Chatswood will shortly call Agnes's carrot top a 'strawberry blonde'. Indeed, these lovely compliments will hold up a mirror to another world. Agnes isn't aware she suffers because it is all she has known. Living in a combat zone, she is overly vulnerable to the worth of a few crumbs of affection that need no repayment, for they are the normal expression of civilised natures.

When the day eventually arrives for her to get out of bed, the doctor will ask her mother to leave the room as he wishes to speak to her daughter in private. Madge will chide him in a haughty tone:

*There is nothing you need to say to my daughter that can't be said in front of me.*

*Please Mrs Keen—with respect. Don't make this awkward.*

Madge will reluctantly leave the room and Agnes will always remember how he closed the door firmly behind her:

*Now, my pretty. I'd like you to tell me how your parents treat you. Don't be afraid, you can trust me completely.*

The idea of telling on her mother and father will strike Agnes with horror. The maternal ear must surely be pressed to the door. She will feel like a worm being cut in two. Why had Doctor Finnegan put her in this position? She has never been asked for her opinion on anything. She is terrified to say the wrong thing. Yet, when he asks her about physical abuse, for a moment she will hesitate. But fear of more violence will stimulate an emphatic denial. Desperately confused, she will shout out loudly, so her eavesdropping mother can overhear:

*I have no complaints against my parents!*

Had she known what lay ahead, she might have responded differently.

Eric Keen was away on business in Brisbane while his daughter lay fighting for her life. Neither parent mentions the beating in the dining room again, but it is merely the first of other senseless physical punishments her mother will impose and which her father will carry out. Punishments caused, if caused at all, by trumped-up stuff that has far more to do with the chemistry between the self-absorbed pair than with their daughter's behaviour.

Agnes views her father as a victim like herself. She feels sorry for him. She believes her mother has put a spell on him and he is not responsible for his actions. In Agnes's teenage years, her mother will insist in a distasteful tone:

*Your father loves you.*

She will say it as if it is something she would like to alter. Agnes suspects it is not normal to beat someone you love without giving them a chance to explain themselves. Yet, whatever happens to her, whatever punishment is meted out over her growing-up years, Agnes will never blame her father.

Adding to Agnes's confusion, her mother will suddenly call her Darling, or Possum. Unexpected endearments her baffled daughter adores. But they also make her doubt if what she is experiencing is actually happening. Nothing is named and she doesn't have the complicated language to explain 'hypocrisy'. During the weeks recovering her health, the atmosphere inside the ungainly white timber house will seem rinsed clean. Agnes will sleep soundly and wake to the sound of music on the radio and the scent of frangipani flowers floating in through the open window. The nightmare over, again, she has survived. Yet, at gut level, she will know she has been changed forever by what has happened.

She will keep out of her mother's way and be liberated from the embittered woman's ravings as, with the timely installation of a phone, Madge's gripes will be redirected to Aunt Marnie.

Henceforth, the line pulses hot for an hour a day as the two women trash their relatives, along with all the ubiquitous trollops and harlots that have the temerity to steal other women's husbands.

## CHAPTER 8

# THE FARM

Is it divine intervention? Nobody knows what prompts Grandma to leave St Joseph's church after early Mass wearing her flamboyant red hat with the feathers and, instead of returning home for breakfast, drive into the country in the Humber to buy land. In shocked amazement, Eric, Ben and Parry, corralled in the cotton factory boardroom, receive the news that a hundred acres have been purchased for a polo base. Excitement increases as they bump over potholes on the dirt road in convoy after the Humber. Up and over a hill speeds the matriarch's beast of a vehicle, kicking up a whirlwind of dust before stopping, abruptly, at the decreed site for the stables. Four years on, the dream of a polo dynasty that died with Mack's betrayal is resurrected. Rumour has it that Mack now sells encyclopaedias door to door. No one mentions his name, although Parry relays a recent call from a desperate man, vowing in a drunken slur everlasting vengeance against Eric. It is a threat that neither Parry, nor anyone else, takes seriously. It's in the past. The file closed. The page turned. An hour's drive from Sydney, situated between Liverpool and Camden, the hundred acres will be known simply as—The Farm.

A workforce of family and friends mobilise to build the stables over weekends. With hard work threatening, Madge puts a picnic basket for her husband and sons in the boot of the car and remains at home. Agnes stays at 'Rosemont' on weekends and accompanies Grandma back and forth in the Humber. It is a happy, festive time and Agnes imagines it like the communal effort of medieval towns to build the great cathedrals Dora Chadwick once told her about. Uncles, aunts, dogs, and children tumble out of cars, laughing, making faces and shouting. Most of them city kids, they revel in the space to chase each other and roll down the grassy hill above the burgeoning stables, where Grandma plans to construct the grand homestead in the country that Madge constantly pines after.

Agnes can't wait to hear the blare of the horn that announces Jean Pales and her husband Richard's arrival with their three small girls and a few friends. Scottish-born Richard will take Mack's place as the fourth member of the polo team. Alongside the rumbustious, swarthy uncles, refined Richard Pales looks straight at you calmly, and with a clear gaze. He listens patiently and can alter himself like a chameleon to match others. Agnes likes his Scottish accent and is in awe of the way in which he captures trees and landscapes in his sketchbook. She watches avidly as his pencil flies over the small page and will forever treasure the guardian angel he has drawn for her, which hangs over her bed.

The group joins Grandma with spades and picks to clear the low-lying scrub for the stables. Bent over on hands and knees, they move like a swarm of locusts in formation until, by the end of the first morning, they can peg out the new buildings. A line of stables and a feed room will occupy one side, and an equipment room with a front porch—called the tack room—will emerge at the top of the slope. It will look down on the stables and beyond to the new polo field in the distance. The combined structure will create an L-shape that will be squared off with a fence on the other two sides. Further discussion provokes alteration of pegs and string. Uncle Ben has technical knowledge from his engineering training. Richard Pale and Eric Keen know carpentry and Uncle Parry is a competent handyman.

A contractor digs two dams—one on the paddock inside the entrance gate and another on the plateau above the stable block, where a local builder will erect a small timber house for a groom to live in and care for the horses during the week. Fleets of trucks with materials arrive in such quick succession, and the acceleration of the structure is so fast it looks like a film on fast-forward.

Because of Madge's hostility to even a single nail being hammered in the walls at home, Agnes's excitement to be part of a construction project is palpable. Her world has come alive. She *loves* making things and will, in future, never miss a chance to look through a hole in the fence of *any* building site. She joins the other kids in painting the timbers for the new stables with a harsh-smelling wood protector that stains exposed skin iodine yellow.

Sausages, chops, hamburgers, and steaks sizzle on the barbeque grill at lunchtime. The smell is intoxicating. Potatoes in tinfoil are rolled into the hot coals, the pulpy flesh drenched in butter and pepper and eaten piping hot. The workmen are ravenous. Bottle tops fly in the air. Uncle Parry can cleverly open one top with another. The amber liquid fizzes and spills down the cold glass bottles. The group fans out around the fire to eat—some on picnic rugs on the ground, others propped on building materials. All are encouraged to savour the communal salads and delicacies from one another's picnic baskets. And then it's back to the fire for afternoon tea, where the billie is boiled for the brew, and the women hand around delicious homemade cake. They all call Agnes by name, and for a short time she feels like she belongs to a family of people who *care* about each other.

The exception to the general family enthusiasm is Sill O'Connor, who takes no interest in The Farm. Sill is a thoroughly urban animal who shuns places with snakes, or spiders and flies. And she hates polo.

As for Grandma, and despite the exciting building initiative she has orchestrated, most of the grandchildren continue to find her aloofness intimidating. It is amazing to Agnes how little individual interest she takes in her souls for heaven, having given birth to so many herself. But, because she is used to her grandmother's silence, while the cousins hold back timidly, Agnes volunteers to work alongside her.

Together, they clear the scrub off the flat site for the polo field. She watches Grandma closely. Bent over and quietly concentrated on the task in hand, Agnes has never seen her so content. She doesn't seem to care about laddering her nylons or the legion of paspalum seed heads clinging to her skirt. Apart from the occasional refinement such as wiping sweat off her powdered face with a perfumed, embroidered handkerchief, her grandmother looks like a hardy pioneer you find in the Westerns at the pictures on a Saturday afternoon.

Scythes cut through the brush and recalcitrant roots are dug out with picks. At the end of the day, Grandma gives Agnes the honour of striking the match to set the bonfire mound of cuttings alight. Red, yellow, blue, the flames soar upwards. The evening mist descends to freeze the blurred background of tall gums into rainbow magic.

Parry ploughs the bare ground with a tractor and removes loose stones, ready to plant hardy grass seeds. The kids fight over whose turn it is to ride on the tractor and stand on the running board of the Humber whenever the uncles drive to the store for supplies. And then, one day, the work is miraculously finished. With the goalposts in place on the field, the gates hung, horses installed in the stables, the farm is ready for polo.

Madge appears like the Queen of Sheba and gives orders for a line of poplar trees to be planted and fenced in along the outside yard of the stable block. In future, the sound of rain on a corrugated iron roof, and the wind rustling through poplar leaves like women dancing in taffeta skirts, will forever take Agnes back to The Farm.

Once the Sunday practice matches are in full swing, and new players gradually join the club, Grandma stops coming. The uncles' restraint in her presence degenerates into larking around like schoolboys in her absence. Two children's ponies arrive: a chestnut called Paddy and a grey called Snowy.

Sighting Agnes slopping around in the saddle on Paddy, Uncle Ben decides to teach her to ride properly:

*Toes slightly out and heels down… reins crossed over in right hand above the pommel... sit straight... shoulders down and cling on with your knees. No, not like that – you look like a sack of potatoes... bottom out of the saddle when you trot. You can do it!*

*No, I can't! It's too much to remember!*

She yells at him in anger, having bitten her lip as she is bumped around on the trot. Then suddenly something clicks, and it becomes as natural as walking—one two, one two, up down, up down:

*Wow! I've got it! I can feel it! Look I'm doing it!*

Ben is running down the stable yard from the porch of the tack room to open the gate, chuckling happily to himself. His curved eye teeth seem to infuse a tenderness into what can often look like a silly grin. He is grinning now as she trots out of the yard. She is counting *one two, one two, one two*. But Paddy isn't keen to leave the stables. He stops dead on the other side of the gate. Agnes kicks him in the ribs, but he turns to stone. She urges him on:

*Come on, Paddy! Come on, old boy!*

She doesn't see it, but she has heard Ben's whip connect with Paddy's rump. He is laughing uproariously as Agnes shoots off over the hill. Paddy is so stimulated that he breaks from a trot into a canter. It's sublimely exhilarating. The wind is in Agnes's face. She merges into the animal's body—streaking forward as if in a dream. She's Elizabeth Taylor in *National Velvet*—training her rambunctious pony for the famous race.

Once they arrive at the main farm gate, Paddy stops in his tracks again. Agnes pulls the right-hand rein to steer him down towards the creek in the far paddock, but her steed refuses to budge. He has a mind of his own alright. She increases the pressure on the reins, but Paddy is rigid. She wonders if he's only capable of two directions. Out of the blue, as if he has heard her thoughts, he springs to life again and stubbornly charges back to the stables. The canter to the gate was fast, but now galloping Paddy sprouts wings like Pegasus. She's flying. She knows now what it feels like to be a jockey moving at full pelt to a finishing line.

When she arrives back at the yard, Uncle Ben booms:
*Who is the master? You or the horse?*
She has lost her helmet and Paddy is foaming at the mouth. She shouts back:
*Can't you see? The horse of course!*
*Is that so, my girl? Well—we're going to change all that!*

Agnes loves the way he announces this, as if he is committing himself to her improvement when no one else has ever done so. And, indeed, he teaches her not only how to ride but how to jump, so she can enter the local hunt. And when she is older, Ben says, he'll teach her how to drive a car. He treats her like one of the blokes, unselfconsciously, not remotely aware of his drooling mouth as he points out to her the finer points of a female curve he has spotted:

*Fair crack of the old whip, get an eyeful of what's going on in the cardigan! My fanny aunt, I've never seen a pair quite like that!*

As her Uncle Ben graphically and vocally imagines himself as a netball goalpost, or an athletic horse in contact with naked female flesh, she finds herself wondering at her obsession with this warm-hearted man. His ramblings might make him sound a bit dim-witted, but she always feels relaxed with him—never intimidated or uncomfortable in the way she feels with her father—or Uncle Parry. She smacks Ben's hand playfully and tells him not to be rude. She doesn't have tits and wonders about all the fuss. At 10, she is on the same scatological level as Ben and can't wait to share a rude joke with him. His explosive, boisterous laugh is compensation for the silliest tale.

Ben plays 'back' on the polo field, sitting solidly on the big horses he favours. Unlike Eric who loves his horses, Ben has no warm feelings for his mounts, often roughly yanking and pulling on the bit till their mouths bleed. Compared to Eric's smooth seat in the saddle and riding finesse, Ben looks like an overheated steam train. Although he is eager to please, she has worked out that his blindness to the feelings of others leads them to dismiss him as a buffoon. It's a puzzle to her why he favours her and ignores some of his own children. Also, how he remains blithely unaware of Madge's antipathy towards him, no matter what diabolical trick she cooks up. He chuckles at complaints others voice about her, all the while in denial that she is anything less than a devoted sister.

Ben is in high spirits on the Sunday morning Agnes accompanies him in the utility truck to look at a horse for sale at a pony club in Camden. He rejects the horse, but convinces Roger McFarland Mead, who runs the club, to invite Agnes to join the hunt. Agnes nearly dies when Ben tells Roger what a cracking good rider she is: a judgment he has seemingly based on seeing her canter across the polo field the previous Sunday. His praise seems to be coupled to his pride in being her teacher.

Roger stares at her uncle from under eyebrows resembling pulled threads of steel wool. Ben towers over the other man, his glance intermittently flashing towards the stables. Agnes knows he is hoping for another look at Sandra, a well-endowed and pretty girl who is on a working holiday from Wiltshire. She is wearing a T-shirt with no bra.

McFarland Mead claps Ben on his lower back, which is as high as his short arm will reach:

*That's settled then, Ben old chap. Jolly good. Splendid. Couldn't be better. I'll put her name down. Yes, I'll put her name down as soon as I go inside.*

Ben gives him a playful army salute, filling the paddock with his familiar guffaw. He is impressed by McFarland Mead and the other polo people, but he doesn't deify them like Agnes's parents, nor put on another way of being around them. He is his same uncouth self with everybody. A toot of the horn, a wave, and Agnes and her uncle charge off in a tornado of dust. She feels excited and scared simultaneously. What has convinced her to have a go at the hunt, despite grave doubts, is the welcome chance to surprise her father. She pulls at Ben's shirtsleeve urgently.

*Know what, Uncle Ben? I'm not going to tell anyone, so I can surprise Daddy. We'll keep the hunt a secret just between you and me. He won't believe his eyes when he sees me.*

*Okay, young Agnes, it's a deal. My lips are sealed.*

Ben lends Agnes a horse called 'Jake' that she exercises for him on weekends. He is a nervous, finely made black gelding with a gleaming white star on his forehead—his coat so dark, it looks purple in the sunshine. Ben tells her that 'Jake' is too small for polo, but that he would make a perfect equestrian jumper:

*If he performs well, I'll sell him to McFarland Mead. That'll be a turn-up for the books, eh? Ha-ha-ha! We go there to buy a horse and end up selling him one!*

Ben schools Agnes in what he knows about jumping. So that she can practise, he places some recently cut saplings from the woodpile between petrol drums out in the yard. She spends hours and hours going over them, getting out of the saddle time after time to put them back in place whenever 'Jake' kicks them off. Ben applauds her efforts, and she feeds off his optimism to secure a place in her father's heart. There is a little nagging doubt, however—perhaps she should wait a bit, for she's never ridden out with a pack of riders. Yet she remains determined to prove herself.

On the morning of the big event, Ben drives Agnes to the pony club with 'Jake' in the back of the float. Agnes is carrying her best jodhpurs, a white shirt, and a wool tie she has nicked from her father's wardrobe, all secreted away in a bag. She changes at the Pony Club. The long brown leather boots, pink coat and black helmet they lend her fit perfectly. Well-endowed Sandra from Wiltshire plaits a black velvet ribbon through her long hair. To Agnes's delight, everyone who sees her exclaims how sensational she looks.

At the starting line, with the other horses and riders milling around her, Agnes's confidence swells. 'Jake' looks just as good as the other mounts. It's a crisp autumn morning, the sun held back behind a thick cloud. As condensation billows out of the warm mouths of horses and riders, she leans forward to pat her mount's neck. 'Jake' is trembling, and he stomps his hooves erratically. His ears are flat as if pinned back. He is overstimulated. She tries to soothe him by gently repeating his name. Ben approaches, and she whispers to her uncle urgently:

*Jake doesn't like it here...*

Ben squints at her through shrewd narrowing eyes:

*Nonsense. They're all frisky at the start. Once you get going, he'll be fine. Don't be scared, stay in posture, cling on with your thighs. That's it. Don't forget elbows down, reins firm. Anticipate the jumps by getting ready to move forward.*

She grasps the double reins tightly as Ben takes off his hat. Then he smacks her leg in a crass gesture of good luck. At the unexpected impact, 'Jake' flares sideways. As she struggles to control him, Agnes is shocked to spot Uncle Parry, Richard the Scottish uncle, and some of the cousins dotted in the crowd at the starting line. She hopes no one has told her father and spoiled the surprise.

She could never have imagined what would happen next. She wonders if it is down to Uncle Parry, as she is wary of his continual pranks. It might even have been Ben. In the terror that follows, a lot gets blurred. All she knows is that, suddenly, shockingly, a rogue whip has come down hard on the rump of her horse and 'Jake' has taken off like a rocket. She will forever be haunted by the sound of that single lash that sent him into such a frenzy.

She clings on, bending down over his mane like the cowboys at the pictures to avoid a bullet in the back. Pulling on the reins with all her might makes absolutely no impression on him. She has lost all confidence. The creature is in a flat-spin panic. She breaks all the rules of riding etiquette by hanging on to the pummel with both hands like a buck jumper. She manages to stay in the saddle over two jumps. She is in the firm grip of sheer terror.

Mercifully, the nightmare ends when Jake unseats her at the third jump, and she lands, head-first, in the mud. She lies there, motionless, seeing all unfurl around her in slow motion. Horses' hooves thunder perilously close. The lovely pink riding jacket, long boots, and the black velvet helmet look like they've been lodged in a stormwater channel for months. While mortified by the state of the borrowed clothes, she is grateful the ordeal is over. As she has such little concern for her own wellbeing, it never occurs to her that she might have broken her neck.

She is carried to Camden Park House in a blanket. A lady shears away the legs of her jodhpurs below both knees where sharp branches have cut in, then gently cleans around the cuts, and bandages the wounds. Uncle Parry, Richard, and two of Richard's daughters arrive in an open Jeep to ferry her to hospital. Richard drives, while Uncle Parry cradles Agnes in his arms in the back. They all sing silly songs, chanting the choruses again and again to cheer her up.

At the hospital, Uncle Parry holds Agnes's hand while the doctor gives her a local anaesthetic and proceeds to stitch the torn flesh on her knees with black thread. Dread begins to fill her throat. What will happen when she gets home?

She might have guessed. Back at home, there is complete silence. She has tried, in vain, to explain herself:

*Someone hit 'Jake' on the rump with a whip! That's why he got a fright and took off!*

Her knees are swollen like footballs and sting like hell. She is covered in bruises and her body aches all over. Unable to tolerate the tension, despite the pain, she finds herself squatting down next to her father's armchair:

*If that had happened to any of the other riders, their horse would have done the same. If I hadn't been sabotaged, Daddy, you would have been so proud of me!*

*Get her away from me!*

Eric Keen has shouted to his wife who is in the kitchen. Agnes knows her father is avoiding addressing her directly. As usual.

*I can't hear any more of this rot, Madge! She's a disgrace. Why Ben ever let her enter the hunt is beyond me. Her performance makes fools of us all!*

At this, Madge finally emerges from the kitchen:

*Go to your room, Agnes, and don't upset your father. You can't imagine the shame he felt when people he's known all his life, professional horse people, described your ridiculous behaviour!*

Her mother is looking triumphant. It's clear Agnes's tale of truth is unwanted, and she is starting to suspect that, had she been seriously injured and, perhaps, put on life support, neither callous parent would hesitate in giving permission to turn off the oxygen. She wonders, too, if they aren't also punishing her for fraternising with Ben—who is now the well-established silent enemy.

The humiliation of the hunt will set the ball of change rolling even faster. Richard Pales' time as fourth player of the team will be brief. He and his family will depart Sydney to revive the depleted fortunes of a sheep farm miles away in the Northern Tablelands of New South Wales, an enterprise once run by the notorious Mack. Agnes will really miss the fun around the barbeque, the games, the shared picnics, and the cakes with tea, for The Farm will feel horribly deserted when they leave.

And, within another year, Eric Keen will lose the ameliorating influence of Uncle Parry. Weary of brother Ben's scheming for ultimate control of the factory and having to further put up with him at weekend polo meets, Parry will resign his job, sell his horses, and never come back. He will join his wife's family in the pub business, buy a boat, and take up golf.

Losing Parry's support will deal a serious blow to Eric Keen's stability. Devoid of the relief of airing his frustration over Ben's misrepresentation at work with Parry, his exasperation will pierce the silence of the early morning hours in Agnes's parents' bedroom. Night after night she will be woken by her father's impassioned lament. How, Agnes will hear him demand, can he deal with the lies that Ben constantly drips into his mother-in-law's perfumed ear?

He will endlessly implore his wife in a voice so saturated with despair it will tug at Agnes's heart:

*Why don't we break away, Madge? Like Parry!*

While assiduously ignoring his proposal, Madge will swear everlasting vengeance:

*First thing at nine sharp, tomorrow—on the dot—I'll ring Mother and have it out. Without fail tomorrow. The old lady's eyes will be opened to the skulduggery around her!*

This vitriolic pledge to action finally soothes her husband into sleep and, before long, loud snores will replace the anxiety.

Nine o'clock will come and go, however, and her mother will remain in bed, humming to herself while she cooks her pearls against her skin. The following day Agnes will wait expectantly for her mother to make the promised call. But Madge Keen never will.

CHAPTER 9

# ROSEVILLE BATHS

Agnes develops the habit of going to Roseville Baths on the bus on her own. A rectangle of submerged wooden planks cordons off a section of Middle Harbour to protect swimmers from the great whites, bronze whalers, bull and tiger sharks that roam the waters. The entrance is through a turnstile with a sloping roof. It is a miniature replica of the roof on the bandstand, on top of the building below. A steep wooden stair leads from the entrance on Babbage Road to the changing room facilities under the bandstand, near the water's edge.

The pool is submerged in a national park surrounded by native bushland. Tall red gums, shaped like prehistoric creatures, cover the hill above where Agnes gets off the bus at the last stop on Babbage Road. A mixture of banksias, wattles and scribbly gums—so-called because of the pattern left by burrowing insects—grow in pockets along the shoreline. This display is interspersed with low-lying vegetation that shades striking rock formations covered in rich green moss. Roseville Bridge, which links the peninsula with the rest of Sydney, is the only man-made structure in sight.

Agnes likes to get there early in the morning so she can gaze over the water from the timber platform that circles the perimeter of the pool. She has figured the path northwards would join the national park area at the end of Lennox Street. Magpies, parrots, honeyeaters and wrens swoop by her. They may well have perched on the self-same trees she used to climb near their old house. Early sunbeams break through the mist from across the water at Frenchs Forest.

The smell of salt in the air and the chatter of feeding birds make her feel close to God—through his creation. She begs Him to change all that is ugly and unhappy at home. Squinting through the blinding glare, she marvels at the illusion of thousands of shimmering, white-feathered creatures flapping their golden wings as they skid over stars and under diamonds.

It is the school holidays and, as the morning progresses, the pool gradually fills with shrieking kids who, clinging to the railing, tumble down the steep stairs. They abandon their bags on the grass at ground level and dash into the water—dive-bombing, running, jumping, and doing mad, twisting gyrations. Some older kids, with no money, sneak down the steep rock face under the wooden slats behind the stairs, get a toe-hold in the cracks and climb over the wire fence. Free entrance being small compensation for the perilous efforts to avoid paying. Nobody seems to mind.

Agnes can't remember how she learned to swim. She had taught herself to dog paddle in the snag-infested creek at the farm, where the muddy water was a minefield of unseen danger. And kids at the pool show her stuff which she copies. Today, she settles on swimming breaststroke because she can't master the breathing that goes with the crawl.

Having watched a middle-aged bald man—whose head sits on a long neck between startlingly wide shoulders—give a group of boys a diving lesson, she develops a sudden fierce desire to learn to dive. The instructor has a whistle around his neck and wears a pair of lime-green sunglasses. He blows the whistle:

*Okay you lot! Rule Number One! Never, never, never dive into shallow water! I know a kid who broke his neck doing just that. I'm not here to scare you, but to underline the importance of calculating the depth of the water before you take off. Always—and I mean always—check for yourself that the water's deep enough. I'm not nurturing sheep. I want you to think for yourselves and make your own decisions. All clear so far?*

He concludes his orders, searching each boy's face for a reaction. His deep voice sounds as if it's coming up from his toes. The boys nod in unison. He assumes the diving position so they can all copy him:

*Important point boys! Imagine your trajectory before you hit the water! Understood?!*

He goes down the line checking the position of each boy. A dizzying assembly line display follows. Each boy dives when he blows the whistle, swims back, pulls himself out of the water and re-joins the line.

One casualty of the lesson that Agnes is observing is a thin, scraggy blonde-haired boy who manages the dive reasonably well but with a weird jerky style. He ends up with red-rimmed eyes. The instructor, who all the boys call 'Mr Lawson', soaks cotton wool in water from the tap and gently bathes them.

An endless supply of medications and lotions seem to spill from the pockets of Mr Lawson's shorts. It's impossible not to be struck by his kindness.

That night, in bed, Agnes goes over the diving instructions in her head. She is almost the first one at the pool the following day, intent on putting the borrowed tuition into action. Like the fat boy yesterday, she loses her nerve, hesitates at the last minute, and goes splat on her face from the poolside. Despite the protection of her Speedo top, her chest stings like hell. Gradually though, as her body relaxes, she succeeds in dominating the jangling nerves that habitually strangle her whenever she tries to learn anything new. She improves. Then, resolved to test herself, she climbs the steps to the diving board. From the top, the water below looks like the distance between the deck and the level of the sea on an aircraft carrier in the war pictures she loves so much. She almost loses her nerve, but she can't possibly go back now. No way of chickening out—not with a bunch of kids already lining up behind her.

Taking the chance pays off. Cutting into the water headfirst feels so sensational that she's instantly back in the queue to prove she's not a 'one-dive wonder'. She copies the little jump the boy in front of her executes and, after the second or third time, absorbs the practical use of invoking the spring in the board that gives those extra few seconds to tighten the stomach and point the toes before moving off. She also adopts the practice of swinging her arms up with the jump, which adds more lift-off.

She can see Mr Lawson from the corner of her eye, and steels herself to complete one of her best dives. Agnes desperately hopes that they will connect one day. She likes him so much.

She dives in and is satisfied with the effort. She eases her body out of the water:

*That dive you did was a bobby dazzler!*

Mr Lawson *had* been watching!

*My only comment is push further out from the diving board like you're flying against gravity before letting the descent take hold. But, well done, girl! You look like a natural!*

Agnes melts when he pats her on the head and asks her name:

*Well now, Agnes. If you can repeat what I just saw, I think you can learn all sorts of tricks.*

*Can I do another dive for you, Mr Lawson?*

*Sure, go right ahead. I'm watching.*

Her knees start to shake as she mounts the board. No... no... don't mess it up, she cautions herself. The horror of the accident at the hunt comes back. With each step she climbs she is assaulted by the almighty fall, the cold terror of mud, tangled stirrups, and the agony of humiliation that followed. She always feels jinxed when seeking adult approval. She closes her eyes at the top of the board to try and calm down and, when she opens them, is assailed by hundreds of colliding multicoloured dots that swim across her vision:

*Take your time, don't rush it!*

A slightly authoritarian tone in Mr Lawson's voice further

unnerves her. He sounds a bit accusatory but, worse, she senses he may be feeling sorry for her.

Agnes is in the water, knowing the distractions have made her bungle her effort. She has hit the surface in a loose-leg splash. She is so disappointed that she feels like drowning herself. She pictures Mr Lawson walking off in disgust. Struggling with a lump in her throat, she decides to run to the changing room and catch the next bus home. How embarrassing, after all the false bravado! She wants to slither away from the baths and never come back.

Her head down, she's already dripping her way in the direction of the changing rooms when she feels a tap on her shoulder:

*'Hey! Where are you off to? You're not abandoning ship after one go, are you?'*

Mr Lawson's eyes are kind. There is no malice in this statement. She is so relieved that she runs back up the stairs to the diving board. The kids in line smell her urgency. She moves like a car with a blaring siren through traffic, and they step aside to let her pass. Running along the board with a new sense of freedom, she sets the bounce with one foot and surges forward. Nothing else exists but this dive. When she surfaces, she hears clapping. She looks up from the water and sees Mr Lawson's heart-breaking grin.

He continues to give her loads of helpful pointers as if he has all the time in the world for her. His enthusiasm is contagious. Diving fever grips the pool. Now *all* the kids want to learn. She knows Mr Lawson teaches for money but doesn't know how that works. She chooses to see his presence there that day as divine intervention—as she does anything good that happens to her.

It seems that God has not only sent Mr Lawson to the swimming pool but installed him a short walk from Agnes's house. They are neighbours. A left turn at the bottom of Edmond Street and there he is in Nicholson Street in a big two-storey square brick house—on the corner with Havilah Street overlooking Beauchamp Park. She has walked past his place hundreds of times on the alternative route to school. She remembers the house because all the windows are always open and the garden full of the sound of children. He and Mrs Lawson have five kids—three of their own and two adopted. She discovers that not only does he live nearby but owns a sports shop in Victoria Street. He has even swum freestyle for Australia in his youth.

With school about to start, Agnes regrets only getting to know Mr Lawson halfway through the summer holidays. Before leaving the pool on their last day, she goes over to thank him. It comes out sounding a bit stilted, like anything she rehearses too much, but he puts her out of her misery:

*Delighted to hear we're neighbours, Agnes. I'll tell you what. Now school's about to start and I've got to work in the shop, we'll be coming here early morning to swim. There's a place in the van if you'd like to join in. You're ready to learn some advanced dives. We could start with a jack-knife, if you like the idea?*

Learning to do a jack-knife! Who would believe it! But, on the appointed morning, Agnes is overcome with doubt. It's been a week since she saw Mr Lawson so he may have forgotten. Children, business, teaching—he's got a lot on his plate. Maybe he didn't mean it. Just saying it to be nice. As nothing happens in her house without a good deal of shouting, his casual manner had felt insubstantial to her. He had said the van was due to set off at 6am. The more doubts that take hold, the more Agnes dallies but, to her amazement, when she walks down Edmond Street half-heartedly, she sees they're all in the van—waiting for her:

*Oh, Mr Lawson I'm so sorry! I didn't know if you really meant it!*

*What do you take me for, girl! Of course, I meant it! Now hop in—and if you're not on time tomorrow we'll go without you!*

The following day she is there by the kerbside before they have all tumbled out of the house. The eldest boy, Matt, is fifteen. He was a very good swimmer, already entering competitions. There are twin girls, about Agnes's age, called Sadie and Rose, and two boys—John and Alan—twelve and thirteen, who the Lawsons had fostered before adopting them into the family. Agnes thinks how good it would be to live with them all.

One Saturday morning, she shows Mr Lawson how she has improved the jack-knife. As she emerges from the water, he leans down to pat her on the head:

*You're a star!*

For days afterwards, Agnes is walking on air, Mr Lawson's compliment singing in her head. The desire to show her father what she can do in the pool grows inside her. She can expunge, once and for all, the bad impression from the hunt. Gratifyingly, Eric does seem quite enthusiastic at the prospect of a regular swim. He's an early riser, so says he can easily adapt to a quick morning trip to the pool before he leaves for the cotton factory.

The early summer mornings become full of joy and promise. Agnes is happy to unite the family and proud to show Mr Lawson she belongs to one. Entrance to the baths is free until the talkative blonde lady arrives at 9am to take the money.

Agnes is proud, too, to discover that her father is a good swimmer, and enjoys introducing him to Mr Lawson, who winks at her encouragingly:

*Show your Dad what you can do on the diving boards, Agnes.*

Although very nervous, she dives, and feels she has dived well.

Her father's reaction—and what happens next—fragments. She knows she is drying herself on the grass away from the others, after a shower at the poolside. Her father's face is blocked out by a shaft of sunlight. She doesn't need to see him to recognise that familiar rough hand moving between her thighs and then his finger, under her Speedo, pushing up inside her and starting to twirl around. She supposes he must have pulled his hand away eventually. She knows he says nothing. She knows he walks off.

Her stomach is turning over. Her mind reels in confusion. What does it mean? The sky darkens. Her skin crawls. In the car on the way home he is acting as if nothing has happened. He even whistles as he drives.

The next morning, when her brothers clamour to go swimming again, she says she has a headache, so they all go without her. She never goes back to the baths—or dives—again.

Agnes has always been haunted by her father's act at the pool. It did—and didn't—happen. Was—and wasn't—his hand. She reasons that, as he is a good man and all fathers are good, there must be something bad in her that has provoked it. It is—and isn't—a concrete fact. And what does it mean anyway? Thoughts splinter apart. Had he done this before? Yes. Once. When they had listened to the Davis Cup broadcast on the radio in his bedroom. But she can't unite the Davis Cup incident with the incident at the baths. She can't categorise them as similar as she can't grasp either. Any effort at recall leaves her crippled with doubt.

Her father returns to ignoring her. She hears her mother tell Aunt Marnie that her vexing daughter sees things that aren't there all the time. Is this a trick to undermine her credibility? But something wrong *has* happened because, in the pit of her stomach, she feels bad and dirty in a way she never did before. Why didn't God protect her? Is it because she's not worthy? She is ashamed for somehow provoking the whole thing. She goes on seeing herself in the wet green Speedo against a black sky.

Now, when she wakes early out of habit, she goes to 7am Mass and takes communion at the parish church in Archer Street.

Agnes never knows whether her brothers are aware of her father's continual angst, as she never confides in them. She presumes that, like her, they try not to listen and keep their distance. However, it amuses her brother Bert to challenge the Mad Woman—as he calls his mother. Avoiding the whole Lennox Street tragedy somehow gifts him with the power that is denied Agnes and Jim to defend themselves. Thus, the beatings Agnes endures bypass Bert and land on six-year-old Jim. She only knows that something terrible must have happened at home to make Jim steal £10 from Madge's purse and run away. She does not know what it is. He had caught a train to Hornsby but, when he tried to cash the £10 note in a shop, the attendant rang the police. Agnes had not been at home when two social workers brought him back.

One day, Jim will be rushed in an ambulance to the Children's Hospital at Randwick. He will be bleeding to death. His spleen will have stopped producing platelets—an essential ingredient for blood clotting. Blood transfusions will eventually save his life, but Jim will remain seriously ill in hospital for several months. His mother, who likely caused this severe damage, will relate events outside the house and bathe in sympathetic responses from family and neighbours. However, inside the house, the subject will be forever taboo. Which is why, when neighbours ask Agnes for updates, she will have none to give.

In the days that follow Jim's admittance to hospital the phone will constantly ring, and the new post box will be crammed with Get Well cards—none of which will reach Jim as his parents don't visit him. When Agnes reveals a plan to go by train to Town Hall Station and, from there, to catch a bus to Randwick to see her little brother, Madge will clip her across the ear with such force that she will never dare to broach the subject again.

The powers-that-be at 'Rosemont' will enrol both of Agnes's brothers in boarding school, and Jim will be liberated from further beatings when the doctors at the hospital send a warning that, under no circumstances, is he to be hit—either at home or at school. Nor should he be allowed to play sport for the foreseeable future.

As for Agnes's fate, 'Rosemont' will decide to sacrifice her on the family altar. She is to keep her mother company when her father is away on business.

The formal decree will be: SHE IS TO REMAIN A DAY GIRL AT SCHOOL.

CHAPTER 10

## DAVID JONES

Nurtured by a few wise young nuns, Agnes has enjoyed three good years at Our Lady of Mercy Convent.

The sight of a beautiful woman gliding down the school path, wearing a lipstick-pink halter-neck dress, turns heads in the playground. Agnes realises, with pride, that it is her mother. Slim, imperiously erect, Madge looks bewitchingly glamorous. Agnes is playing basketball on the court at the far end of the school ground when Madge arrives, and she manages to score a goal—much to the delight of the team. Her mother has shown up just before half-time. Agnes hopes she will look over at the court and see how well she is playing. But, if Madge does glance across at the court, she never mentions it.

One of the girls in the team hands around a plate of orange segments. Madge raises a manicured hand in disdainful refusal—a gesture that displays her exquisitely painted pink fingernails. Agnes worries her mother might be rude to someone, as she has no sympathy for the least blemish or human oddity. As a result, she stands in front of a girl in the team who has a face full of explosive pimples lest the unwholesome sight robs Agnes of a rare moment in the spotlight. Thankfully, although utterly indifferent to her surroundings, her mother appears to be on her best behaviour. In fact, she is leaving a dazzling trail of glitter in the impressionable minds of Agnes's schoolmates:

*Is that really your mother? God—she's gorgeous!*

Agnes keeps hearing it repeated around her:

*God—she's gorgeous.*

*God—she's gorgeous.*

It makes Agnes feel guilty for ever hating her. She instantly forgives her mother for not coming to any school she has ever attended until now. Agnes is constantly searching for the least fragment of evidence to excuse both parents. She has single-handedly invented their great love—an all-consuming passion for each other—that justifies their neglect. This one-off appearance serves to intensify her mother's exoticism and makes it all the more memorable for never being repeated.

One of the young nuns rushes up to Madge. She is gushing with enthusiasm:

*I never saw such a miracle, Mrs Keen! When she first arrived here, she was like a limp rag. Such a sad little face. Lips pressed together, eyes on the floor. The least angry word would bring tears to her eyes. She just stared out the window in a kind of a trance. I decided that discipline would be a further burden on a soul in pain, so I left her to come around of her own accord. So wonderful to see her blossom! She pays attention in class. She's one of our best basketball players, you know! She likes Botany and English, does lovely needlework, and recently got 100% in Religious Knowledge!*

Such praise might have pleased Grandma, but is of no interest whatsoever to Madge. She doesn't need an earnest nun bothering her with talk of improvement. Her children's unread school reports keep company with unpaid bills in the drawer that once housed the architect's plans. She hasn't visited the school for a progress report, but to tell the nuns she'll be taking Agnes out a day early for the Easter holidays. But Agnes will not be going to the dentist—as Madge has deliberately misinformed the nuns. Instead, she will be accompanying her mother to 'David Jones' department store where Madge hopes to bump into all the polo wives who are due in town for the Royal Show. For two weeks every Easter, town and country dwellers rub shoulders in a miniature walled city at Moore Park on the edge of the city. Agnes's attendance at 'David Jones' is intended to be a kind of backhanded rite of passage. She is to be presented as the well-educated daughter in a new frock.

Madge wakes Agnes the following morning. She is holding up a coat-hanger which is draped with a sleeveless green cotton dress. It has a white lace collar, like a decorative nun's bib. A new pair of black patent leather strap-over court shoes, and a pair of short white socks with a frill on top, are displayed on the white chest of drawers with the ceramic roses. Agnes finds herself pulled and pushed into the dress and her hair is pinned into kiss curls around her face and sprayed with lacquer. At this last indignity, Agnes protests:

*I'm not going looking like a kewpie doll!*

*Don't get me churned up with your likes and dislikes on an important day like this, Agnes!*

Arguing is futile. Agnes decides her mother will soon forget about the curls, which she surreptitiously straightens with her fingers as they move along the street towards 'David Jones'.

The ground floor of the store is a shimmering wonderland. Agnes's head spins with the large silver baubles as they swirl in mesmerising circles from the ceiling. The cosmetic concession counters—Max Factor, Elizabeth Arden, Helena Rubenstein, Yardley—are attended by well-groomed, glamorous shop assistants radiating elegance from every skin pore. Enlarged photos of beautiful screen idols dominate each counter.

Dressed in a ravishing, well-cut, pleated yellow linen dress under a yellow and white striped linen jacket, Madge could easily take her place with film stars. Agnes observes her mother's inherent irritation evaporate as she drifts dreamily from counter to counter, fondling the latest skincare and make-up product, pausing to spray her wrists with a new fragrance. She sees the tightness around her mother's mouth soften and her heavy, dictatorial step become carefree and dainty. Agnes tags along behind her, not sure what to do. She's on tenterhooks like a maid waiting for instructions from a temperamental mistress. The buzz of the ground floor is soothed by the sound of a Chopin Polonaise being played on a grand piano by a lady dressed in black. The performer is raised on a dais in the centre of the floor.

Madge settles her preferred custom on the Elizabeth Arden counter, choosing three or four items for which she signs the account. Purchases completed, she then dashes for the lift—forgetting Agnes, who runs behind and just manages to squeeze in behind her mother before the door closes. A short, tubby lift driver, with hair growing out of his ears, announces the availability of goods on each floor in a sing-song voice, before opening the lift door:

*Fourth Floor: Furniture, barbeques, Venetian blinds, curtains, etcetera… Fifth floor: Electric domestics, including washing machines, stoves, fridges, radios, and gramophones, etcetera…*

He opens the doors to the sixth floor in silence. Agnes thinks he must have lost his voice. Then she twigs that the sixth floor is so exclusive that any direct reference to barter would be offensive to the pedigree ladies who alight here. The sixth floor is no place for casual browsers. Only the initiates sink their high heels into the acres of plush red carpet.

Nose in the air, Madge strides into her favourite playground, with Agnes making a snail track in her wake, dragging the new patent leather shoes through the deep carpet pile. Compared to the ground floor bustle, the hush on the sixth floor is ecclesiastical. It wouldn't have surprised Agnes to see a holy water font appear from behind one of the bedecked mannequins. No other space, apart from the sideline at polo matches, appears to tranquillise her mother so effectively.

Feeling rather like a stray cat, Agnes watches a few well-dressed women survey the latest imports from Paris, London and New York and marvels at how secure her mother seems amongst them. Madge would normally treat shop assistants with contempt, but here she bows to them as if they are sanctified beings dwelling in a heavenly cloud. One so anointed spots Madge and sails forward. Regulars luxuriate in hearing themselves addressed by name. In no time, all three ladies who swanned in from the lift are claimed in person:

*How are you, Mrs Keen? It's been too long since we've seen you. I must say, you're looking radiant in that lovely yellow linen. I remember parcelling it up for you last year.*

'Valerie' clasps the gloved hand Madge extends, holding her gaze in mascara-hooded emerald eyes as she draws her close and intones the words Madge has longed to hear:

*Wait till you see what we have for you!*

En route to the promised speciality, which awaits Madge in a wardrobe at the far end of the store, 'Valerie' pauses briefly to straighten a black jersey knit with a cowl collar back onto a wine-red satin coat hanger. As she turns to collect Madge, who is admiring a pink wool dress on a store mannequin, she catches sight of Agnes, who is hiding behind a fluted pedestal that supports a Grecian vase containing a bunch of long-stem red roses. 'Valerie' smiles at her magnanimously:

*I seem to remember you play the piano.*

Madge quickly chips in:

*She could end up performing. Mrs Grierson says she shows great promise. The problem is that she has to practise at school as we don't have a piano in the house. As we're spoiled for space I said to my husband, we must buy the girl a piano! Nothing lovelier than piano music in the home! But, for now, all plans are on hold as Eric is playing polo at the show and what with the horses currently stabled at the ground, I can't think of anything else!*

Agnes is always dumbstruck by her mother's shameless outdoor personality. She wishes the floor would open and swallow her up. She manages to muster a limp smile for the benefit of 'Valerie' as she winds her non-musical fingers awkwardly around the clasp of a cheap white plastic handbag. She is praying this torture will soon end. She has had a mere handful of piano lessons at the convent and knows nothing more than the position of Middle C and a few scales. What is more, her mother has never heard her sound a note.

*You'll be in seventh heaven, Mrs Keen, when you see what I've hidden away for you...*

The velvet tones of 'Valerie' seem to have mesmerised the normally tyrannical woman like a magician's pendulum. The astute shop assistant moves on, gently guiding her captive towards the treasure. Superlatives flow in admiration of her eager client, who is soon parading in a Norman Parkinson fine pleated wool and silk dress in pale grey and pink tartan, with a short tailored matching jacket lined in pink satin.

The next purchase to be swaddled in tissue paper is a fine Charles Creed yellow and blue tweed pencil skirt with matching three-quarter jacket, pockets and collar trimmed with blue velvet. 'Valerie' deftly prolongs the banked purchase of the two outfits by extending Madge's passion further. Agnes observes her besotted mother as the assistant seductively trails an Emilio Pucci short crêpe evening dress in gold with a flowing skirt, long sleeves, and a crossover bodice along the spotlessly clean carpet. 'Valerie' casts her spell bewitchingly:

*It's got your name all over it, Mrs Keen!*

It truly is a perfect fit, and the colour a wonderful complement to Madge's raven hair and searing dark eyes. As Madge signs her name to the last docket without even glancing at the price, Agnes is already anticipating her father's fury when the extortionate bill arrives. Immune to the reality of cause and effect, Madge has no fear of the consequences of her actions.

Upon completing her final purchase, Madge's longed-for social cachet moment arrives, for there is Janie, the polo wife she adores. Mrs Janie Marble Flood, wife of the Captain of the Goulburn polo team, is floating out of the lift and heading towards her.

Madge drops the carrier bags and rushes to fling her arms around her idol. The serene country beauty appears startled but quickly regains her composure and beams a perfectly restrained white-teethed smile at Madge. Agnes watches as her mother gushes nonsense at the faintly bemused woman.

Agnes is in as much in awe of Janie Marble Flood's appearance as her mother. The woman's smooth, lightly tanned complexion melts into a natural pink blush over high, rounded cheeks. A sprinkle of tiny dark freckles across a pert nose adds an impish touch to her classical beauty. She seems to be a person who never has a hair out of place, for Agnes can attest to having seen the thick, naturally curly brown mane unruffled in all conditions. Whilst other women wrestled with scarves on the windy polo field side-lines, Mrs Janie Marble Flood's curls would remain unfazed. Agnes knows all too well that her husband, Mr Dan Marble Flood, is the fourth generation of the family to live in a stately country house, with its very own ballroom, and dating back to the original land grant.

Madge's adoration of Janie has the intensity of a schoolgirl crush. She is as possessive of her as she is of her husband, surreptitiously intercepting approaches to her by any outside intruder. She even takes exception to her sisters and sisters-in-law daring to stand near Janie at the polo. Such impertinences could provoke a spiteful pinch, or a shove in the ribs. Where this woman is concerned, Madge abases herself without encouragement. Her obsession extends to Janie's three children, upon whom she lavishes the breadth of attention of which her own offspring can only dream.

Now Janie utters the words Agnes dreads hearing. Words that stab her with guilt for harbouring hateful thoughts:

*Agnes, how lucky you are to have such a wonderful mother!*

Struck dumb, Agnes can only nod. As Madge gabbles on, her daughter watches the underside of Janie's crocodile high heel poised for a quick getaway. Her mother just cannot stop talking. Her mouth gallops like a racehorse to a finishing line that never comes. Janie is beginning to look exasperated. Agnes squirms with embarrassment. Her mother never knows when to stop with people she puts on a pedestal. She lacks any awareness of others and, just like Uncle Ben, is utterly oblivious to a snub.

Unable to stand it any longer, Agnes courageously finds her voice: *Mummy, Janie's short of time. You'll see her tonight.*

After this unexpected intervention, her mother looks more bewildered than angry.

Janie flashes another toothpaste smile before dashing away. Happily, there are no repercussions for Agnes speaking up, as Madge remains dazzled by the fortuitous encounter with her idol. In fact, since the 'Rosemont' decree that Agnes was to be sacrificed to care for her mother, she has dutifully acted as prompter and interventionist lest Madge put the wrong foot in the wrong fiction. She knows people laugh at her mother behind her back but, although painfully shy, manages to defend her with a boldness she could never exert on her own behalf.

Back home, Madge transfers the tissue-paper-shrouded dresses onto satin hangers, hiding them at the back of the wardrobe. She orders Agnes to dispose of the tell-tale carrier bags in a bin in another street, as the mere sight of them has the potential to turn her husband into a raging bull. Eric never comments on what his wife wears, although he is clearly proud of her appearance. Agnes suspects he maintains an out-of-sight-out-of-mind attitude to what lies behind the wardrobe door. Tonight, under floodlights, he is to play in a high goal polo team at the showground – a pinnacle in his polo career – and is consequently in an above-average temperamental state when he dashes in the back door. He ignores Agnes, as usual, settling on the back step to clean his long riding boots until they shine like tinted glass. He showers in the tub, cleans his teeth, greases his fine hair, and puts on the standard white jodhpurs and club T-shirt under a tweed coat with a member's tag displayed in the lapel.

Although Madge is itching to show off her new clothes, she exercises restraint, aware the sight of an expensive new outfit could ruin the whole evening. Bathed, hair done, made up and perfumed, she wriggles into a coral pink wool suit.

Fully aware they don't want to take her along Agnes hears herself insisting she will be fine at home. She is trapped yet again in the horrible cycle of having her mother cling to her in her father's absence, and then resent her presence when he returns. Now she overhears a brief exchange that horrifies her. Her father speaks first:

*Does she have to come?*

*Now Eric, Mother said we must take her with us.*

Eric drives fast, swerving around corners, shooting daggers at Agnes whenever their eyes meet in the rear-view mirror as if she is the source of his present frustration. When he turns off the engine in the showground car park, he jumps out of the driver's seat, gets his stuff out of the boot, and slams the lid. To her astonishment, he and her mother run off—like two robbers leaving the scene of a crime. It feels pre-planned. Agnes knows her father will be heading to the stables and that Madge will be joining Janie and the other idols in a small exclusive members' stand. But why did they just suddenly desert her, and without even saying anything? Do they expect her to wait in the car? She watches them emerge out of the dark distance and into the brightly lit street without looking back. In these moments she fervently hates them and wishes they would die. In numb despair, she clings to the door handle outside the car to steady herself.

The car park is filling up. Doors are slamming shut and voices are swirling around as people walk away from parked vehicles. Agnes is feeling cold. She didn't bring a coat. Her green jumper is thin and her legs under the tartan skirt are bare. She had expected to be with her mother in the Special Members stand, where she would be protected from the weather.

Her mouth is dry. She can't swallow. She is abandoned by prayer, too, as she can't seem to remember the words of the 'Our Father' or the 'Hail Mary' that she parrots at school every day. Sudden memory loss will, from this point, become a permanent disability in Agnes's life.

A bearded man with bulging eyes walks between the cars. He is shining a powerful torch on the ground as he picks up litter with a spike and puts it in a plastic bag. He is suddenly alongside Agnes and is forcing his cracked lips onto hers. The putrid smell of his foul breath is nauseating. She runs from the car park, dashing wildly towards the crowd on the brightly lit street, her eyes blurred with tears. She collides with another man who shouts at her. She is swept along like the ballerina in *The Red Shoes*, compelled to keep moving. She floats through display halls with intricate carpets of vegetables, woven tapestries of fruit and fabulous displays of plants, crafts, cakes, fabrics, and flowers. Men wearing official badges are standing around chatting. She snuggles up close to family groups, pretending she belongs to them, but panics when someone suddenly turns and stares. She can't bear anyone to know she is not wanted.

The mounted police pass in formation on the road, followed by horses and riders, cows, Shetland ponies, goats, sheep, dogs, and pigs, graded in size, and led by attendants wearing long dustcoats. Purple, blue, and yellow ribbons are draped around the necks of the winning animals. She is aware, from previous visits to the show, that this is the Grand Parade exiting the main ground but, tonight, she sees it all in a blur, just as she does the buck-jumping and bull-dogging. She's afraid to return to the car. Her parents will attend a drinks party in the exclusive stand after the match, but she doesn't know where it's located, let alone have the heart to chase after them. And so, she watches the polo match alone in a crowded stand, hardly seeing a thing.

Exiting the stand, she is pushed along in a thick crowd, like one of a herd of sheep, and finds herself in the middle of the dazzling lights and loud music of the entertainment area. Shrieks, cries, screams, and laughter saturate the cold air as pleasure seekers jostle each other at the wheels of dodgem cars. People are spinning in the big dipper or riding up and down on the horses and chariots of the carousel. She looks on from the street, as she has no money to buy a ticket for a ride, or a sideshow. Promoters fight to lure customers to see a woman cut in two or to gaze at acrobatic midgets. There are freaks with two heads and contortionists who lick their own backs. Hysterical laughter leaks out of the entrance to the ghost train. She passes shooting galleries, dart throwers and contestants rolling balls into the rotating mouths of brightly painted clowns.

A motley line of Aboriginal boxers, dressed in white singlets and shabby satin shorts beneath worn silk dressing gowns, bounce up and down in thin lace-up boots. They are punching right and left hooks mindlessly into the air. A fat-bellied man with a pork-pie hat and vacant stare bangs a huge drum that sounds like the accompaniment to an execution, while a short tubby fellow in a check suit, with a friendly weather-beaten face, shouts in a monotonous voice into a blurred microphone, inviting men from the crowd to try their luck against one of the boxers. It is an intensely dark night with no moon and, standing still now, she realises she is freezing cold.

A rumble of thunder explodes in the sky, followed by huge spidery arms of lightning extending out like the roots of great trees. People gasp and scream as a lightning bolt hits a huge wooden post near the elevated boxing stage. People stampede for cover. The strike has cut a line in the post, which explodes into sparks like a firecracker. Numb with horror, Agnes feels as if she is living the Lennox Street electrocution all over again.

As if programmed to put out the fire, the heavens open and rain pours down. The remaining intact floodlights illuminate knife-like raindrops as Agnes runs off towards a road that looks familiar. But, tripping up in her haste, she lands, spreadeagled, on the sodden ground.

Strong hands lift her up by the waist and she finds herself looking into the concerned face of a policeman. Her voice sounds feeble, plaintive, in her head:

*I'm so cold…*

He carries her gently, wrapped in an army blanket, to a tent full of people where she gulps down a hot cup of tea with lots of sugar. As she dozes under a pile of blankets on a camp bed, feeling comfortably warm for the first time that night, she hears the police report that an ambulance has taken a few injured people from the lightning strike to hospital. It seems there were no fatalities.

She is fully woken by another voice. The voice she does—and does not—want to hear:

*Darling! What on earth are you doing? Your father and I have been frantic... looking all over the ground for you! Thank you, Officer! We've been worried sick! I'm so glad you found her!*

Mercifully, the next night of the show, her parents let her stay at home. Alone, she seeks comfort in her mother's wardrobe, curling up in the foetal position under the illicit clothes. She imbibes the perfume in the fabric as she had once done in Grandma's wardrobe at 'Rosemont'. The inside of her mother's wardrobe is a constant wonder. It could easily be a display cabinet in an expensive woman's boutique: satin underwear and nylon stockings in cloth envelopes, woollen jumpers kept like new in plastic bags, drawers with jewellery in boxes wrapped in cotton wool, creams and perfumes with unopened reserves—worthy of a Hollywood star. Agnes knows the clothes in her mother's wardrobe so well that, if they had been a subject on the school syllabus, she would get a hundred per cent—to match her score in Religious Knowledge.

The bill from 'David Jones' arrives in the first mail after Easter. The familiar houndstooth check logo on the envelope inevitably incites tension between husband and wife. Along with other bills addressed to Eric, the longer it sits on the dining table, the more this tension grows.

On the day Eric Keen summons up the courage to rip the envelope open, he is already trembling. The amounts stated on the account inside send him into a predictable frenzy:

*I can't believe it! How could you do this! We can't afford it! Where* the hell am I going to find the money? Just when I'm getting ahead, you throw me back into debt! Always the same story! It's unendurable!

He smashes his fist into the top of the walnut table:

*Can't I ever get through to you?!*

Madge's continued silence incites him to further fury:

*Well, say something woman! You promised your mother you'd exercise restraint, but you bloody well double the spending! I'm ruined and you don't give a damn!*

Despite the cold evening air, sweat is pouring down his red face. He kicks a chair and splinters the seat. Agnes knows her father is defeated before he has even begun. She searches her mother's face for some relief—an apology, contrition, empathy. But there is nothing of the kind available there. What Agnes does see, however, is the angelic look of a ham actress, masking a bare wisp of a triumphant smirk.

Eric Keen tears the account statement to pieces like a petulant child, throws them in the air, grabs the car keys on the table and creates a fresh snowstorm of plaster as he smashes the back door behind him. A screech of tyres indicates that he is off to find solace at the pub. But his daughter knows that he doesn't need a 'David Jones' bill as an excuse to indulge in a drinking binge. Any pub is more of a home to him than the ugly ramshackle house his fractured family now rattle around in.

Agnes will feel sorry for her father for the rest of the day. She will already be in bed when he staggers up the hall to a restless sleep. He will leave the house early the next morning, seemingly ashamed of losing his temper the day before. She knows that Eric Keen is a proud man. And it is clear the forces assembled at 'Rosemont' contribute to his dilemma. Madge's unruly spending now forces Agnes's Grandma and her son-in-law into conspiratorial huddles, like the parents of a delinquent child.

In fact, Agnes has watched her father flirt with all the 'Rosemont' women and Grandma is no exception. It is, she deduces, almost as if he could be married to Grandma, rather than to her problematic daughter.

## CHAPTER II

# THE DRESSMAKER

The matronly local woman in garish florals who sews.

This is how Agnes's mother refers to their new dressmaker during one of the marathon character assassinations by phone with Aunt Marnie. The three children are being fitted for new clothes to wear to the wedding of the oldest of the three young aunts—the fabulous Charlotte. Charlotte—the 'Rosemont' daughter who has done everything right: school head girl, university degree, engagement to a wealthy country grazier, planned European honeymoon. It will be the only family wedding Agnes ever attends and, today, she can hardly contain her excitement.

The last-minute decision at 'Rosemont' to include the Keen children as guests has caused a rush to find a dressmaker and Mrs Ryder is the only one in the area prepared to accept the tight deadline. Two further fittings follow the initial measurement day and then, miraculously, the wedding outfits are ready to go.

Mrs Ryder never makes clothes for Madge. There is no way Agnes's mother could be weaned off the designer labels on the exclusive sixth floor of 'David Jones'. Agnes overhears her mother telling Marnie that she would never contemplate having cloth draped around her body by the likes of a woman who grew up in an English bed-and-breakfast next to a common funfair in Blackpool. It amazes Agnes how someone so ignorant of the world finds ammunition to feed her snobbery in a chance remark about a town, and a country, which she has never seen.

You would have thought that the Keen family lived in a mansion, the way Madge scorned the Ryder house. Starting with the broken entrance gate held permanently open by the tentacles of a morning glory vine, she would spill out her bile:

*Be careful! Stay away from the gate! You children will get a good clip across the ear if you catch your school uniforms on those spikes! Why doesn't Mr Ryder do something about it? I'll tell you why—because he's in bed all day! They're a dirty bunch, these Poms! Never shower! They leave their squalid tenements in England to sail here on luxury liners for ten pounds and expect to have it all laid on—gates and all! They live like pigs!*

This is crisp talk coming from someone who has never fixed anything in her life and spends a good part of the day comatose in bed. The wooden gate to Madge's own side entrance had long ago disintegrated into a pile of broken fragments that the council removed from the pavement without either she or Eric even noticing. The proverb 'people in glass houses shouldn't throw stones' obviously didn't feature high on the 'Rosemont' list.

For Agnes, the wild garden, the broken gate, and the dark hiding place in the thick berry hedge all add to the delicious mystery of the inhabitants, who are made the more intriguing for being both foreign *and* non-Catholics. It is when seated on the earth floor and hidden from view in the front hedge that Agnes, and Mrs Ryder's daughter, Rita, will hug each other and vow eternal friendship. The mingling of the blood on their arms will signify nothing can ever part them. Through Rita, Agnes will fall in love with the ballet and for the next few years the two girls will remain inseparable. Agnes will also develop an all-consuming interest in Mrs Ryder's skill as a dressmaker—from the first cut of the material to the production of the final article.

When Agnes first surveys the intriguing interior of the Ryder premises, where rows of completed garments hang on a moveable metal rail, ready for collection, she recalls Dora Chadwick's beautiful ceramics and painted pictures, and it occurs to her that women could make their own living instead of waiting for the uncertain arrival of an inebriated husband. Like the form within the clay, potential resided in every roll of cloth.

Her fascination with Mrs Ryder's dressmaking creations is at odds, however, with the indifference of their creator, who only receives payment on completion and always seems to be short of money. This is the reason that the dressmaker accepts any imposed deadlines as, apart from supporting herself, her child, and an elusive husband, she must find the money for twice-weekly ballet classes in preparation for Rita to become a prima ballerina.

Agnes has also spotted that the original side door on the inside of the workroom is screened off with a white sheet which is covered in magazine cuttings, tailor's patterns, and bits of sample material. She suspects the door is locked. In this new world of female industry an unspoken prohibition exists against mentioning Mr Ryder, the mysterious husband, who, Agnes has come to discover, inhabits the front of the house, and works at night. Thus, the noise of falling objects, or shuffling furniture behind the mysterious curtain during fitting visits, pass without comment. So much so that those present end up wondering if they have imagined it.

A quick natural smile makes Mrs Ryder's tired green eyes sparkle, while pink cheeks appear to question the dark circles under them. She is dignified in manner and, Agnes notices over the ensuing visits, rarely irritable. The pressure of deadlines may mean she has little time to attend to her appearance, yet there is a beauty in the fine-featured, unblemished skin, and the dimple in the centre of her fleshy chin gives her an air of cheeky defiance.

Madge's mindless name-dropping will reach new heights when she locates a *Women's Weekly* photo of Janie Marble Flood, and other similarly adored personages, at a picnic race meeting. Mrs Ryder will nod politely as Madge gushes, but Agnes will see that the dressmaker is clueless as to who her mother is talking about. Interestingly, she will feel less embarrassed about her mother in front of Mrs Ryder, who will shoot her the occasional knowing look over a pair of pink batwing glasses. A look as if to say—there are lots of silly people in this world, Agnes, and that is *their* problem, not ours.

Boredom with the fitting sessions will get the better of Madge, who will avoid further contamination with the Blackpool Poms by issuing instructions by phone, using Agnes as go-between.

Agnes senses that she and Mrs Ryder share an unspoken way of seeing things. She loves the dressmaker's funny mannerisms: the way she twitches her nose when she pushes the flamboyant glasses up to her eyes, sighs, and looks heavenwards, as if attempting to engage a passing angel.

As Agnes has missed out on basic parental instruction specifically identifying north and south, and left and right, she will struggle when Rita initiates her into the five basic ballet positions. Finally eliminating the need to make the sign of the cross to differentiate her left from her right, these two directions will magically enter her feet and arms. Rita has such a large bedroom that the girls can twirl freely, without bumping into anything. They jump on the beds, stand on their heads, roll over and spin around holding hands till they're sick with happiness. Mother and daughter's bedrooms are alongside each other in the old section of the house. Agnes guesses there is a connection into Mr Ryder's domain through a wardrobe in Mrs Ryder's bedroom, although she has never actually seen it.

The real wonder in the house is the ballet studio on the ground floor. It is called 'George's Room', as Rita's Uncle George apparently paid for the whole extension. A full-length mirror covers the back wall of the studio, with a ballet barre in front and a sprung wood floor—considered essential—compliments also of Uncle George, who plans on visiting one day before too long.

Rita attends her ballet lessons in the 'School of Arts' building in Victoria Street, next to Chatswood Town Hall and has already reached an advanced level in the Trinity College London exams, which are held in Pitt Street, Sydney. Margot Fonteyn is Rita's idol.

Ballet posters, sent from London by Uncle George, cover one whole wall of the studio. Agnes falls in love with all these images. Perhaps most stunning for its pure physicality is a depiction of a blonde-wigged Margot Fonteyn, captured flying through the air in the Ballet Imperial choreography by Balanchine. However, Agnes has decided that her favourite dancer is Moira Shearer. She stares for minutes on end at the wonderful photos of Shearer dancing the first act of *Cinderella*, complete with headscarf and broom.

Agnes becomes obsessed by the ballet, spending hours in front of the mirror practising her foot positions before moving into *pliés* and *battement*, positions which are designed, Mrs Ryder tells her, to give strength and flexibility to the whole body. Rita shows Agnes how to fix a point to return to when doing a *pirouette*. Slowly, gradually, Agnes even manages to do the splits. After hours of excruciating practice, she performs in front of Rita and her mother for correction.

Rita willingly shares the studio space with Agnes, but there is a limit to the diversion of her mother's attention from herself before Agnes spots a note of sarcasm creeping into Rita's voice. Yet, Agnes knows that when she has done well, a kind of raw joint enthusiasm succeeds in sweeping the two friends back together. Thus, the better part of Rita's nature usually triumphs, and both mother and daughter clap and cheer as Agnes takes her bows at the end of her demonstration. She knows her weak point is her hands. Unravelling her fingers, long constricted in anxious fists, is a challenge but, gradually, the music persuades her rigid muscles to open like reluctant buds coming into flower.

Rita is a few years older than Agnes and lives in fear of outgrowing the petite physique of a ballet dancer. She constantly fights a mop of unruly blonde curls. Sharp features—apparently inherited from her father—are softened by heavy-lidded green eyes, polished rosy cheeks and full lips that are identical to her mother's. Rita is the most sophisticated, self-assured girl Agnes has ever met. She can toss off criticism that cripples Agnes, as if swatting a fly off a windowsill, but can also make Agnes feel that no challenge is insurmountable. Rita can mimic English accents and the speech and mannerisms of American screen stars like Lauren Bacall and Veronica Lake. Cloistered in the red berry hedge hole, she and Agnes sing Frank Sinatra songs at the tops of their voices.

As for Mrs Ryder, she is delighted to find a proxy sister for her daughter, particularly one who is besotted with ballet. One day, she hands Agnes a pair of pink ballet shoes which fit perfectly. Agnes loves them so much she keeps them close in her school bag. In return, Agnes persuades Mrs Ryder to let her help her with the hand-sewing in the workroom. Henceforth, many a hem sails out of the morning glory gate, happily sewn by Agnes.

At some point Rita will confide to Agnes in the secret hedge that after a bombing raid in Germany, her father sustained burn injuries when his Spitfire crashed and caught fire in a badly lit English airfield. It will be a subject Agnes instinctively knows not to mention again. She will discover too, over time, that Mrs Ryder has even more reason to feel sad, as her parents were both killed in a German bombing raid in London. She and her brother were saved by a street warden who shepherded them into an underground railway station, miraculous minutes before the raid began. Agnes will think it strange the way mother, father and daughter live in the split-up house, but gathers that they seem happy. When his wife and daughter do visit him through the secret entrance, Agnes sometimes hears Mr Ryder's big belly laugh and his lusty baritone banging out popular war songs on an out-of-tune piano. His timetable is clearly organised to avoid people. He apparently leaves for work in the late afternoon and returns home in the early morning before anyone is up.

Any doubts Agnes might have harboured about devoting her life to ballet will be swept away when she accompanies the Ryders to a production of *The Nutcracker* at Her Majesty's Theatre in the city. In the afterglow of the performance, Mrs Ryder declares Agnes is destined to be a red-headed ballerina like Moira Shearer. Thoughts of working in a leper colony instantly vanish; Agnes will do God's work by training the body he has given her. But she can't ask her mother for money to buy toe shoes, as Madge knows nothing about her daughter's clandestine ballet training, and wouldn't approve. And asking her father would be out of the question, as months continue to go by without him even acknowledging her existence.

One day soon, when Agnes spots a policeman's helmet on the dining room table through the Venetian blind, she will retrace her steps and go straight to the Ryders without going into her own house. From that point, if she ever sees a police car parked nearby, she will stay away. She will be forever grateful to the solicitous policeman for taking care of her mother on a regular basis, as it gives her more time to help Mrs Ryder in the workroom and to practise her ballet in the studio.

When Madge ignores the fact that her daughter doesn't turn up at home at the usual time, Agnes will know she has done the right thing. She also knows never to mention the policeman, in the way that she never mentions Mr Ryder. Encouraged by her mother's prevailing good mood, she will ask her to buy her a ballet book for Christmas. As her mother never remembers a promise, Agnes will remind her continually and so, one day, upon finding the policeman in proximity to her mother in the dining room, she will mention this in front of him to evoke his support and force her mother's hand:

*Oh! Hello! They can only hold Barron at the Ballet for another week. Mummy's buying it for me for Christmas!*

Then she will beat a hasty retreat.

Agnes did not really need to be quite so vigilant in hiding her ballet passion from her mother as, due to the friendly policeman, Madge will be showing less interest in what her daughter gets up to than usual. This maternal good mood will last long enough for Agnes to get not only *Barron at the Ballet* for Christmas but *Barron Encore*—three months later—for her birthday. And, when the moment to buy some new toe shoes arrives, Mrs Ryder will take Agnes to a shop in

Strand Arcade and Agnes will, for quite some time, consider this to be the best year of her life.

When Eric Keen returns from interstate business, instead of going to the farm on Sundays, Agnes will stay home and convert the dining room into a ballet studio where she will dance to her records. As the yellow and green lino has been thrown out, she will have the advantage of a wood floor to dance on. She will imagine her audience seated on the other side of the big window where the cat and canary continue to conduct their absurd relationship. The dining table is the low barre and the sideboard the high barre. She will cover the dining table in a blanket to avoid scratches. After her workout, she will plug in the little record player and the room will fill with Prokofiev. With a scarf around her hair and broom in hand like Moira Shearer, she will immerse herself in the dance and lose all sense of time. Exhausted, she will flop on the old carpet in the hallway and float up to heaven.

She will work hard to improve, but no need to dig deep to conjure up the character of Cinderella for, after all, Agnes *is* Cinderella.

\* \* \*

With the arrival of a small Japanese piano for Christmas from Uncle George, Rita's time is absorbed during the summer holiday with piano and singing lessons. Mrs Ryder maintains that a girl can never have enough strings to her bow and, as her daughter is shooting up like a well-watered bamboo in the monsoon rains, she can always aim for a career in music should she exceed the corps de ballet required height.

Rita has been working hard for the Trinity College ballet exams scheduled for the coming autumn and her dedication pays off. She is cast by Odette, her French ballet teacher, to dance Swanhilda in the second act of *Coppelia*. The eponymous Act One solo of *Cinderella* will also feature.

Rita persuades the ballet teachers to let Agnes sit in on rehearsals for the gala. She is completely enthralled as she watches fluid routines emerge from fixed initial steps and positions. She longs to have lessons at the ballet school, but her mother categorically refuses to pay for them. 'Rosemont' forbids all stage activity, sanctioning only what forms of education lead to university, the caring professions, teachers' training college, or secretarial training—all the approved stopgaps for girls before marriage.

As the big night advances, every usable space in Mrs Ryder's workroom is covered in material to be made into costumes. As Swanhilda, Rita will wear flamboyant red satin to symbolise her jealousy when her fiancé, Franz, falls in love with the motionless girl on the balcony. Agnes knows that Swanhilda will sneak into the toyshop. Trapped inside, she will discover the truth about the doll and will change into Coppelia's blue dress with its marvellous puff sleeves and gleaming satin sash. Seeing his doll dance, the toymaker will believe he has brought his creation to life.

Rita's flair for comic acting enables her to master to perfection Swanhilda's deceptive pretence. With her abrupt, stiff, staccato head and doll movements, together with her startled blinking eyes, she uncannily resembles the tiny ballerina in the music box in Mrs Ryder's living room.

As for *Cinderella,* Agnes never misses a rehearsal. She masters the choreography in her mind during her solitary Sunday vigils. And, at the end of each day's dancing practice at home, her imaginary veranda audience clap and cheer as she takes her final bow, after which she rushes to put the room back in order before her parents return from The Farm.

The miracle happens on a stormy night. Violent thunder and huge seizures of lightning herald sheets of rain that lash at the glass louvres of the Ryder home. Rita is playing cards through the wardrobe with her unseen father, and Madge is at home being looked after by the policeman. Mrs Ryder and Agnes are stitching costumes when Odette, the ballet teacher, bursts through the workroom door, sobbing. Black curls dripping raindrops, lipstick smeared across her cheek, streaks of mascara under her eyes, she can barely speak:

*Janet 'as ze measles. Her maman rang me 'alf an hour ago. Absolument no Cinderella for le gala! And no time to teach anyone else. What are we going to do?!*

Mrs Ryder looks at Agnes, whose heart is thundering. Something exciting permeates the air. A great change is about to occur:

*Surely, Agnes can dance the role? I've seen her do it. Here is your understudy, par excellence!*

And this is how Odette comes to work with Agnes in the Ryder's dance studio in the week leading up to the performance. Mrs Ryder will alter the dark blue satin dress to fit Agnes. And, on Saturday night, when her parents are dining with Parry and Marnie, with scarf around head and broom in hand, Agnes will leap onto the stage in blue toe shoes to match the satin costume. Sick with nerves in the wings, her body on stage will feed on the confidence of knowing the part well. That magical night, intoxicated by the beauty of the music, Agnes will become 'Cinderella'. The applause—when it comes—will no longer be imagined, but real and thunderous. The beautiful bouquet of flowers handed to Agnes will send her rocketing to the moon and she will whisper her thanks directly to God who, she believes, has granted her the greatest night of her life.

Shortly after their joint triumph, Rita's insistence to see the second *Barron at the Ballet* book that Agnes has received for her birthday pushes Agnes close to breaking her long-running embargo of letting friends come to her house:

*No. I'll pop inside and fetch you the book. Please, Rita—you can't go in with me. My mother's sick.*

*You're always saying that. You make her sound chronically bedridden! Wait outside and I'll bring you the book and you can take it home with you!*

It would be a huge mistake to let anyone she knows come into the house. A maternal grenade or bomb could explode any minute and what would Rita think?

Agnes's mind is buzzing. Despite her aptitude for dance, Rita is quietly furious about having outgrown the stipulated height for ballet by several inches, though Mrs Ryder has constantly cited the example of Beryl Grey (who was well over the stipulated height when she made her debut during the war at the Royal Opera House) but this has done nothing to console her daughter. Agnes is frustrated for her best friend, but it isn't her fault that Rita is too tall.

Because she is so out of sorts, Rita is being horribly persistent:

*You've stayed hundreds of times at my house, and I've never been in yours. Wouldn't you say that's a bit out of proportion, Agnes?*

Rita's nasty sing-song tone is frightening Agnes. She feels the familiar pang of panic. Neither of her parents has any clue she has danced 'Cinderella' and Rita could well spill the beans out of spite. Agnes could not explain her parents' hostility to outside interference, nor how her mother would fire up her father to bring his belt down on her for the most minor indiscretion. She couldn't explain it because she didn't understand it herself. But, as they arrive at the Keen's back entrance, Rita was not about to be dissuaded:

*Wait till they hear what a little star you are! They'll be applauding like everyone else!*

*Please don't talk like that, Rita. I hate it when you talk like that. Aren't we friends anymore? Just wait there and I'll come straight back with the book!*

But then Madge suddenly appears on the veranda above. She is wearing an extremely figure-hugging frock. Amazingly, she appears to be waving at the two of them to come in! She guesses her father must have arrived home early afternoon from his last trip, but as she spends so little time at home these days, she has lost track.

Agnes finds herself standing awkwardly next to Rita in the dining room. Suddenly, her father runs out of the bathroom with only a towel around his waist. He grins at them and opens the towel, so they can see his sausage dancing from side to side with the movement of his gait. Madge, who is leaning against the sideboard, lets out a brief, humourless laugh. The flasher turns on the step up the hall and wiggles his hips, giving a final wave of the sausage before disappearing into his bedroom.

Unsure what to do next, Agnes can only think to drag her friend by the hand into her bedroom, where they lie on the floor and flick through the ballet book. Neither mention the wiggling sausage. They come to a whole section on Beryl Grey, who Rita's mother constantly cites as an inspiration for her beanpole daughter, and soon they are laughing and chattering like magpies again.

Rita's friendship is of monumental importance to Agnes, and she will do anything to maintain it. But change will strike hard and without warning when Grandma enrols her in a prestigious new school. Henceforth, she will travel each day by train to Milsons Point and will be wearing a new grey check uniform. It is the school where she will spend the next five torturous years.

After a heated period between Agnes's parents of fierce arguments and sly remarks, her father will temporarily suspend his interstate travelling and, coincidentally, the policeman will stop coming.

\* \* \*

Three weeks of the enforced new school routine have gone by when it strikes Agnes that she has not seen Rita for ages. Today, Saturday, having completed her household chores, she has finally found some time to go and see those who are dearest to her in the whole world. She can hardly contain her excitement.

But the frontage of the Ryder house is completely transformed. She hardly recognises it. Confused, she walks up and down the street outside. The morning glory has disappeared. Gone, too, is the high hedge and with it the cubby house where she and Rita once swore eternal friendship. In its place is a new fence and gate with

*Chapter 11   The Dressmaker*

a padlock, too high to climb over. Agnes is locked out. The front garden has been cleaned up. A line of orderly shrubs stands in place of the former mess of tangled weeds—each bush neatly attached to one of the old bamboo supports. No more mulching leaves with sprouting mushrooms. The glass in the front doors of the porch, and the windows either side, are so clean they look as if they are newly installed. Freshly washed curtains open out and swing in the breeze.

As Agnes looks closer, she notices new straw chairs on the porch and realises the recently painted clean door is partly open. She stands up on a rung of the new gate and calls Rita's name. And she keeps calling for her until the porch door opens further and a tall, slim man, leaning on a stick, slowly comes towards her. This must be Mr Ryder! His twisted face looks as if it has been caught in a door. Lifeless, plastic, cobbled skin distorts his right eye, forcing his nose upwards and exposing a pair of flat nostrils like a pig's snout.

Agnes now remembers what Rita said about a plastic surgeon in England grafting skin onto burnt noses to grow down like an elephant's trunk, which was then cut and remodelled into a new nose. It seemed too extraordinary at the time to be true. Mr Ryder's remodelled nose looks like putty crudely stuck on with glue. His upwardly twisting mouth is set in a permanent sneer. And yet the left side of the face he seems to favour putting forward looks almost normal. The awful story of his wartime accident Agnes has heard in snippets now comes together. She is spellbound. She can't look away. She stares at his face, trying to find the handsome young officer in the photo on the sideboard in Mrs Ryder's living room underneath the scars. But what comes out of his twisted mouth chills her more than his appearance:

*Dear Agnes—Rita and Mrs Ryder can't see you anymore.*

*But why?*

Her head is spinning.

*No more, Agnes. The friendship is over.*

Tears well up in her eyes. She struggles to be strong. She can hardly swallow for the lump in her throat. The proclamations from the twisted lips are low and determined. But she cannot grasp the meaning of what he is saying to her:

*But it can't be! Rita and I made a vow to be friends forever! We exchanged blood and everything! We made a pledge!*

*My dear girl, you will find other friends. It's not because of anything you said or did. My wife and daughter remain fond of you, but things change. Your adventure together is over. Life is like that. One door closes and another opens.*

Agnes feels a searing pain in the vicinity of her heart:

*But I don't want to open and close doors! Please, please, please let me see them! Just one more time!*

She is sobbing uncontrollably. But instead of responding, Mr Ryder turns his back on her and hobbles away back into the house. He closes the door firmly, shutting her out once and for all.

Agnes is shattered. She stands there, stock-still, going over it. A horrible possibility occurs to her. Is this terrible banishment because her father showed off his sausage? Had Rita told her parents about it? About how her mother had laughed and said nothing? She is glued to the spot, lost in her frantic thoughts. Minutes pass and she cannot move.

For the next few days, when Agnes arrives home from her new school, she will drop her bag, do the shopping for her mother, and sit on the wall of her old school opposite the Ryder house. She will wait for Rita and Mrs Ryder to come out. Everyone else she knows in the neighbourhood will pass her, but the Ryder mother and daughter will not be seen.

It will be on the fourth day of her desperate vigil that the two people she yearns to see emerge from their front gate. But Mrs Ryder will put her hand up in a stop sign and Rita will hang her head as they accelerate their pace to avoid her. Agnes will run after them, frantically calling their names as they cross the road to avoid her. There will be a screech of brakes and Agnes will find herself sitting in the gutter. A wild-eyed man who has swerved to avoid hitting her will scream curses at her out of the driver's window. Agnes will stare at him as he drives off, still shaking his head, and she will finally realise that Rita and Mrs Ryder have disappeared from her life. Their rejection having hurt her so deeply, she will stop her patient vigil. It will be years before she fully absorbs the profound effect that Rita's doubtless fulsome description of the showing of the sausage must have had on Mr and Mrs Ryder.

As a last resort to regain some sort of happiness, Agnes will plead with her mother to let her have ballet lessons, but it will be to no avail. After consulting 'Rosemont', it will be decided that elocution lessons would be more appropriate. But nobody will ever tell Agnes *why* it would be. And so, she will put the ballet shoes and the Cinderella dress into a painted shoebox, and they will join the graveyard of dead dreams she keeps under her bed.

# Part Three

If you repeat a lie often enough it becomes the truth.
—*1984* by George Orwell

## CHAPTER 12

# MOTHER MIRIAM

The head nun bellows:
*A child of the devil walks amongst us!*
Agnes's name is obsolete. Everyone knows it is her. From the top step of a veranda that leads to the classrooms, Mother Miriam, the school Superior, scrutinises her pupils—like cells under a microscope—in the courtyard below. A nudge, a smirk, a raised eyebrow or even a frown can provoke the head nun to swoop down from her perch, grip her unsuspecting victim's shoulders, and shake her like a washing machine on spin dry.

Mother Miriam is on Satan's trail and so can't be careful enough, for any moment he could slip by unnoticed. Constant vigilance is therefore imperative: broom cupboards, storage areas, dark annexes, basements, boiler rooms, behind blackboards, even the narrow gap between the walls of the school and the classrooms, the location matters not. Like a gardener searching for snails, she has even been seen scouring the bushes alongside the main drive. Diabolic innuendos cling to the tail of any sudden, unexplainable flash of light. The innate goodness of the middle-class girls from comfortable families who attend the school only pressurises her to delve deeper into darkness. It is not clear what she plans to do with the devil when she does apprehend him.

Mother Miriam has the habit of abruptly changing tack, like a sailing boat, in mid-sentence, but nothing alters the mean curl of her upper lip, nor the twitching pulse in the right reptilian eye. Now Agnes is exposed, the nun proceeds, in a less strident tone, to discuss preparations for Sports Day and a fête to raise money for the black babies in India. The sudden change of subject heightens rather than alleviates the group discomfort. Girls shuffle their feet and look bewildered. Agnes bends her knees and tries to hide behind a tall girl with a head full of black curls like a maze of miniature caves. She wishes she could disappear. It is a bad beginning. Formerly, school had been her respite from the combat zone at home. Now, her whole world has turned into a theatre of war, and any chance of escaping the front line looks remote.

She struggles for reasons. If not for her devil-red hair, then did Mother Miriam single her out because she slunk in alone after the beginning of term like a stray dog? Or is it because, unable to concentrate in class, she throws caution to the wind by constantly amusing her classmates?

Mother Miriam is seemingly unaware of the nervous tic that sabotages her tall, gangly frame. The whites of her eyes enlarge as she rocks backwards and forwards in her worn lace-up black shoes, and Agnes watches, fascinated, as the frenetic pace accelerates until the woman is rocking so fast her face blurs. At this point, the relentless shuddering converts Mother Miriam's stovepipe body into a series of gyrations like a loose hosepipe receiving a sudden gush of water. It occurs to Agnes that perhaps the devil is closer than she thought.

But the mad avenging nun hasn't finished with her yet:

*Look at her cringing in shame and so she should! There'll be no more disruptive shenanigans around here! I'll say no more other than Agnes Keen is a bad influence. Heed my warning, you gullible girls, and stay away from her. One rotten apple in a box can contaminate the lot!*

Agnes dreads those around her will move and expose her. But nobody does. To her relief, some of her new mates from the North Shore inch closer in solidarity. As she braces herself for the nun to swoop, a young novice taps the Mother Superior on the shoulder and whispers something in her ear:

*I'm called away to the telephone, girls! That will be all! DISMISSED!*

With the nun's disappearance, the torture is over for another day. At the sound of the school bell Agnes shuffles into class with the others. The classroom. A place where she is finding it increasingly hard to listen, absorb, and comprehend what is going on around her. At this new school she feels defeated before she has even begun, struggling to navigate the labyrinth of corridors in a huge building that resembles Government House, and slowly finding her way through the enormous grounds that eventually lead to tennis courts and playing fields. Yet, as if granting her a reward for her endeavours, she will shortly discover that the grounds are blessed with dazzling views of the northern harbour.

Agnes's classmates decide that the mad nun 'has a set on her', which seems to mean that Agnes provokes an inexplicable irritation. This is not hard for her to grasp, as she has always had the same effect on her mother. It is hard to know if the nun is singling her out because she happens to be the first unfortunate face the woman sees, or whether she has unwittingly committed a specific offence.

The first assault had happened at morning break, whilst Agnes had been eating play lunch with her friends. As they lounged around, striking sophisticated poses on a bench in the courtyard, Agnes had suddenly found herself submerged in a mass of black cloth as if someone had put a bag over her head. In the process of taking a bite of her sandwich, she had found herself in danger of crunching into one of the wooden rosary beads around Mother Miriam's waist. Thin, sinewy fingers clamped down on her upper arm, and the nun had dragged her across the quadrangle without explanation, plonking her into the middle of a bunch of startled youngsters from the junior school. Then the savage voice had sieved through long, discoloured teeth:

*Stay there! Impudent girl!*

Giggling small girls had fallen silent as they moved apart to accommodate the order, wriggling away awkwardly in an attempt not to look at the culprit. Agnes had stayed put, though yearning to be back with her own group, especially as she could now see their doe-eyed prefect who all, including Agnes, had a crush on, and who had just sat down with them.

But none of the teenagers had looked her way. She had felt glad of this, as recognition would only have added to her humiliation. Agnes had watched in growing dismay as Mother Miriam put an arm round the prefect's shoulder and smiled down at her. The intimate gesture had felt like a further slap.

Marooned in purdah, Agnes saw nuns fly in and out of the mysterious door to the convent at the end of the veranda. This entrance was firmly designated 'out of bounds' and, consequently, the girls were hugely curious to see inside. Talk of underground tunnels leading from the convent to the Jesuit priests—streets away at St Aloysius Boys' School—kept the girls fascinated. Aware of the pupils' obsession, the nuns only succeeded in adding to the intrigue by snapping the mysterious door shut, like the release of a mousetrap, behind them.

Unable to bear her isolation any longer, Agnes had run around the corner, up the stairs, and straight out of the school gate. Her chest collapsing into forceful sobs, she had clung on to the outside wall of the school to stop herself from falling, grief-stricken, to the ground. Then moving on, eyes blinded with tears, she had sent a pile of empty garbage bins scattering in all directions. The clang had been deafening and she had to chase one of the bins down the hill to catch it. As she rearranged the bins back into a neat row at the main gate, she had felt the sky darken and fall upon her, exactly as when Jesus asked his father why he had forsaken him in the Garden of Gethsemane.

Unlike Jesus, Agnes knows she can't be forsaken, because she's never been claimed. That morning, when she had been ejected from her little group of new friends, it had not been the first time she had thought of leaving home—and school—but she didn't know where to go. As a result, she had decided that her faith was being tested.

The devil can assume any guise, after all. Could he be cunning enough to tempt her to lose her faith by inhabiting the hosepipe body of the Mother Superior? In all honesty, she doesn't know *what* to think anymore.

After that miserable event, she decides to keep out of Mother Miriam's way, ducking around corners, standing behind others, and sliding surreptitiously under the desk if her nemesis ever comes into the classroom. Agnes can always detect the nun's imminent arrival— the swirl of the long black habit which sends the beads clanking against the strap around her waist and which amplifies her step is unmistakeable. But what she can't avoid is the uniform inspection. Agnes tries to tell herself she is exaggerating this madwoman's grudge against her, but just the way she waves the others on with scant interest, settling instead on Agnes, makes it hard to deny. There always seems to be something to engage her predatory eye. Regularly forced to stay behind to darn a hole in a glove, or sew up a sagging hem, she frequently misses the train and is forced to catch a later one, all alone.

Agnes remains as resilient as she can in the face of Mother Miriam's persecution by falling over, doing hare-brained tricks, balancing on one leg, jumping like a monkey, and generally being very silly to amuse the others. At least half of her class live on the North Shore and get on and off at different train stations, starting with those furthest up the line who live in big houses with leafy gardens, swimming pools and tennis courts. Not that the kind of house a person lives in makes any difference, thinks Agnes, for they are equal and united in Catholicism. It is the Protestants who are inferior.

The train ride back and forth is, in fact, the highlight of her day. In the mornings, by the time she steps into the carriage with two other girls, there's a rowdy group congregated near the door where they huddle together, chatting and laughing. Agnes absorbs her classmates' anecdotes: family outings and holidays, older siblings' tennis and pool parties, birthday surprises, practical jokes, endearing parental idiosyncrasies, menageries of animals, and descriptions of shows from those who possess TV sets. She cobbles together what she hears and invents a life in tune with her peers. She makes up fictitious visits to see her brothers at boarding school, bearing her beloved siblings delicious birthday cakes which mother and daughter have slaved over together. She invents a loving father, who saddles her pony and calls her pet names like 'Pumpkin' and 'Precious'.

Even Grandma is reinvented. Ever keen on the sensational, Agnes elevates her parents' great love to a fictional level—equivalent to that of Anthony and Cleopatra, Paris and Helen, Queen Victoria and Albert, Jane Eyre and Rochester, Bogart and Bacall, as well as Grace Kelly and Prince Rainier.

Imitating her teachers is the only benefit available to Agnes from their efforts to educate her. Her impersonations provoke gratifying spasms of mirth from the other girls, Agnes having learned that nobody argues with a person who makes them laugh. The train carriage has become her stage. Striding to the station each morning, she edits her inventions, honing bits of her script. She never disappoints her audience, and their pleasure transports her every time. An impersonation of Mother Miriam is her greatest hit—she has even mastered the nervous tic. Her only problem is to get through the performance without collapsing with laughter herself.

Mother Miriam's onslaught will come to an unexpected and abrupt end one day, shortly after the rosary service in the chapel. Given Agnes has pride of place in the nun's crazed state of mind, she knows she really should be more careful but, instead she will hand Mother Miriam the perfect gift by winking at a friend on the opposite aisle of the chapel while they await the signal to file into the pews.

Mother Miriam will spot the transgression instantly, drag her roughly by the arm out of the row of girls, and fling her into a prayer chair at the back of the chapel—recently vacated by a deceased nun:

*Disrespect in a holy place, Agnes Keen!*

It will be a Friday—when benediction follows the rosary. The priest, wearing sumptuous gold and green vestments, will glide out of the sacristy and cross to the altar to officiate. The scent of incense combined with the singing of 'O Salutaris Hostia' at the top of her voice have never failed to lift Agnes's spirits, and this day will be no exception. But the respite will be brief. The service over, Mother Miriam will attack from behind, ordering Agnes to stand next to the stair-rail where maximum humiliation can be guaranteed as pupils walk past when exiting the door of the chapel. Agnes will stare defiantly ahead. Most girls will avert their eyes. As the last voices fade and Agnes waits to be dismissed, Mother Miriam will wage yet another assault. Grabbing at Agnes's arms, she will start to shake her violently, and Agnes will feel a cold fear rise inside as the nun hisses:

*Why do you persist in this boldness? And in the house of the Lord!*

The nun will continue to rant—her face scarlet. The frantic muscular movement behind the heightened complexion will look to Agnes like the internal workings of a clock. An explosion is imminent. Anything might happen—and does. The madwoman will push Agnes's head back over the stair rail. Aware of the three-storey drop looming below, Agnes will see the ceiling above whirling as long thin fingers close around her neck. She will think the nun is going to kill her and, in a survival reflex action, will bring her arms up and jerk the sinuous fingers from her neck, duck low, and race down the stairs:

*Come back you impudent, wicked child!*

Agnes will hear rosary beads and leather strap clash together like an African tribal dance as the nun pursues her. On the ground floor, she will run into the school and, turning hard into the toilet block, lock herself into a cubicle. Mother Miriam's fist will hit the wood of the cubicle door with a resounding thud:

*Wicked, evil daughter of Satan, come out at once!*

From the depths of Agnes's being will emerge a commanding and unwavering voice:

*Go away, Mother! You've gone too far! This is madness!*

There will be a pause, and upon hearing receding footsteps Agnes will be utterly astonished to realise the nun has left. After a short time, to make sure, and still trembling a little, she will dry her eyes, wash her face and run to the lunch-room, where she will collect her tray, sit down at a table on her own and eat in silence. For some reason she will resist confiding in the comfortable goodness of those seated around her. She is desperately confused about who she is, and who they are. She yearns for sympathy yet keeps her distance. Her energy at school has been dissipated into continually showing these girls she is just like them, and so worthy of being part of the group. But the truth is she has never formed a close friendship, like the one with Rita Ryder, with any of them. The inner turmoil of her life has left no space for anything more than a struggle to survive.

But perhaps meagre miracles exist on occasion for, after naming Mother Miriam's erratic behaviour out loud as madness, it will miraculously cease. The nun will, henceforth, ignore her completely.

One day, the psychotic Mother Superior will no longer dominate the school. Nobody will mention her sudden disappearance. Agnes's colourful reputation as 'a naughty girl', however, will be further established and, in the hopeless years that follow, no humiliation meted out by Mother Miriam will compete with the agony of the consistent non-appearance of her parents at prize-giving, and at every other school function.

\* \* \*

The weekly elocution lessons commanded by 'Rosemont' are coinciding with Agnes losing concentration. Gradually, relentlessly, comprehension of the various texts she is obliged to read diminishes. For one horrendous hour, she finds herself scrutinised by a series of bemused voice teachers as she degenerates into mouthing words, without meaning, like a parrot. Words, once dear companions, have turned against her—hovering, smudging, and vanishing from her reach. The downward slide at school coincides with strange levitations in bed at night, when her body seems to rise to join the Guardian Angel in the treasured drawing Richard Pales gave her, that hangs above her bed.

She can no longer read fluently and, to avoid ridicule during sessions of reading by turns aloud in class, she tries to calculate in advance the paragraph she will be designated so she can rehearse it. Sometimes this works but, more often than not, she anticipates her turn incorrectly and is left stuttering and tripping over unfamiliar words like a small child with a severe handicap.

God in his mercy organises a teacher to make Agnes feel better about herself. This octogenarian nun, who teaches English, possesses less power of concentration than Agnes. Unpinned starched wimple seriously skew-whiff, the nun shuffles into class looking as if she is wearing a battered white box on her head. Age has drained her lips of elasticity and her gaping mouth no longer closes properly. A cruel addition to what is already an ugly appearance is the proliferation of hair around her chin. If a passion for literature ever burned inside this woman, it has long been extinguished as the syllabus sends her to sleep within minutes. As each girl reads in turn, the teacher's eyes begin to droop and, gradually, her head flops forward until her own open book becomes a pillow. Once cushioned comfortably, a light snore is audible. The English class waits, motionless, until she suddenly raises her head like a jack-in-the-box and point an arthritic finger at a non-specific face:

*Next, next, next!*

As the teacher's desk is on a raised podium, Agnes takes advantage of the decrepit nun's bad eyesight to sink low over her own desk and so avoid reading altogether. After all, there are enough girls more than keen to oblige, so by abstaining she is giving them a chance to take another turn. Agnes's classmates remain loyal, for nobody ever points out to the teacher she is being missed out. Yet, regardless of her deteriorating ability to read, Agnes still loves to hear a story. The one book she can't forgive the teacher for desecrating with snores is *Great Expectations*. Unlike the soporific crash-landing guaranteed with Shakespeare's *Twelfth Night*, it takes a little longer for Dickens to send the old nun off to sleep. Consequently, as the class are burning with curiosity to know what happens next to Pip and Estella, they gradually edit out their snoring teacher and go on reading.

At the end of the story, when Pip recognises his pretentions, makes amends and embraces Joe Gargery's love, Agnes always wonders if her parents will eventually have a change of heart and value her as much as they do the polo crowd. Yet, she knows in her soul that her educational development is in decline, for she increasingly seeks refuge in the passing clouds and is grasping less and less of what happens around her.

One day, fortunately not in class, the nameless old nun will drop her head onto the New Testament—open at Saint Paul's Epistle to the Romans—and never lift it again.

Mother Miriam may have been the tallest nun Agnes has ever encountered, but her reluctant successor—Mother Jude—is the complete opposite. Closer in size to a midget, she seems to swim inside her capacious habit. Not only is she physically diminutive, but everything about her—from her delicate white skin to the pink blush on her cheek— resembles a saint on a holy card. The devil-crazed tyrant has been replaced by an angel! But this allure of sanctity is reduced when Mother Jude dons a pair of oversized beige glasses. They magnify her pale eyes to the point of cartoon comedy, all the while reducing her tiny nose to a knob.

Agnes comes to like everything about Mother Jude's manner; she puts the girls at ease and doesn't play one off against the other. Named after the patron saint of lost causes, the little nun's soft voice and shy, retiring demeanour can't help but give the impression that she herself may soon be in need of assistance from the very saint whose name she has taken. But her gentle aspect is not confined to voice or nature.

## Chapter 12   Mother Miriam

Instead of rousing assemblies and public humiliation, Mother Jude favours the noticeboard and personal consultation. She makes it known to the pupils that she is always available to listen to their concerns, privately, in her office. Naturally, Agnes is desperate to talk to someone. And so, she hovers outside the new Mother Superior's office with longing. More than once, she resists the temptation to unburden herself for fear any complaints will inevitably reach her mother.

In less than a year, however, Mother Jude will no longer be the head of the convent. It will be decided that her saintly complexion and sensitive demeanour are more suitable for teaching Art. Decades later, all Agnes will remember of her brief initiation into art studies with Mother Jude is the gentle nun's prudish defilement of the school's art books. His delicate masculinity hidden under a toga of pink tissue paper, Michelangelo's 'David' will look like a marcher in a gay parade, and countless will be the variegated tissue clumps adorning the timeline of marble and bronze sausages from the Renaissance to Rodin. Although she has no technical knowledge of art, after her years as the self-appointed keeper of 'The Art Book', Agnes will be further distressed to discover works she has long admired with added extras—particularly Rubens' 'Three Graces' who, under Mother Jude's auspices, now sport clumsy white tissue nappies. And the relaxed fold between the legs of various reclining nudes will be stamped with a single gold star, as if Mother Jude has elevated Giorgione and Titian to the top of the class.

Agnes will long imagine Mother Jude, alone in the privacy of her chaste cell with her tissue paper, like the shy professor in the Marlene Dietrich film, *The Blue Angel* when he blew on a postcard of Lola—secretly titillated by a sudden glimpse of what lay underneath.

By the time Miss Josephine comes into her life, Agnes will be weary of authority figures. A recent graduate of psychology now working as a lay teacher, Miss Josephine will have a target: that of improving Agnes's deteriorating ability to read. Inevitably, Miss Josephine asks the key question Agnes dreads:

*Are you happy at home, Agnes?*

Miss Josephine will fix Agnes with her piercing sapphire eyes. It will be impossible for her to answer sincerely, as the invented life has fast taken over. There will be no option but to go on lying:

*Oh, yes, I'm very happy at home.*

She will try to be diplomatic, for her parents still haven't got over the social worker's questions after little Jim ran away all those years ago. When summoned to the school by Miss Josephine, Madge will taunt her daughter:

*I'm going to ring and cancel!*

But, like the promised pillow-talk call to Grandma, she will never activate her threat. The call to come to the school will have Madge cornered. She will waver, but her vanity will not be able to resist a golden opportunity to give the yellow mohair coat—the one she has knitted specially to take to the Scone polo tournament—its first social outing. This will be her first and last visit to this school and, unlike her deceptive trip to the Mercy Convent, will end in disaster.

Madge will arrive, looking gorgeous in her daughter's eyes. Having had her hair done, her nails will be painted coral pink and the soft yellow mohair will perfectly compliment her shiny dark hair. Hovering in the doorway, Agnes will watch as her mother engages in animated chatter with Miss Josephine. A young, nuggety, bright-eyed nun—also studying the impact of learning difficulties—will be in attendance too.

Agnes will enter the room, sliding awkwardly onto the seat beside her mother and, as the experts talk briefly between themselves, Miss Josephine will turn to address Madge:

*We think Agnes 'sees' words differently to other children. It's a disability that impairs a child's reading fluency and comprehension. Words look 'different' to Agnes.*

Miss Josephine will utter this sentence in a courageous effort to elevate Agnes from difficulty to uniqueness. If, at this stage in her young life, Agnes knows one thing for certain, it will be that she sees more than the *words* in her world differently. She will keep a close eye on her mother for any sign of irritation as Miss Josephine presses on. And then, soon, very soon, the eruption Agnes accurately predicts will come:

*What are you talking about! She's a perfectly normal child!*

*Yes, indeed that's true, and absolutely is not in question. You'll perhaps recall what I pointed out on the school report—about Agnes's short attention span.*

As Madge never reads school reports, she will dismiss this with a wave of a manicured hand. Miss Josephine, unaware of the deadly heat building under the mohair, will plough on:

*Let me point out the three cognitive subtypes—auditory, visual, and intentional...*

She will go on to explain these categories in depth, assuming the listener's interest. The one thing Agnes has always been able to read, without impairment, is her mother's moods. Her survival has depended on it. On this day, as she observes Madge's lips tighten and her voice become strident, and knowing the tipping point would soon be reached, she will brace herself for the inevitable explosion:

*No child of mine is retarded! How dare you!*

Madge will flounce from the room, the assembled experts watching her departure in shocked amazement. When Agnes runs after her outraged mother as she struts indignantly up the drive, Madge will turn on her and snarl:

*I'll deal with you later, young lady!*

## CHAPTER 13
# TRUTHS AND LIES

Agnes hears Eric Keen late at night—when only cats stalk the pavements. He slams the back door and lumbers up the hall as he bounces off the walls on the way to the front bedroom. He is usually mumbling to himself these days. Concern for her father's well-being has stimulated in her close observation of drunks in the street. What drives them to drink? And, lately, the incoherent, dead-of-night pillow talk is sounding even more frantic:

*Let's make the break, Madge, before, it's too late. Let's split with the family, like Parry. Buy our own place in the country. Why not? What's stopping us? Work for ourselves. No bastard telling us what to do. I know sheep and cattle, Madge. I could train horses. Sell them. Get a polo team together. Go to America. I've still got contacts. We'd be free. What do you think?*

Madge's reply is, as usual, inaudible, and Agnes knows, as heavy breathing fills the small space between their rooms, that the sorrowful pleas in the next room will be swept away with the morning light.

Her chances of rehabilitating her father become even more remote on the day he ignores her in front of her classmates. It happens on the side-line before he is about to play polo as a member of the NSW's team at Warwick Farm. They are up against a visiting English side that includes the Duke of Edinburgh. Agnes strolls towards her father, where he is signing autographs surrounded by fans—some of whom are her pals who have unexpectedly turned up to watch the match. She stands with these girls on the outer circle.

They all see Eric Keen turn his head and look straight at his daughter, without showing her any recognition whatsoever. No acknowledgement at all. The empty connection with his eyes is indisputable, along with the snub. The pain is so intense, Agnes feels as if she has been stabbed through the heart. She stays, riveted to the spot, until she fully realises that he really does have no intention of greeting her, or of meeting her school chums, who remain standing uncomfortably beside her.

Shrugging her shoulders in front of them, she tries to cover it up by telling them that she and her father had a fight that morning and that he obviously has not forgiven her. They nod kindly, yet she senses they smell a rat. Perhaps they even doubt he really *is* her father, and not just someone she has invented—like everything else.

The agonising pain lingers, but she cannot hate someone she wants to save. These days, subject to a belligerent hell-fire priest every Friday in the school chapel before Benediction, and relieved now of Mother Miriam's persistent persecution, she lives and breathes saints and miracles and prays constantly and fervently to the Blessed Virgin to send her a sign. Her efforts are gratified when the Virgin Mary obligingly appears on top of the flowering wisteria vine in the back garden as Agnes kneels on the rough ground below, saying the rosary. Wearing a blue mantle over a white robe, Our Lady matches the blooms perfectly. Agnes offers the pain in her knees up to Our Lady and asks her to save her parents.

This apparition had occurred at twilight, precisely when day merges into night. All around Agnes had been silent, as the disruptive Cleary children were indoors getting ready for bed. Ribbons of thin white clouds, like hundreds of merged feathers, had swirled above the vine. As the perfume from the flowers intensified in the evening calm, Agnes had been filled with a wave of pure joy, for Our Lady was whispering to her:

*Have courage. Trust in God and you will find the grace to intercede.*

And, of course, there were the levitations. Although keeping these events to herself at school, she has started to reveal her nightly experiences to Monsignor Harrington in the confessional at the local parish church. When he had revealed to her how Saint Teresa of Avila had such powerful levitations that the nuns in the order had to hold her down, Agnes had eagerly unburdened herself to him:

*One minute, Father, I'm in bed asleep and then the next I'm leaving my body. It's not imagined, but real. I float up to join the guardian angel in the picture above my bed. Is God calling me to bring my parents back to the faith? I'm worried they'll go to hell. They don't go to Mass on Sunday. My mother has forgotten it's a sin to eat meat on Friday. She is so furious when I remind her. I leave the meat on my plate and just eat the vegetables. What's the matter with you, wasting good food? she says. You should be shot. She chastises me, Father, but I remain silent. My mother goes crazy at the mere mention of sin!*

Monsignor Harrington had reassured her that they would work together to restore her parents to God. A surprise visit to the victim of the devil was, apparently, the first step. Thus, the fatal die was cast.

Agnes and the priest having discussed the best afternoon for him to visit her mother and the day had finally arrived. He seats himself on the worn beige two-seater lounge chair, and gazes up at the giant framed picture of three wild horses, their nostrils enlarged, necks straining, manes flowing, as they galloped across an open plain. A recent thunderclap is evident in their terrified eyes and a jagged flash of lightning has just severed the bruised clouds above them, threatening an imminent deluge. Two pale green patterned ceramic vases, encircled by a ring of thin glass teardrops, sit either side of the fireplace shelf, as if weeping for the plight of the horses above. Apart from the guardian angel hovering over Agnes's bed, the horses and the teardrop vases are the only ornamentation in the house:

*Do you like the picture, Father? It might be a scene from the Last Judgement, mightn't it?*

*It is certainly a powerful image, Agnes, yes.*
*Are you interested in painting, Father?*
*Oh, yes. I've been to Rome and seen Michelangelo's work in the Sistine Chapel.*

At this, Agnes had rushed up the hall to retrieve 'The Art Book'. She meant to open it at the Sistine Chapel ceiling but stumbles nervously. Instead, it falls open in the priest's lap at Goya's 'The Third of May 1808'. This page is dog-eared because Agnes is so fascinated by it. The priest gazes down at the ragged queue of terrified men behind the central figure in white who, waiting to be shot, has his arms flung open wide like Jesus on the cross. And there, of course, is the stained earth below, drenched in blood from those executed.

But Monsignor Harrington is handing her back the book in silence. Keen to maintain his interest, and delay her predicament, she shows him Goya's 'Saturn Devouring his Son'. The priest glances down at the huge, demented figure, its eyes like cooked egg yolks, its teeth buried in the half-eaten head of a child:

*What do you think of that, Father? A monster eating his own child!*
*Horrible, my child! Horrible! It's his black period. Goya was out of his mind. You'll upset yourself looking at images like that!*

And, with that, he clamps the book shut and, frowning, hands it back again. Agnes regrets her choice, worrying that he might think her morbid.

When Madge finally joins them, she is wearing what, at first glance, looks like a First Communion dress. To Agnes's huge relief, she is more than gracious to the visiting priest:

*Thank you for coming, Father. This is indeed an honour.*
*Excuse my neglect, Mrs Keen, in not calling on the mother of one of our dearest parishioners sooner.*

Hearing this hopeful start, Agnes departs the room to make the tea. As she boils the water, she thinks of the early slaughtered Christians piled up in the catacombs in Rome. She coughs politely to alert them she is returning with the tray. Then she lays out the best willow-patterned cups and saucers, silver sugar pot and milk jug alongside the pot of tea, together with the basket of little cakes she had bought from the bakery for the occasion. Emboldened by the priest's support and her mother's seemingly even mood, she ventures:

*Father? Do you think you could bless our house?*

*Yes, of course, Agnes my child.*

Madge scowls at her daughter:

*Why don't we ask Father to come and do the blessing after the cleaner has been?*

*Quite so, Mrs Keen, although Almighty God doesn't mind a bit of dirt!*

*Well, he mightn't, Monsignor, but I do!*

There is no cleaner except Agnes. Her mother told so many lies, she despaired of her path to redemption. She had hoped the ceremony of sprinkling holy water and reciting special prayers with a raised cross would purify the atmosphere in this ugly house. This pointed remark to the priest was a bad sign. Indeed, Madge's wrath, once the Monsignor has enjoyed a cup of tea and departed, will be predictably terrible:

*Not a word to anyone—even the Pope—about what goes on inside these walls! Do you hear me? No dirty linen aired in public! You're a nasty little troublemaking tittle-tattle! I'll have no social workers or teachers with new-fangled ideas coming here or summoning me anywhere! And you'll invite that priest back here over my dead body! Have you got that through your thick skull!?*

The only novelty about this tirade will be that Madge Keen will stop threatening Agnes with a beating from her father and give her a clout across the ear herself.

A few days later, when Monsignor Harrington asks in the confessional about life at home, Agnes will be beyond telling the truth.

\* \* \*

Agnes has put her age up by a year to 16 and, in the run-up to Christmas, has landed a job in the children's department of 'Mark Foy's Department Store'. Catching the train each morning to the city is proving to be heaven. She is really loving being usefully employed and pleases the manager so much that he gives her a bonus on top of her wage. She has decided to use this extra money to give her parents breakfast in bed 'Hollywood style' on Christmas morning. Her brothers have agreed to help prepare their parents for this surprise while Agnes makes the special breakfast.

This morning, she is arranging two narrow-necked white vases, containing long-stemmed red roses cut from the garden, and placed on two white fold-out trays with linen mats. With their mother and father firmly anchored in bed, Agnes and her brothers are enjoying the freedom of having the kitchen to themselves. The salt and pepper sets, from Woolworths, sit next to the roses, along with curled butter in white bowls beside tiny jars of imported English marmalade. She has polished the good silver cutlery with the crest so well that the contents of the tray are reflected in the blades of the knives. Tumblers of fresh orange juice and half grapefruits—with the flesh severed from the skin—are sent up the hall with Agnes's brothers. They are smirking their heads off as they pose as straight-backed formal waiters. A second course of fried tomato, mushrooms, ham and eggs is to follow, to be rounded off with hot crustless toast displayed in little toast racks—also from Woolworths. She has wrapped the racks in a tea towel to keep the toast warm, and there is copious hot tea to wash it all down, just the way her parents like it.

Yet, apart from the pleasure of watching the parental jaws in action, the grand breakfast evokes none of the 'oohs' or 'ahs' of delight Agnes has anticipated. After gulping down the last of the tea, the indulged pair stare with bemused disinterest at the three expectant faces of their offspring, who are seated on the bedroom floor patiently awaiting a word of praise or thanks. Regardless, Agnes, ever the optimist, congratulates herself on the seemingly peaceful outcome of the Christmas breakfast project.

Given the blank atmosphere at home, Agnes is easily drawn into the warmth of the Armenian house across the road where Natasha Arziani lives. Sprawled on a Persian rug immersed amongst layers of soft cushions on the living room floor, Natasha and Agnes are treated by Mrs Arziani to mugs of mint tea accompanied by *baklava* drenched in honey and chunks of melt-in-the-mouth Turkish delight. Agnes imbibes the exotic offerings like a visiting ambassador while Mrs Arziani targets her with the task of luring her beautiful daughter—who spends the holidays avidly reading everything from true romance to the classics—from her luscious rosy bedroom and out into the fresh air for exercise:

*She in there all day. She get fat and silly. You, Agnes, make her run... jump... yes?*

In anticipation of Natasha's transformation, Mrs Arziani has had two posts cemented into the ground on the flat strip of land at the side of her house, between which she has hung up a badminton net. She hands Agnes two rackets and a shuttlecock. Agnes believes she is probably the only neighbourhood child who has yielded to the immigrant's entreaties to prise the reluctant Natasha out of her room.

It duly does prove to be a tug of war to get Natasha into the open air and Agnes is, admittedly, more drawn to dally with her in the melting wonder of Rhett Butler and Scarlet O'Hara's tempestuous relationship in *Gone with the Wind* than to drag her outside. In truth, Agnes would like to hide in her friend's cosy and rosy room forever. When Rita Ryder introduced her to the ballet, Agnes had claimed it as her own. Now floundering with the written word, she can only experience Margaret Mitchell's masterpiece through Natasha. It isn't just the inability to read that has stalled her, but devoid of any concrete prospects for the future of her own, she is drawn to tagging on to the lives of others—her reaction to any stimulus, a pastiche of their reactions. She is turning into a second-hand person as the residue of her former self slips away.

No expense is spared on the party for Natasha's 17th birthday. Agnes herself has recently turned 15. Standing alongside her curvaceous friend, she looks like a stick of celery. But, within the space of what seems like the blink of an eye, Natasha has shed her puppy fat, much to Mrs Arziani's delight. She has emerged like a butterfly out of a chrysalis, transforming into a great beauty. Natasha knows exactly what happened in the bedroom after Rhett Butler carried Scarlet O'Hara up the stairs, whereas Agnes still doesn't have a clue. She wants to ask Natasha about sex but doesn't know how. Gradually, she stops struggling to understand, accepting that she is not meant to know things like other people.

The beautiful Natasha will waft out of Agnes's life forever after the holidays, when she commences studying medicine at university. After her daughter leaves the district, her lonesome mother will attempt to describe to Agnes the massacre of Christians by Muslim Turks in Armenia—an event too early for Agnes's mother's knitting bag cuttings:

*Natasha Australian girl. She never see killing. Me and sister… children… see terrible things Agnes… no forget.*

Agnes finds these horrors hard to believe. Armenia is an unknown quantity—on the other side of the world. Yet she knows that Mrs Arziani still feels wary of being spirited back there. She watches her as she fervently kisses an icon of the Virgin Mary to ward off danger. The icon, illuminated with tiny candles, resides in a small room, decked out like a miniature chapel. And the danger, it seems, is not imaginary, for Natasha once confided to Agnes that her father, the sallow silent man with a face like a whippet—and rarely seen—was still wanted in the old country for some kind of sabotage.

Agnes allows herself to be inaugurated into the ritual of the icon. She hopes it is not blasphemous to kiss it, but she can't risk offending such a kindly and generous neighbour. She presses her lips unashamedly to the image for, deep down in her soul, she knows she needs all the celestial assistance she can get.

After Natasha's departure, Agnes's memory continues to fragment. She struggles for chronological order. Tiny snippets remain of accompanying her parents to a polo tournament after her recent 15th birthday, but she doesn't know how she got there, nor does she recall the matches, spectators, players, or gracious Janie in her sixth-floor finery, nor the fabulous Federation House and Museum with its antique buggies and carriages. Madge tells her how lucky she is to be received at Springfield, as if she's going to be presented at Buckingham Palace itself, but Agnes retains no memory whatsoever of Janie Marble Flood's ballroom—or anything else.

All that remains in her brain is the sense of running from a man late at night. She sometimes wonders if this man is her father but, when she struggles for clarity, the face retreats like a tortoise into a shell and stays hidden. Sometimes a blur of features, the mouth set in an ugly grimace, comes back, but she doesn't know why she must escape him.

Agnes now locks herself in the den so her mother can't force her to go to the polo practices at the farm on Sundays, especially as Madge insists her daughter now wear high-heel shoes and stockings like her. But Agnes has to be alone. She has nothing to say to anyone. She doesn't unlock the door of the den until she sees her mother and father drive off, after which she wanders listlessly around the house. The heavy mahogany table with the clumsy pineapple feet and the sideboard opposite have seen it all. Here she had dreamed of being a ballerina. Why had the Ryders abandoned her when she loved them so much? She had been prepared to go on dancing until her toes bled—no sacrifice would have been too great. Her dreams of success are dead. Death and endings increasingly occupy her thoughts. She imagines herself at the funeral of her parents. Once, when girls and teachers at school consoled a student over her mother's recent death, Agnes found herself secretly wishing it had been Madge.

In the weeks following the polo tournament, she finds it

hard to breathe. Clouds clog her mind. She continues the dizzy, disconcerting levitation in bed but tries to ignore it. She is a tiny ship tossed in rough seas, but a safe harbour will soon appear in the form of a home of a school friend.

\* \* \*

It is only one train stop up the North Shore Line, yet the crossing into Roseville via Boundary Road at the top of Archer Street is dramatic. Small houses on cramped blocks give way to dwellings with massive gardens, tennis courts and swimming pools.

White-painted windows and a double-sloping roof soften the solid vertical lines of the chocolate-coloured brick bungalow belonging to the Kellys. The family which lives there get on with their lives without explaining themselves. They are the Kellys, and that is good enough.

Mr Kelly seems as wide and tall as the house, lumbering around like a parody of a military sergeant, giving orders that nobody takes any notice of. He is a self-made man—a successful importer of textiles into Australia from America and Japan. He doesn't *kowtow* to a 'Rosemont' power base as Agnes's parents do, nor does he bother about scoring points for heaven or the state of his immortal soul. He lives in the moment, works hard, and keeps getting richer.

The days float by at the Kelly house like the melody of a familiar song. For Agnes, the underprivileged child, visiting the well-appointed Kelly home is like moving from the servant's quarters to the main house. But her desire to belong can never be more than a pipe dream. In truth, she slides into the household as a charitable replacement for Maria Kelly's former best friend, who has decided that being bullied by Maria is too high a price to pay for lavish Kelly family holidays.

Agnes doesn't deem Maria to be a bully exactly, but the girl is very direct to say the least. Agnes is bewildered when she asks her *why* the nuns pick on her, *why* she stutters when she reads, *why* her parents don't renovate their house, and *why* they don't care where she goes. Agnes wonders all the same things, so has no answers. It is like asking someone with a crippled leg why they don't walk straight. Intriguingly, Maria has started standing up for her at school, but Agnes intuits that her new friend's indignation smacks more of affectation than conviction. It never occurs to her that if she had a supportive family and a rich father, like Maria, her life might be better. She has increasingly come to accept that she just isn't worth much.

Maria and Agnes ride their bikes together over the autumn holidays. Agnes doesn't have a bike, so borrows one of the many spares in the Kelly's overstuffed garage. But the bike riding will end when Maria is cast in the lead role of a lavish end-of-year school musical and her spare time taken up with extra singing and acting lessons.

On Maria's 'Big Night', Agnes sits on stage, like a prop, in a formless green satin dress and watches her friend's vocal cords vibrate in her neck. She is fascinated, too, by the minute bell-like bulge of skin between the gap in her front teeth, which somersaults like a punching bag. She will have no idea what the musical is all about, her objective simply being to avoid arousing anger, as any kind of human aggression now makes her tremble like a violin string. In a semi-daze, she will accept her position as an extra in Maria's life. She misses kissing the candlelit icon, and the gastronomical delights enjoyed while lounging on the Persian carpet with the Armenians, but since Natasha went away to university, that friendship is long redundant.

Observing Mrs Kelly's passivity is like being bathed in velvet. She sits, still as a sphinx, in a grey wing-back chair opposite the front door, waiting for someone to come in. Her abnormally small head, thick wrestler neck and straight body devoid of curves make Agnes think of the Henry Moore stone lady in 'The Art Book'. Because Mrs Kelly has a cleaner who cooks, and three sons in boarding school, she is never pressed for time. Agnes obligingly worries with her over how to manage the fine baby hair Mrs Kelly says she has inherited from her mother. She attempts to add extra volume with a tight perm that doesn't suit her, and wears hair nets in a host of different colours and textures. She favours one embedded with glass beads that twinkles like tiny stars in the sunlight but, indoors, looks to Agnes like a milk-jug cover protecting against flies.

Over time, Agnes gets to know all the anecdotes attached to the various photos of Maria that are abundant, and even encourages continual re-showings as an excuse to stay close to this calm woman with the gentle voice and manner. But she does feel awkward when Mrs Kelly quizzes her for information about Maria and sometimes wonders if she is only being nice to her so that she can find things out about her taciturn daughter. It seems that, of all Mrs Kelly's four children, Maria, the only daughter, is her favourite.

When a pretty girl with a blonde ponytail and curly wisps around her ears arrives at school halfway through term, Agnes holds her breath a little. Jacqueline is from the New Hebrides and is fluent in French as well as English. When Maria captures Jacqueline as a proper best friend, Agnes finds herself turned into a tag-along. Disconcertingly, Mrs Kelly seems just as smitten with this new friend as her daughter. As Agnes herself was unexpectedly consigned a position in the Kelly household, and is still grateful, she can listen without envy to Mrs Kelly's praise of Jacqueline and her arrival, as if she has parachuted into their lives from heaven. But Jacqueline will soon meet a boy and turn her back on Maria, and so Agnes's status will be elevated once more.

Desperately shy, Agnes is intimidated by Mr Kelly, making herself scarce when she hears his booming voice. He has a bulbous, open-pored nose like a pincushion and sees the world through a pair of thick horn-rimmed glasses. He spends much of his time overseas. Mrs. Kelly says he is accident-prone.

Agnes notices that Big John Kelly's family talk more about him than to him, and although he often provokes riotous laughter and is genuinely much loved, the house is always more peaceful in his long absences. Homecomings from his travels abroad are made all the more spectacular as he always returns laden with gifts. Maria's classmates are in awe of her imported dresses from America and more than a few of them have confessed to Agnes that they feel like tripping her up out of pique.

When he is home, Big John enjoys sailing his boat. Because Mrs Kelly prefers her shadowy wing-back chair to sitting on deck with her husband in the full sea glare, Maria and Agnes become Big John's mariners. With his Captain's hat pulled over his ears, he extends loud nautical greetings to other weekend sailors as they traverse the network of inland waters from the mooring at Bobbin Head. At 'Rosemont', they have a word to describe people like Mr Kelly, dressed like an English Admiral as he strides the deck of his shiny new launch: 'common'. Aunt Sill, in her new-out-of-the-box shoes, refers to the Mr Kellys of the world as 'nouveau riche'. As Australia is only two centuries old, Agnes wonders how long it takes to sanitise financial success.

Agnes longs to belong. To be fully part of the light-hearted Kelly banter. But she will never be more than an observer—a stray cat drinking a bowl of milk at the back door.

When Maria's parents decide to host the very first mixed evening party for their daughter, it will be the first such party Agnes has ever attended. The long, wide wooden-floored back veranda with its aspect over a vast back garden makes, in Agnes's estimation, a perfect dance floor. Agnes's parents have been invited but have sent their excuses. Parents who do attend will watch their daughters cross the floor to dance with boys—often for the first time.

On the evening of the party, the wooden planks of the veranda pulse as girls in full skirts, bolstered with layers of petticoats, spin like Ferris wheels as they jive to the beat of Chuck Berry and Bill Haley and the Comets. Later, when the lights are turned low, couples shuffle around to the slow rhythm of crooners' torch songs. Most of the girls have teamed up with boys from the two Jesuit schools—St

Aloysius and Riverview—where many of their brothers are pupils. Agnes assumes they will probably go on to marry them, thus avoiding the pitfalls of marrying outside the church.

Agnes's Aloysius boy is called Don. She is entranced by his soulful doe eyes and wistful smile and admires how his pithy remarks cut through the usual soppy sentiment and mindless chatter. Don says what she herself thinks but doesn't dare to say. His intensity manifests a lack of ease that matches her own. No one has introduced them. She had just found herself sitting next to him on a bench at the party, as if it was preordained. Normally she would avoid eye contact, her gaze stuck no higher than anyone's neck—so it is thrilling, this evening, to stare candidly, like an equal, into Don's eyes. Lost in his gaze, the laughter and chatter on the veranda disappear entirely until there are just the two of them, in the world. She likes the clumsy way he holds her when they dance together awkwardly at the end of the evening.

Don will drive her home in his car and invite her to be his partner at the Cadet Ball. They will share what will become an impossibly short first love.

What is still very strange to Agnes is how oddly her father had behaved when Don had arrived to pick her up to take her to the Ball. She was wearing an off-the-shoulder dress, its pale green satin underskirt shining through the white, slightly transparent, overskirt and clutches a white, silver-threaded mohair stole, tastefully draped around her shoulders. Agnes's mother had answered the door, directing Don to wait in the lounge room in front of the storm-crazed horses.

As Agnes eagerly rushed out of the bathroom, she had collided with her father just as he entered the back door. He was, yet again, in an inebriated state. Used to being ignored, she had been shocked when he stopped and spoke to her:

*Where do you think you're going dressed like that?*

Before she could answer, Don, who had heard her father's voice, walked out into the hall. He was looking so handsome in his army cadet uniform that Agnes had held her breath. She had never introduced her father to anyone, so she initially stumbled for words:

*I... I would like you to meet my father, Eric Keen. Daddy, this is Don Burns.*

Don had greeted Eric Keen confidently, stepping forward to shake his hand:

*Good to meet you, sir.*

To the young couple's utter surprise, Eric had brushed Don's hand roughly aside and pushed past him, still holding his briefcase. Agnes and Don had no choice but to retreat to the dining room, where they silently listened to his raised voice as he spoke to his wife in the front bedroom:

*Where does she think she's going dressed like that?!*

*Your daughter and Don are off to the Cadet Ball, Eric.*

*Why wasn't I consulted? She's too young to go out with boys—wearing dresses that fall off her shoulders!*

*Now, Eric, you've lost track. She's turning 16 next March and most of her classmates will be there.*

And then suddenly there was Agnes's belligerent drunken father standing above them on the step into the dining room. He was swaying on his feet, but Madge was quickly by his side. Turning her husband around lightly, she had waved Agnes and Don away with a brief nod.

A few weeks prior, Agnes had heard her mother boast proudly to Marnie, by phone, of the upcoming Cadet Ball with 'the Aloysius boy' and it had made her wonder whether, because of the way her mother saw the world, she was no longer deemed a dangerous single woman simply because a man had invited her out.

Hand in hand, Agnes and her beau had run out of the back door to Don's car. How different her life might have been if she had gone on running and never come back.

Agnes has spent her life worrying about what people think of her dilapidated house but, with Don, she feels no compulsion to apologise. Somehow, she knows he does not care what kind of a house she lives in. Not having to pretend is liberating. And, to his great credit, Don has made no comment about her father's churlish behaviour and drunken outburst. To Agnes, it is as if she and Don have jumped into a safe cocoon and can now float over any storm by simply not acknowledging it exists.

But Don will never enter the Keen house again for Agnes dare not risk a repeat performance. The remainder of their relationship will be sensibly conducted outside those problematic walls.

She soon discovers that Don has his own family sorrow, for he is mourning the recent death of his mother and a subsequent estrangement from his father. An only child, he isn't unwanted like Agnes, but shares an incomprehension comparable to that of Shakespeare's Hamlet over his father's too-hasty relationship with another woman.

Father and son live in a hilly backstreet in Lindfield. Only one stop further up the line from the Kelly's place, their two-storey house is so overgrown with trees and shrubs that only flashes of red brick peek through the smothering jungle. Agnes never goes inside, but happily keeps Don company like a fellow surveillance officer, observing the house from his parked car. Don has a pair of binoculars which he trains on the house whenever he knows 'the girlfriend' is there. Out of respect for his mother's memory, he has vowed never to be at home when she is visiting his father.

Once the scarlet woman's car leaves, Don drives Agnes home, pleased to have staved off any unwanted contact with the interloper. In the sanctuary of Don's car, they kiss and cuddle, pulling apart when passion overtakes them—at which point they listen to the car radio. It is as if they are living out a story from the pictures. To avoid her father, Don drops Agnes in Archer Street. Like Romeo and Juliet, the young couple live a clandestine adventure between two contaminated houses.

Membership of the school debating team has helped Don to see both sides of an argument and articulate his thoughts, and Agnes longs to emulate his erudition. She talks with him every day by phone in secret, from the handset in the den, and from public phone boxes, and soon realises that bereavement has made him mature for his years. He loves jazz and, when there is no sign of the scarlet woman invading his home, introduces Agnes to Dave Brubeck, Shelly Mann, Gerry Mulligan, John Coltrane and Miles Davis. She loves the way he loses himself in the music, watching avidly as he mimes playing individual instruments. Decades hence, memories of Don will remain embedded for Agnes in the melancholic sound of 'Around Midnight.'

Don will never tell her she is stupid, as others have done. At this time in her life, he will be the only person she can be frank with about her prevailing state of mind. Yet, although she trusts him as if he is part of her, she will never—*can* never—value him properly because she doesn't value herself. Still haunted by nightly levitations, she will lose the ability to recall even elementary arithmetic. She will fall asleep over her books and will not recall how to spell simple words—formerly known well. She will be like an old lady with dementia, her mind seemingly programmed into forgetting. In lucid moments, she will realise she has to fight for a future and, at other times, will wonder if she is actually losing her mind.

She will pray before entering the exam room in Willoughby but, despite a seismic struggle, concentration will evade her. Her head will turn into a radio stuck between stations. She will write a great deal, and then lose track of the question. Sweat will pour off her. The clock will be ticking. She will wrestle courageously, but will know she has lost the battle.

After the exams, Agnes will feel estranged from Don as she can manifest no ambition. Her lack of fluency will inevitably hamper future secretarial work and she will be barred from any jobs requiring good reading and writing ability. She will try to put a brave face on a chronic disability.

The tension at home will become explosive and neither her

prayers, nor the pledge of total abstinence, will have any effect on her father's increasingly heavy drinking.

On leaving her school, her final act of rebellion will be to wire a Real Estate 'For Sale' sign she has found onto the academic establishment's imposing front gates.

CHAPTER 14

# THE INQUISITION AT ROSEMONT

Agnes has no memory of the months that follow, yet undefined fragments remain, rather like the sight of a familiar dress in a crowd with no inkling of why it strikes a chord. Time disappears from her. She cannot recall leaving the house on the corner of Rose and Edmond Street. Nor of leaving her white chest of drawers with the ornamental ceramic roses made for her by Dora Chadwick. Nor leaving her picture of the guardian angel, 'The Art Book', the ballet books, the toe shoes, and all the other lost dreams hidden away in shoeboxes. In the summer of her sixteenth year, everything is swept away, and with it, Agnes loses contact with what defines her.

She hears that she has failed her exams. Her parents' hostility is palpable. She is standing outside a familiar red-brick building with them so it must be serious, as she never accompanies them on an outing for pleasure. They are mounting the steps at 'Rosemont'. The familiar amber letters above the entrance swirl before her eyes. This is her first reference point in months. She doesn't know where she lives. She has so many questions whirling in her head but stays silent.

However, the wonder of the mahogany-panelled entrance remains, along with the line of letterboxes into which she imagines the postman slipping letters addressed to educated inhabitants who read classics like *Middlemarch* and *War and Peace*. It is a summer afternoon in early January 1959 and the red carpet in the foyer is spotless.

Aunt Sill opens the door abruptly and scowls at Madge and Agnes.

Primped, ironed and coiffured, she reserves her smile for Eric. Her perfect, just-out-of-the-tissue-paper medium-heeled navy shoes sink into the carpet as she strides ahead like an office receptionist— leading the way to supreme command.

Grandma is seated on a low tapestry chair in the small antechamber at the end of the living room. She smiles when Eric goes down on one knee and kisses her hand. What a crawler! For all her confusion, Agnes can still see straight through her father. He accepts the offer of whisky and Agnes and Madge agree to take tea.

Aware of his princely status, Eric wanders into the living room and pours himself a generous slug of Johnny Walker into a cut-glass tumbler, adding ice cubes with tongs from a thermos. He swirls the amber liquid around approvingly, before taking a serious gulp. The Grand Matriarch is keen to quiz him on his news, for he is one of the last two of the dynasty managing to keep her beloved game of polo alive:

*Hope all's well between you and Ben?*

Madge pulls a face at the sound of her brother's name, but Eric replies without a second's pause:

*Oh, yes, all goes well.*

He is seated on a low chair next to his 'boss' and is jiggling the ice cubes in his glass. Agnes notices that Grandma is wearing her favourite red hat. In fact, she reckons even more feathers might have been added to the adornment on top. The hat sits on Grandma's head at a jaunty angle, as if asking for a compliment. Eric obliges:

*You're looking wonderful today, Ellen. Red is decidedly your colour.*

*Oh, thank you, kind sir!*

Grandma is smiling foolishly, like an aging coquette. Agnes spots that she has lipstick on her teeth. She wants to tell her but expects such an intervention would be deemed impertinent. Eric extends his arm around the back of his boss's chair and makes a corny joke that isn't funny but the three ladies chuckle in unison, in compliance with the rule that all male contributions, no matter how inept, must always be responded to favourably.

Sill has spotted the teeth problem too, placing a warning finger against her own lips, and handing her mother a tissue. Grandma takes the hint and rubs them with the vigour of cleaning a window. Task completed, she smiles at her daughter, who confirms the 'all clear' with a nod. Grandma continues the interrogation:

*How are you enjoying living at the farm, Eric?*

Madge answers for him:

*Thank you, Mother, it's wonderful.*

*And how do you find the drive, Eric?*

Eric Keen answers this for himself:

*No problem. I'm up early with the light to attend the jobs around the stables before I leave for the factory. There's less work as the horses are out in the paddock. I'm on the road before peak hour, so manage to avoid the traffic.*

Grandma sits back in her chair. A pronouncement is obviously forthcoming:

*Well. Now that you're living there, this might be the moment to put the farm into your names. My solicitor can transfer the property into all four names as tenants in common. But he'll include a clause giving you both sole rights over the cottage, which means you'll be able to reside there, and make improvements, without consulting Ben and Beth.*

Sill appears again. She is wearing a white apron over her navy-blue shantung pleated dress and is obviously headed to the kitchen to make tea. Responding to her mother's prod, Agnes offers to help. In the spotless kitchen, under Sill's brusque direction, she puts four rose-printed china cups and saucers, a matching milk jug, a silver sugar bowl with tongs and teaspoons on a tray, all the while struggling to stop her hands from shaking.

Sill lifts down a box of cakes from a shelf, opens the lid and holds the contents up for Agnes to admire:

*I bought these at a new bakery in Double Bay. Aren't they divine! I've cut these round paper doilies so we can put one on each of the three tiers of the cake tray. Now! How will we arrange them?*

Agnes knows this is a rhetorical question, as Sill never delegates arrangement to anyone.

She watches her aunt as she fills the silver teapot with hot water and proceeds to carry in the tray. Agnes trails behind her with the cake plate. Something is amiss in the room. Things have been said about her in her absence. Agnes closes her ears to avoid listening and stares out of the window at the earthenware pots full of red geraniums. She has always admired the way they adorn the flat roof of the building opposite. The sun on the horizon is still so fierce it looks as if it might melt the boats on the harbour. The sea is drained of colour. The sound of her name draws her back:

*Agnes, I've arranged for you to start school at Rose Bay Convent at the end of next month. You will board, so we need to get you fitted with uniforms.*

Grandma has dropped this bombshell in a matter-of-fact tone. Agnes is shocked to the core. It is too late for this! Four years ago, she would have been more than glad to get away from her mother, but the horror of more Mother Miriams and still further humiliation over her poor reading abilities now hit her like a brick in the head. She believes Grandma is sincere in her belief and convictions, but she is no Henry Fonda in *Twelve Angry Men*. She will have no reservations in pronouncing Agnes 'GUILTY' along with the rest.

Madge speaks for her daughter, as usual:

*Thank you, Mother. This is just what needs to happen. Agnes thinks she can run her own life. She's too self-willed for her own good.*

*Grandma, thank you, but I can't possibly go!*

*What do you mean you can't go? What is stopping you?*

*I can't concentrate in class. I try, but a terrible tiredness prevents me. I can't control it, Grandma! I'm physically there but lessons come and go, and I don't understand anything. Something has happened to me. I stammer and shake when I'm asked to read. They say I'm a bad influence, a troublemaker, but it's just that I can't remember things. I try but nothing works! I'm giving, and helping, and praying, but it all goes wrong!*

In response to this unburdening, Madge cannot resist a nasty tirade:

*You see, Mother, she's got this boyfriend. That's why she failed her exams. All she can think of is how to see him. She spends all her time in his car, instead of studying for her exams. Imagine, bold as brass, parked near our house! God knows what they get up to! Her father and I can't discipline her. She takes no notice of us. She's a delinquent!*

Agnes sees red in front of her eyes. It is as red as the outdoor geraniums. She has clenched her fists. She has never felt more like punching her mother. The fight may be on, one she will inevitably lose, but she can no longer hold back. It was time for her mother to hear the truth:

*Don't you start bad mouthing me and telling lies when I spend my life slaving for you! You've got the devil inside you! Monsignor Harrington told me you're going to hell unless you come back to God!*

Her mother gapes like a goldfish. Grandma is looking confused, and Aunt Sill is glaring at her as if she is a substance capable of polluting the furniture.

Grandma composes her features, sits back in her chair, and chooses to use her most level tone:

*Agnes, you don't know what's good for you. Nobody will employ you without the leaving certificate. It's time to come down to earth and capitulate. Your parents can't cope with you. You'll make new friends at Rose Bay and in six months you'll have forgotten all this nonsense.*

Agnes is biting her lip trying not to cry. Nobody ever takes any notice of what she says. Grandma has taken off her hat. She has some problematic children and now they are producing grandchildren with issues. She has no tolerance for individual differences. She is a black and white thinker. A child is either good or bad, and Agnes is clearly the latter.

Eric Keen has remained silent during this heated exchange. Agnes is vaguely aware of him wandering backwards and forwards between the closed balcony and the whisky bottle. But she has no doubt that he will be annoyed at her rebellion, for Grandma is offering to take his vexatious daughter off his hands and, what's more, pay the bill. Agnes tries one final time to be heard:

*I'd rather die than go to that school, Grandma! I can't bear it. You can't make me. I won't do it!*

Blinded with tears, Agnes runs out of the front door and slams it hard behind her. She jumps down the stairs two at a time and then dashes through the swinging door onto Rosemont Avenue. It crosses her mind briefly to run out in the road straight in front of a car, but she keeps going along the pavement. It occurs to her she is close to Aunt Beth and Uncle Ben's flat. Beth has always been kind. She runs up the stairs to their door and knocks frantically.

When Beth opens the door, Agnes flies into her arms, howling like a baby. She gasps with emotion as she tells her about boarding school and why she can't go. She searches Beth's pretty, distressed face for a solution, knowing in her heart that this poor, mild-mannered woman is incapable of anything more than laughing at her husband's bad jokes and writing polite thank-you letters. On this terrible day, one thing is crystal clear to Agnes. She is crippled inside. She is also aware, although a desperate need to belong blinds her to the truth, that none of the people to whom she is related can possibly help her. Sweet, ineffectual Beth can only dry her tears, offer tender words, and send her on her way.

Predictably, Beth rings 'Rosemont' and within half an hour her parents pick Agnes up on the corner of Ocean Avenue. They drive in silence through Centennial Park, turning at the showground, then on past the cotton factory, before moving into the setting sun. They are on their way to their new home at The Farm. Agnes leans on the front seat between her parents, her head in her arms, desperate for some human warmth.

The shade is down over the windscreen to block out the blinding rays of the western sun. Her father simmers with annoyance. He has forgotten his sunglasses. From her between-the-seats vantage point,

Agnes stares at him. Liberated from the glare at the Liverpool turn-off, he has finally stopped frowning. His bloodshot eyes look like two crushed bluebottles. A noble nose dominates a fine broad face, its high cheekbones tapering to a well-shaped rounded chin. It strikes her that he looks Scandinavian, but of course his red hair points firmly to his Irish ancestry. Of course, he might be a throwback to the Viking invasion. But the application of copious amounts of hair oil has turned his coppery mane boot-polish brown. There is something comical, ridiculous even, about the greasy strands that, like the lines of a child's train set, are now plastered to his forehead. Self-absorbed as usual, he doesn't notice his daughter's sharp eyes on him.

Agnes is relieved that, as they approach The Farm, neither parent has mentioned during the entire journey what has just happened. Perhaps, like the late-night pillow talk, the drama at 'Rosemont' has been consigned to the void. Forgotten it might be, but she knows all too well that nothing is ever forgiven.

The car radio has been blaring out the latest music hits, interspersed with news of a crisis in Cuba and Buddy Holly's death. Her father changes the station to catch the racing results. This decisive action seems to bring Madge back from Mars. As if she is reading her daughter's mind, her mother breaks the long silence:

*Don't think your father and I are going to maintain you after you snubbed your nose at your grandmother. Free schooling and expenses rejected by Miss High and Mighty who knows nothing!*

I'll get a job.

Madge's shoulders shift huffily in her seat:

*And what kind of job do you think you can get with no qualifications or training?*

Eric shoots her a lethal glance in the windscreen mirror:

*Will you shut up! I'm trying to listen to the radio! I don't want to hear anything more about her. She's finished as far as I'm concerned!*

She senses a conspiracy between these people—her parents—as if she has been set up. The firestorm inside her rekindles. Her guts are swirling like a wild river. She connects with her father's chlorinated swimming pool eyes in the mirror and shouts:

*I hate the way you suck up to Grandma. You care for no-one but yourself. You ignore me and never defend me! You blame Uncle Ben for lying, but you lie all the time! You're a horrible, sly, whinging, two-faced man with no compassion or pity!*

The mask cracks, and the monster appears. He whips around and slaps her in the mouth with full force. She tastes blood as she lands on the back seat. The car swerves as the monster bellows:

*I'll kill her! I'll damn well kill her!' Christ! Look what she made me do! We nearly hit that ute!*

*Calm down, Eric! Keep your eyes on the road!'*

Agnes's tooth has cut her lip, but instead of showing a vestige of concern for her daughter, Madge slides along the seat and puts her arm around her husband's shoulders. As Agnes watches as her mother caresses the back of his neck with her coral-pink fingernailed hand she knows she is simply a pawn in a diabolical game. They have stolen her life. Their backs unite to block her out.

Her next gut reaction feels instantaneous. Reflexive. She opens the door of the moving station wagon and flings herself out. She rolls over until she drops into a ditch at the side of the road. Her forehead hits the edge of a rock. Blood trickles down her face. Her father drives on. Neither parent appears to look back. Then she hears their car stop suddenly. Agnes can see them arguing through the rear window. The car is only a short distance from the gate of The Farm. Agnes's hip hurts, but her legs are still working because she can wiggle her toes. Shafts of sunlight cut through the avenue of gums on the opposite side of the road. Cloud puffs high in the sky look exactly like ducklings following their mother in a line to a pond. She has landed at the foot of the hamlet that includes the general store. If she tilts her head back, she can see the top of the little Anglican Church of the Innocents up on the hill.

Her mother will spread a towel on the back seat of the car to protect the upholstery from bloodstains. Her father's face will have turned to stone. In less than an hour, he will pull the car up behind an ambulance at the entrance to the casualty department of Liverpool Hospital and, in 10 years' time, Madge will drive to that same spot with her dead husband in the back of a car, cradled in the arms of her youngest son, Jim.

\* \* \*

The rosy-cheeked girl at the hospital entrance desk has a miniature nurse's cap perched on top of a tall chestnut bouffant, like the summit marker on a mountain. Overwhelmed with shame, bloody, barefooted, Agnes has hidden her face under the blue towel retrieved from the car, like someone avoiding the press. Her dress is filthy, and she has left her sandals in the ditch.

The beehive nurse shuffles her large body around the desk and gingerly lifts a corner of Agnes's towel:

*Hang on, sweetie—we're here to help. I know you're poorly, darling, but we need a few details.*

She rubs the back of Agnes's hand as she writes with the other one, beaming intermittently, her pleasant mouth full of metal teeth braces.

No physical wound can touch the gut-wrenching shame Agnes experiences, knowing she is unwanted. No stranger must know this sad fact either. She mumbles her name, followed by the address at Chatswood as she doesn't know the new one at The Farm. She thinks of ringing Don Burns. It never occurs to her she might have been killed. She remains obsessed with the sight of her mother invading the space she vacated just after her father hit her in the mouth. Neither of them has ever cared about her education and she has now gifted them the justification to abandon her, once and for all.

Still drowsy from a sedative, Agnes awakes on a narrow bed in a small, curtained cubicle. Everything appears elongated and distorted, including her mother, who has not just one, but three, ugly faces.

Before Madge can lay into her, a young doctor with enormous dark eyebrows on his several faces pulls back the curtain and asks how she feels:

*She's much better now, Doctor, so perhaps we could go as my husband's waiting in the car outside. He's in shock.*

The doctor gently grips Agnes's shoulder as her eyes start to focus. He addresses her directly:

*I've put four stitches at the side of your head, along with a couple in your lip. Your mother has said you won't be coming back here, so any medical centre in Sydney can take them out. No more falling out of cars, young lady! I hear the door wasn't properly closed, so when you lent against it, out you went. Go home and relax. I told your mother not to blame herself. Accidents happen.*

He concludes this advice by winking at Agnes and squeezing her ankle reassuringly. If she couldn't live with the kindly nurse with the bouffant beehive, this jolly doctor would do fine, she thinks with longing. She thanks him but is unable to smile due to the revulsion she feels of being party to yet another of her mother's devious lies.

As she and her mother walk out of the hospital, Madge makes a grim pronouncement that doesn't surprise Agnes in the least:

*Your father wants nothing more to do with you. What you said will never be forgiven.*

Arriving at The Farm, Agnes flings the car door open, hobbles barefoot to the bathroom and locks the door. She showers and washes her hair, taking care to keep the water away from the stitches. She eases the last gobs of roadside tar off the side of her leg with her father's hair oil and dabs the thick layers of iodine painted on her legs at the hospital with cotton wool. Leaving the dirty spotted green dress and stained towel on the floor, she wraps herself in a fresh towel and limps her way to a small, only dimly familiar bedroom, clutching the little bottle of disinfectant and cotton swabs they gave her at the hospital. She locks the door, towels her hair and brushes it into a ponytail. She puts on clean underwear, a blue cotton dress, clean socks, and an old pair of sandshoes she finds in an unfamiliar wardrobe. The dress is long enough to cover the bruise on her thigh. She still feels wobbly but forces herself to prepare to leave.

She packs a few clothes into a small suitcase, together with her old white plastic handbag, and a little purse containing her secret savings squirrelled away from her holiday job. They will have to be enough. She retrieves a large torch from the back of the wardrobe. It occurs to her that she has no memory of the Christmas or New Year just passed.

Although she does not recall seeing either of her parents again, she remains conscious of their eyes burning into her as she opens the front door. Harbouring the admittedly vain hope that one or other of them will run after her she saunters at a snail's pace down the path between the rose bushes and out the front gate, but neither mother nor father have followed her.

As the house disappears behind the hill, she is infused with a sudden miraculous flood of energy and quickens her pace along the dirt road. The poplars standing sentry along the dairy farm fence shake their heads in a sudden breezy farewell as she crosses the cattle grid onto the Bringelly Road.

Glorious gold, purple and pink lines merge into a sunset sky. She isn't wearing a watch but imagines it could be seven or eight o'clock. She crosses the road out of the shade to where the light is brighter and sets out for Liverpool.

The road looks different on foot. Until now, she has always travelled along it by car or on horseback. She regrets her outburst now. What came over her? She really didn't intend to hurt her father. The words leapt out of her mouth without even thinking. So little traffic on the road, she could be walking on the moon. But no. She is not wanted.

She must accept it. She must plan ahead now. Once in Liverpool, she will catch a train to Sydney.

Agnes enters a stretch of road flanked on both sides by a thick forest. There is no moon. The air is black as soot. She could be walking down a subterranean tunnel. But God has directed her to leave and so she marches forward like a soldier on parade. With a firm grip on the suitcase, she tries not to think of the strange restless ghosts blowing their icy breath in her face.

A dull light appears in the distance and she runs towards it, her heart racing. Heaving for breath, she has arrived at the turn-off to the old polo field where the team would practise before Grandma bought The Farm. Feeling safe in the well-lit street, she relaxes her pace. The road surface is damp, but the sky is clear and full of stars. The underarms of her blue dress are soaked with her efforts.

Eventually, she comes to Uncle Mack's abandoned cotton factory. She will rest here briefly, and then walk on, but coherent thoughts from this point in her life will be as scattered as dry winter petals. They will not blossom back into memory until many years later.

*By the side of a narrow crossroads, I sit on a bench, put my head on my suitcase, and fall asleep. I do not know how long I have been out until a set of headlights, shining in my face, wake me up. The car is moving slowly towards me along the side street. It stops beside me. A woman with a wrinkled face like an old road map calls out from the driver's window: 'Leaving home, girlie?' she shouts. She is taking deep drags on a cigarette. I think of making a run for it, but my fear is obliterated by a heavenly whisper that help might be at hand. I reply in a jokey voice to match hers: 'Yes! That's right! My parents don't love me anymore!' The woman smiles: 'I'm going to Liverpool if you want a lift?' Her words all run together in a drawl. I hear myself say: 'Oh, how perfect. I want to catch a train to Sydney'. 'Well,' she says, 'just you bundle your cheeky self in the car and let's get going!' I am so relieved I could hug her. I jump into the passenger side and sink my bottom deep into the broken seat, my suitcase tightly clasped on my lap. The car looks as if it has come from the dump and sounds like a lawnmower. It kangaroo-hops along the main road.*

*I must have fallen asleep again as I come to with a shock to hear: 'Next* stop Liverpool Station!' The woman has called out in a high pitch like a train conductor. 'What have you been taking, girlie? You went out like a light!' Her voice crackles, and she covers me in a blast of cigarette smoke that makes me cough. I splutter my thanks to her. 'Now that's enough of that. I've got you here, and that's my good deed for the year!'

I buy a ticket and step straight onto the last train to Sydney. There are a few inebriated workmen swaying through the carriage, but they ignore me, and I ride safely. The hands on the big clock at Central Station are pointing at midnight when I arrive. I head down the slope towards George Street. The path submerges into a dark, deserted underpass. I emerge in the dull light at a junction of Cross Street and lose my bearings. Unsure, I turn in circles. When I hear footsteps advancing quickly behind, I run straight ahead and find myself in George Street. To my right, in the direction of Town Hall, I see an illuminated neon sign advertising 'Rooms to Let' peeping out of a side street. A woman with thick glasses, seated at a desk inside, is absorbed in an old film on a small TV. She looks annoyed when I bound up the stairs. 'Sorry for interrupting you,' I say. 'My parents are arriving tomorrow from Melbourne, and I want to surprise them at the station.' The woman pauses for a second, then: 'That's all right, love. If ya got a quid there's one left on the first floor, bathroom down the hall, check out by midday.' She doesn't look at me again, keeping her eyes on the TV screen. I fumble through the contents of my suitcase and hand her £1 from my savings. Hardly looking up, she slides a key over the desk. I scramble up squeaky stairs to the floor above, locate the room number, insert the key and double lock myself inside. I feel a sense of huge relief. There is a sink in the room, so I can pee into it and flush it away with the tap. I take off my shoes and socks and slide between musty sheets.

I must have slept. I can't remember. But I am looking up now at Central Station clock. I am catching a train to Wynyard. I believe I will feel more relaxed back in an area I know well.

I turn up Martin Place, just past the Cenotaph, where a scattering of office workers perch on the steps of the General Post Office. There must be an American ship in the harbour, as sailors with their tell-tale white caps *are milling around as they chat up the girls on lunch break. This is where my mother might have met her Yank, years ago, if she hadn't had me.*

*Entering the ground floor of 'David Jones' is like floating into an embrace. The pianist in black plays 'Moonlight Sonata' on the raised platform. I watch her fingers float over the keys. I ride the escalator and check my suitcase into a locker in the Ladies Room on the first floor. After using the toilet, I luxuriate in washing my hands with a piece of scented soap and drying them on a clean white hand towel provided by an assistant. Gazing at myself in the well-lit mirror, I look like I've staggered out of a field hospital in a war zone. There is a chocolate milk stain on the front of my crushed dress from a bottle I gulped down at Central. It adds to my overall dissipated appearance.*

*Summer frocks on the first floor are draped in red sale labels. As if preordained, a shop assistant, dressed in black, has draped several over my right arm and is whispering in my ear in a way that reminds me of Valerie enticing my mother up on the sixth floor: Try these, she says, I'm sure they're your size. In the dressing room, I slip my arms into a green shirtmaker with white buttons and a belt that fits perfectly. I daren't try on anything else. The money has to last. With each twirl in front of a full-length mirror, I feel better: 'Gorgeous! Perfect colour with your red hair!' I hear the assistant exclaim. I ask her if I can wear it now and she tells me no problem: cash or account? Account, I reply, holding my breath, and I give my father's full name like I have watched my mother do a hundred times. A quick call to the Accounts Department and I am signing a docket in vague disbelief. Emboldened, I sign for some make-up to cover my black eye, a wash bag, toothbrush, toothpaste, new sandals and a white leather handbag. Back in the Ladies Room, I complete the transformation by slipping into the new sandals, transferring my things into the new bag and throwing all the discarded stuff into my suitcase.*

*At closing time, suitcase in hand, I saunter across Hyde Park to St Mary's Cathedral where I unburden my heart to a statue of the Virgin Mary. Devoid of simple choices, I'm without a wish to go with the candle that I light in the brass stand beneath her. I stroll across the park trying to keep my head clear. At Town Hall station, I buy a ticket to Roseville, but get off out of habit when the train stops at Chatswood. Now I can see myself walking slowly down Victoria Street past all the closed shops as if in a dream. I pause outside the Town Hall where I danced Cinderella. Now I am hiding in and out of doorways, fearful of meeting anyone I know. But I do linger for a while on the pavement outside the Ryders' house. It is still barricaded against me. If I could only find the courage to knock on Mr Lawson's door. But I don't. Now I see myself dragging my feet up Edmund Street to the home I have no memory of leaving.*

*It seems the builder has finally arrived. The side path is full of rubble. My depleted memory retains a picture of the architect's plans that were never used. I keep walking around the block. Round and round my old home. It is growing dark. A pile of junk is stacked in the garden ready for a bonfire. I imagine the future day when the pile is lit, and the bonfire takes hold. I can see in my mind's eye the top drawer of my white chest with the ceramic roses. Dangling over the edge of the drawer are the pink ribbons from my toe shoes curling up and scorching in the heat. It is too late to run and save them. Everything I own is swallowed up in seconds. In my mind, I move closer, searching for all the books I love, but know they are already cinders.*

*The bird of paradise bushes either side of the steps leading to the Kelly's home have never looked so welcoming. The house behind is dark. I creep along the overgrown side path, shielding myself from thorns with the suitcase, and mount the back steps. God must still be with me as I find the door to the veranda open.*

*I dart into the spare bedroom, where I often used to sleep. I take off my new dress and sandals and, knowing I'm safe, slip between the sheets.*

*The bonfire in my mind is quenched.*

## CHAPTER 15

# MAROUBRA

Mrs Kelly has tears in her eyes as she looks down at Agnes in bed the following morning:
*What a fright you gave me, my poor, darling girl! What on earth has happened to you?*

*I fell out of my father's car because the door wasn't properly shut.*

Agnes has told the lie in line with her mother's story. She will be suddenly convulsed with sobs, and Mrs Kelly will gently rock her back and forwards in her arms. But this respite with the Kelly family is fated not to last long, for prescient Aunt Sill will phone Mrs Kelly just two days after Agnes's escape from The Farm. As Mrs Kelly takes the call, Agnes will dread to think of the latest pack of falsehoods circulating the 'Rosemont' grapevine.

Mrs Kelly will allow Agnes to listen in on the extension as Sill states coolly that Agnes's Uncle Parry would be coming to pick her up tomorrow. Mrs Kelly will tell Sill that Agnes was very welcome to stay while she decides what she wants to do, but Agnes will hear the curt woodpecker repeat the statement that her uncle would be arriving tomorrow. At 4pm.

Mrs Kelly will valiantly persist:

*Really, it's no trouble. Agnes wants to stay here. She's spent a lot of time with us, you know. She's like one of the family.*

*That would be impossible. I must warn you not to be fooled by her, Mrs Kelly. Agnes has a violent temper that can erupt unexpectedly at any minute.*

To her great credit, Mrs Kelly will continue to defend Agnes, but the order will be repeated a third time, then Sill will hang up in Mrs Kelly's ear. Agnes knows that the 'Rosemont' judgement is final. Her grandmother, seriously short of empathy, controls what goes on in her family and Sill is her lieutenant. Mrs Kelly is a rank outsider.

Agnes will reflect on her untenable position. Uncle Parry is kind enough, but she doesn't want to be cut off from everyone she knows, living miles away with Parry and Marnie in an unfamiliar place. The North Shore is her lifeline. Her triumphant escape from The Farm will no longer have any meaning.

She will be ashamed of the way Uncle Parry treats Mrs Kelly when he arrives. Rejecting her offer of tea and leaving the cake she has made for the occasion abandoned untouched, he will indirectly accuse Mrs Kelly of brainwashing Agnes against the family. His attitude towards Agnes will be like a policeman returning an escaped prisoner to jail and, when she still insists on staying at the Kelly house, her mother's poison will slide off Parry's tongue:

*The problem with you, Young Lady, is that you don't know what's good for you.*

None of it will make any sense to Agnes as, when she lived with her parents, she had little to do with them. Instead of the victim of a violent physical attack herself, she has apparently become the abuser. Parry will declaim her future like a legal decree:

*You're not to go back to the farm. Your father is deeply injured by your behaviour and wants nothing more to do with you.*

Agnes will answer him back to keep her spirits up:

*Oh yes? So what's new!*

Desperate to seem independent, instead she will feel a brand-new emptiness welling up inside.

\* \* \*

Parry and Marnie live on the corner of a row of identical two-storey red-brick houses, in Maroubra. The properties are built on narrow blocks and enclosed with grey paling wood fences. The plastic pegs on the rotary clothes-line are the only visible spots of colour.

From the fence on the corner, Marnie can be seen, every morning through the glass windows of the living room, dressing her three little daughters on a green carpeted floor in front of the TV. It is here, in a space that runs the width of the house and spills into an L-shaped kitchen, in which family life revolves.

Parry is bumping the car over a set of tramlines so that he can park down a slope on a sandy mound in front of the house. It is like the rough of a golf course. His house looks up, as if in adoration, to a lone tram shed on the crest of the hill above where, in deep despair, Agnes will shortly find herself joining passengers for the long slow journey into the city.

Devoid of tree cover, the row of red-brick houses bakes in oppressive summer heat, giving off a haze like the steam from an old train, in which eerie shapes form and dissolve above their rooftops. Agnes has been dragged to this place in the middle of a heatwave. In the morning newspaper, dated today, February 6 1959, there is a photo of a couple frying bacon and eggs on the pavement in Martin Place. In an effort to be friendly, Agnes has handed this newspaper to her Aunt Marnie upon arrival, and can hear herself reciting in an awkward high-pitched voice:

*Hello Aunty Marnie. What a relief to enter a cool room with so many fans! Look at the newspaper—it's nearly a hundred degrees and people are cooking on the pavement!*

But her aunt, seated on the green carpet floor, goes on folding clothes into a cane basket. She neither greets Agnes nor makes any attempt to take the newspaper, and lets it fall. Parry picks it up, giving his wife a disapproving look. Catching his eye, Marnie changes her attitude:

*Excuse me, but I'm halfway through folding the clean clothes from the line.*

Parry forces his wife to her feet by lifting the basket and placing it on a chair with the newspaper on top. Marnie, tight-lipped, continues with a false friendliness:

*How are you, Agnes? I see you've been in the wars. How did you get that ripe bruiser? I hear you've been giving the O'Connor clan a run for their money.*

Before Agnes can decide if her aunt's sarcasm is intended to be for, or against her, Parry diverts the subject away and onto the children. He is laughing and making honking noises as he scoops up his two-year-old daughter and blows raspberries on her fat tummy. The child squeals and laughs, begging for more and wriggling with delight as her father lifts her up and catches her in the air. Parry turns the child to face Agnes:

*Now, children. This is Agnes. She has come to stay and help Mummy look after you.*

Agnes, unsure how to act, makes a silly face and waves her free hand like someone slightly demented. So, this is to be her role. Mother's helper. Yet again.

Making the best she can of a problematic situation, Agnes initially finds being part of the little tribe on the green carpet comforting: changing nappies, putting on shoes, combing hair and being the eldest little girl's favourite playmate. But she can't put her finger on Aunt Marnie's demeanour. An undercurrent of hostility has continued to emanate from her since Agnes first stepped through the door, and her confusion only increases when she overhears Marnie talking about her on the phone:

*She's off with the fairies... daft as a brush...yet Parry's infatuated with her...*

Agnes is unsure what infatuated means. All she knows is she is suffering the same disorientation with her aunt as she did with her mother. As she doesn't know what else to do, she can only try to be as helpful to Marnie as possible. But even this gambit fails when Marnie makes it clear that she doesn't want her help, and never has, so Agnes will spend many mornings looking longingly at the little family group of mother and children behind the sliding bubble glass doors—now firmly closed against her. She senses she is a pawn in the playing out of some strange kind of 'couple game'. One similar to the type played by her parents. Though this time it's different. Reversed. Her father would ignore her, and her mother would not want her there when he was around. Now it is Marnie who ignores her, and Parry who wants her with him all the time.

Practically every morning since she first arrived, she has accompanied Parry as they drive the short distance in his car to the beach. Holding hands like two children, they run into the frothy water and frolic in the surf. Agnes reverts into a small girl, inventing silly names for him and falling over laughing. She settles on 'Horatio Henry' and can hardly say the words for giggling. He is lifting her in his arms and swimming out with her into the waves on his back. She is falling into his every caress. He is a strong swimmer and has taught her how to identify the shape and curl of a wave so she can body-surf into the shore. She has mastered the technique and finds the sensation fabulous. It is like riding a magic carpet. Sometimes she picks the wrong wave and ends up in a centrifuge of foam, before being dumped with a mouth full of sand on the shore. Yet here in the surf she feels free.

They are barefoot this morning, towels around their shoulders, and are eating hot fish and chips at an outdoor table of a café in the main street overlooking the beach. She watches his pleasant face and remembers overhearing him at breakfast, shouting angrily at Marnie:

*Can't you see she's disturbed?! You've got to get over it and be kind, Marnie! I'm trying to help her!*

Instead of replying, Marnie had slammed the door in his face.

Agnes watches Parry scoff down his food. He is quiet for once. He has started to take her everywhere with him. At this café table, as she observes him eating, she realises she now lives to hear him call out for her. She will wait outside the front door of the house and jump in the car beside him, as eager as a pet dog.

Parry never walks anywhere if he can help it. Only yesterday she had ridden with him in the car through deserted streets to the White Horse Hotel. It is his mother-in-law's pub and is in an ugly part of King Street, Newtown. Jammed between two closed shopfronts with rubbish-stuffed entrances and crumbling yellow-painted cement frontages, the burgundy brick building, by comparison, looks like a palace. The first time he had taken her there, Agnes had counted six front windows facing the street. The middle one, she figured, must have lit the stairs.

She will never see the bedrooms, where she will wonder if guests stay. Whenever she has asked Parry questions about the place, especially the bedrooms, he looks at her in a funny way and puts his arm around her shoulders without answering.

Usually, at the pub, a few old men in singlets would be perched at high bar tables on ugly purple stools, sipping pints of beer and smoking roll-your-owns with nicotine-stained fingers. On their first visit, Parry had told Agnes, as if it was a secret, that the only women allowed in the bar were barmaids. But the gender embargo never prevents him taking her behind the bar to access the huge basement below, where the pub stored supplies. Parry would regularly lift the trapdoor and take her down the basement steps during the heatwave in order to cool off. She would stare up at muscular men in blue singlets who rolled beer barrels on wooden planks down from an opening in the pavement. The temperature change felt good, but Agnes finds the big dark space scary as the only natural light trickles through a small, barred window in the rear wall. The lines of these bars casting shadows on the cement floor give the impression of a prison. Parry has told her that the caretaker sleeps on the old bed in the corner of the basement, he often stretches out on himself to soak up the coolness.

*The summer is over, and my uncle abandons me— just like his wife has done. I think it happens after a visit to the White Horse Hotel and a trip* under the trapdoor into the dark basement under the bar. But I'm not sure. From one day to the next he treats me now like I'm not there. He stops taking me with him in the car. I wait for hours for him at the front door. When I bang frantically on the car window, he waves me away and, one day, he kicks me aside when I grab him. *Get away from me, you… you… you!* He is yelling without finishing the sentence.

It feels like I'm back with my parents in the car on the way to The Farm after the inquisition at 'Rosemont'. I think Parry and Marnie are angry with me because I started a fire in their kitchen. I am not clear on much that happens to me at this time, but I can still see this fire surging up in front of my eyes. Flames rise and lick the walls. Great red tongues eat at the kitchen cupboards and blacken the ceiling. The fire goes on forever, burns forever, in my mind. When I question Parry about the fire, he gets angry and shouts: 'There was no bloody fire! It's all in your bloody head like everything else!' So, I can't be sure, after all, if the fire was real. Or if the strange creatures and eerie sounds that swirl around the hot summer rooftops are real. And because I don't know what is real and what is not, I decide to kill myself. I buy a jar of aspirin at the chemist.

I wander around the beach looking for a place to swallow the pills down and die. It's too cold for swimming, but there are enough sunbathers at lunchtime for me not to stand out. I will die with my face under a straw hat and my sunglasses on. I have brought some beads to say a rosary while I wait for the end. But it seems I am too stupid even to go ahead and kill myself. Either there are too many people on the beach, or I forget to bring water to help me swallow the tablets. Then I start worrying about leaving my dead body behind, like a bit of garbage, on the sand.

The summer must be over, as now the winter months dissolve into images like the frames in an old silent picture-show. There are long rides on an ancient tram that shudders along Anzac Parade to Elizabeth Street. I buy *The Sydney Morning Herald* and read it in The General Post Office building. Responding to advertisements for work and receiving interminable rejections is too much for me.

Crippling despair drives me to another suicide attempt, but a young *couple step in front of me just as I'm about to jump under a train at Wynyard. And I'm thwarted another time when I decide to jump off the Harbour Bridge as I can't get access to the ledge. I'm not capable of killing myself, yet I die a hundred humiliating deaths when a store detective with a hard face is called to a counter because I am freezing cold and have tried to charge a winter coat to the 'David Jones' account: 'Your signature has been cancelled Miss Keen. And if you try and use the account again, you will be expelled from the store'.*

*I decide to lie in front of Parry's car as he is about to drive off. He gets out of the driver's seat and wrenches me up by the arm: 'You're mad! Stark staring mad!' He is screaming in my face. Even my mother hangs up when I ring her and ask her for money. I am dead to her too. It is only to be expected.*

## CHAPTER 16

# COOGEE

Coogee is the Aboriginal word for 'big smell', at least that's what the fish and chip shop proprietor has just told Agnes. She has walked there, out of habit, from the boarding house, which is situated above the beach in Coogee. She has been waiting in a queue to be served. The boarding house sits on a windy northern headland overlooking the Pacific Ocean and is full of old people. Is it also a place for people not right in the head? No chains or straitjackets are in evidence. Agnes has been too afraid to approach anyone and ask. But the question of madness buzzes like a pestering insect around her thoughts. One morning, she had woken up in a room here with no idea how she got there. *Is* she mad? She *must* be because Uncle Parry *said* so. Now, in her tortured state, mad goes with bad, not very bright, and off with the fairies.

She has a little money left in her pockets. But not enough for fish and chips tomorrow. She sits on the beach and devours what could be her last hot meal. She watches the sea being dragged out, as if against its will, and wonders whether she has had madness thrust upon her.

Two days later, after showing Agnes her double-jointed fingers, Jeanette Gibson, a fellow guest, drags Agnes in to sit with her in the dining room for breakfast. This is how Agnes learns that breakfast and a hot evening meal is included with her board and lodging.

After the meagre morning meal, Jeanette takes her by the arm and leads her into her room to see a silver-framed photo of a young man with calf eyes and wavy hair. He is wearing an army uniform, cap in hand over his heart, and dominates a small table venerated with flowers and candles. Agnes obediently kneels beside Jeanette on the cushions placed in front of the altar where Jeanette proceeds to call to God to bring George back to her. The strange ritual is completed with Jeanette's full-throated rendition of 'Danny Boy'. She has a lovely voice which, Agnes will notice, will improve as the days go on. Or perhaps she will become a better listener, as she relaxes into a regular morning attendance at the tribute to Jeanette's dead husband.

Mrs Ivy Forsythe, the manager of the boarding house, enthusiastically informs Agnes that Jeanette's world stopped when she received the news of George's death in the war against the Japanese.

Barred from the 'David Jones' account and the cold now really setting in, Agnes finds herself shivering on the street without a coat and has no money to buy one. But Jeanette comes to her rescue. On a particularly chilly day, Jeanette marches up to her and hands her a good-quality green wool coat with a brown velvet collar that she says she found at a bus stop. It is a little big on Agnes—she has lost so much weight—but it looks good on her. She suspects Jeanette may have stolen it, as it is hard to imagine anyone abandoning such a lovely garment at a bus stop. But at least she is warm now, and secretly hopes the coat won't be spotted in the street and reclaimed off her back.

This wintry morning, with a chill wind rattling at the boarding house windows, Mrs Forsythe has just handed Agnes an envelope. Tucked inside is a map of the area with a tram stop circled in red biro. The map nestles next to a small pile of pound notes. Agnes unfolds a typewritten paper slip which bears the cotton factory's letterhead:

**Be careful with this money as there is no more. GET A JOB.**

This is the first time she has been given money since she escaped The Farm. Agnes wonders if this message has come from her father, or 'Rosemont', but it really doesn't matter as she deems all her family to be simply one giant antagonistic conglomerate. It isn't a huge sum, but it is *something*. Presumably, paying her boarding house accommodation fees is considered adequate help for such a delinquent. Any extra funds, like this, are to be considered a generous bonus. The bullying, unsigned note plunges her into a dark state.

There is a rocky shelf, called Wedding Cake Island, which protects Coogee beach against turbulent seas in rough storms. Perched high on the cliff above the beach, the boarding house receives the full brunt of spray from the huge waves crashing against the escarpment opposite. Such a storm strikes soon after Agnes receives the loveless note. Lashing rain, driven by fierce winds, pounds at her bedroom window and shakes the timber structure of the house, which shudders and creaks like an old boat. The noise is deafening. Isolated indoors, she can sense herself sinking deeper and deeper into despair and, when the vicious wind abates, she exits the building and walks slowly towards the cliff edge, feeling increasingly drawn to jump into the raging foam below.

The sight of Jeanette silently observing her makes Agnes pull back from the cliff edge. She is trembling when she runs towards her friend. Instead of the usual pat on the head, Jeanette puts her arms around her like a proper sane person and holds her tight.

She is not meant to end her own life. Her attempts have all been thwarted. Perhaps God is protecting her after all. Agnes enjoys the rare physical human contact for as long as she dares, then runs down onto the beach, feeling the exhilaration of the wind in her hair. If herself is all she has, then so be it. She would be *enough*. She would *have* to be enough. She would show *all* of them she was enough!

She chants into the roaring wind:

*I don't need permission from anyone to go on living. I will go on living. Living!*

\* \* \*

Agnes is up early the next morning. She feels a fresh determination to regain her own sanity and track down that elusive job. Once again, she washes her long hair—which hasn't been near a hairdresser in years—scoops it into a neat ponytail and covers the elastic band with a length of green ribbon Jeanette has given her. A clumsy woman on the city tram having snagged her last pair of nylons with an umbrella, she decides to wear them with the ladder on the inside of the leg. She stains the bald patches on the fronts of her patent leather court shoes with boot polish, but finds to her dismay that no amount of rubbing alters the textual contrast. While brushing down a caramel tartan kilt Jeanette has also donated, she discovers moth holes inside the pleats. She dismisses this concern as she reckons the holes won't be visible whilst sitting still at an interview. She rolls the long skirt over at the waist, pulls a nutmeg-shaded lambswool jumper over her head, fixes a white detachable lace collar inside the neck and decides that is the best she can do. There is no denying she looks shabby, but with the smart bus-stop winter coat over her arm, hiding skirt and stockings, she might just manage.

As the bus pulls away from the kerb, the smooth motion of the wheels on the newly tarmacked road starts to fill Agnes with hope. She is still digesting the delicious cottage pie from the evening meal last night, and deliberately hasn't bothered with breakfast to avoid any distraction to her renewed determination.

The General Post Office looks sombre, its stonework dark from an earlier downpour. But nothing diminishes the wonder of the colonnade along Martin Place, and resolute Queen Victoria gravely presiding over the main entrance, flanked by allegorical figures bearing the British Coat of Arms. Having bought a copy of the *Sydney Morning Herald* as usual, Agnes's arrival in the city centre is so early that she decides to splurge on raisin toast and coffee in Angel Place. It's the first time she has felt courageous enough to sit in a coffee shop like a proper grown-up—all on her own.

She is utterly amazed when her first phone call from the Post Office, on the dot of nine, and in response to an advertisement for a receptionist/tea lady at an import/export company, goes straight through to a manager:

*Timing is everything Miss Keen. If you're at the GPO, why not come straight to the top of York Street for an interview?*

It is a male voice. A smooth voice.

The atmosphere on the street is electric. Office workers are dashing to be at their desks by nine and the exit from Wynyard station is so congested that Agnes moves onto the road to avoid a bottleneck. The early rain intensifies the sound of screeching brakes and horns as traffic crawls bumper to bumper. Agnes feels elated to be part of the energy powering the city. She is feeling revitalized when she spots the building where he is, apparently, waiting for her arrival.

The owner of the velvety voice is not the rugged Heathcliff, seething with passion, promised on the phone. His short legs only just reaching the floor under the desk, and with visible chest bumps straining under his shirt, obesity will make him look older, while plump cheeks affirm youth. But the laugh lines around his eyes will put her at ease and she will move forward in such a hurry to greet him that she knocks over the umbrella stand. Apologising, she will return the stand back in place, hoping he hasn't got a glimpse of her laddered stocking or bald shoes. He does not seem to be staring at her legs... so far, so good.

*Call me John.*

She will shortly get to know that John is the boss's lazy son—humoured by the staff but ridiculed behind his back. But he seems to like her from the off, and she quite likes him so far. She crosses her fingers behind her back.

*Well, my girl, you went to a good school all right, same as my sister, but you don't have to be Einstein to make the tea and take it around the office. We'll require you to do errands and learn to use the switchboard, so you can fill in when the operators go to lunch. Do you think you can do that?*

*I know I can, Mr... John, I mean. You won't be disappointed!*

Clasping the bus-stop coat in front of the damaged nylons, she will follow him to the switchboard on the other side of the aisle, its red lights already flashing manically above rows of black holes. She will recognise this from office scenes she has watched at the cinema and bends over slightly to get a closer look at it:

*Ah-hah! I see before me a stairway to paradise!*

She turns to see him chuckling as he observes the point where the ladder in the stocking disappears under her skirt. Agnes steps back with a combination of surprise and disapproval. She will learn to keep well clear of his wandering hands over the next few months.

To her astonishment, when he asks her if she can start straight away, sudden waterworks threaten to trip her up simply because a pudgy man with short legs has offered her a lifeline. After so much deprivation, the least kindness has the power to reduce her to a weeping wreck. She pinches her thigh through the skirt to regain her composure.

Her new boss scribbles a note, signs it, and leaves it on someone's desk. Agnes can just about decipher what it says:

*We have a new tea lady called Agnes Keen. Record her details, show her how to use the switchboard, manage the petty cash. And be kind.*

Agnes is somewhat disconcerted by 'be kind' and will wonder if it may also be a request on his own behalf. He smiles at her, and she smiles back at him, still reeling from this sudden change of fortune. Months of rejection are over at the mere passing whim of a small fat man.

## CHAPTER 17
# ACTING THE PART

It is Saturday morning and Agnes has spent one week at her new job. She throws a few things in a bag and catches the bus from Coogee to the city, wearing a new pair of nylon stockings and a pair of red court shoes she has bought with her first pay packet. Next week she will buy a new skirt. The green bus-stop coat reminds her of Jeanette who has, quite shockingly, died from a sudden heart attack shortly after arrival at a psychiatric centre for an assessment. Bereft, Agnes goes on talking to Jeanette in her head as if she's still alive. But Jeanette would want her to be strong, and so Agnes strides up Martin Place with her head high and shoulders back, adopting the posture Rita Ryder taught her for the fifth ballet position.

The warm sun on her back helps to fill her with optimism. Spring has finally arrived, the days are long, and the flowers are out. She waves to Queen Victoria over the entrance of the General Post Office. Details on façades of buildings, the specific garments people are wearing, all jump out at her as her eyes focus sharply on the world around her. Earlier that morning she had phoned Maria Kelly and is now on her way to see her.

As the train speeds over the harbour bridge, she feels the way a prisoner must feel after release from jail. Her lighter heart leaps at the sight of railway stations she knows well. She is to stay at the welcoming Kelly house at weekends and join Maria at her Saturday morning acting classes at the Ensemble Theatre.

Maria is waiting impatiently when she arrives, worried that they will be late for the class. Agnes is briskly informed by her friend that they have less than an hour to get to the 11am session. So, within minutes of dropping her bag in the spare room off the veranda, she finds herself in the back seat of Mrs Kelly's Mercedes, speeding down the Pacific Highway to Kirribilli.

Maria, in the front seat, is bubbling with enthusiasm about the class.

*It's called method acting Agnes and it's fantastic! You know, Marlon Brando and James Dean are both method actors? And wait till you see Hayes Gordon. He's like no one you've ever met. He's been in stacks of Broadway musicals. They blacklisted him in America for being a Communist sympathiser during the McCarthy era and he got no work after refusing to sign the oath of loyalty, so he upped sticks and came to Sydney. He says he's not a Communist but a man of principles. In the class we focus on not just making faces but feeling our way into the part. You don't pretend but BECOME the character. You'll love it, Agnes! It's just so exciting and different!*

As they leave the sunlight behind and tiptoe down a ramp into the hallowed atmosphere, Maria explains to Agnes that the theatre auditorium is 'in the round' like a Greek or Roman amphitheatre. The class already underway, they slide surreptitiously into the first two seats just inside the entrance:

*Don't sit over there! Come closer, so you can hear what's going on!*

For a moment, Agnes has not grasped that the man on the far side with the deep American accent is addressing them. He shouts again:

*Come, Marline! Bring your friend and sit here!*

Puzzled, Agnes follows Maria across the stage to some front row seats directly across from a black-bearded man with a large face. His eyes are hidden behind tortoiseshell glasses and overhung by a shelf of bushy brows. Maria whispers to Agnes covertly:

*Marline is my stage name.*

Agnes has noticed that, compared to fellow students who are

wearing leather jackets, boots, velvet caps and slouching willy-nilly amidst tangles of coloured scarves in the rows around them, Marline, née Maria, and herself, both clad in skirts and twinsets, could not look more out of place.

Hayes Gordon sounds to Agnes as if he could run the world. His presence both mesmerises and intimidates her. A lone spotlight from above encircles him like a halo, and when he looks at her it feels as if he is boring a hole in her skull. She was to quickly discover that most of the group were already devotees of Maria's beloved 'method'. Names like Stanislavski, Lee Strasberg, Stella Adler and Elia Kazan are constantly referred to by Hayes and seemingly familiar to all present at the lesson. To Agnes, the 'method' sounds equally fascinating and bewildering.

In the second hour of her first session, their instructor calls upon the group to team up with partners to play 'actions'. Ten minutes are allotted to integrate a specific action into a story backstage, then to be ad-libbed on stage for the benefit of the group. The audience's task is to identify the action, the motivation, and assess what each performer is trying to achieve.

A young guy wearing a leather jacket, approaches Agnes to be his partner. Fearful of tackling something beyond her comprehension, she quickly suggests they weave their story around buying and selling, as what could be more straightforward than that? Her partner takes the initiative and plays a clothes vendor in a street market rushing to finish the day's trading so he can get home to give his diabetic mother an insulin injection. One more sale will top up the rent due on the house he shares with her. In her head, Agnes returns to the recent cold winter when, without a coat, she used to warm her freezing hands and arms under hot water taps in the 'David Jones' Ladies Room.

The ad-libbing simply flows between them, and Agnes is completely immersed in the experience. The haggling over the cost of a coat reaches a crescendo and Agnes hears herself shouting, her throat all choked up, as if this new acquaintance of only an hour is alone responsible for her life of suffering. Her voice reaches a crescendo of pain:

*I'm going to run off with it and not pay you a penny unless you agree!*

Her partner stops suddenly when he sees her eyes full of tears. He puts his arms around her and hands her a handkerchief out of his pocket:

*Here. Give me £5 and that's the end to it. I'll rob a bank on the way home for the rest.*

Agnes hands over the fictional money, kisses him on the cheek, and walks off the stage to a considerable ripple of applause.

The discussion that follows their exercise is brief, as the 'action' is abundantly clear to all.

At the end of all the performances and discussions, the group individually approach Hayes to pay him for the class. When it is Agnes's turn, she is thunderstruck when he pulls her to one side:

*You have the talent and the looks to go with it. But if you want the stage, you must make the commitment to work on yourself. As Stanislavski says: 'The body is just the instrument.' See you next week.*

In the classes during the weeks that follow, Agnes will shine during one session, and the next will feel out of her depth and fall into despair. The truth is that she has been conditioned to feel comfortable in the shadows, yet she will still manage to reconnect with her ability to amuse, successfully drawing on the comic techniques she once used to entertain her classmates at school. However, during one session she will experience a minor nervous breakdown as she attempts an exercise which Hayes calls 'Emotion Memory'. It is a technique exploring the theory that any emotions necessary for a part cannot be called up to order but will emerge naturally by recalling the setting in which the event that prompted the emotion took place.

Agnes will conjure up her little bedroom in Chatswood: the light, the smells and scents, the atmospheric temperature, the familiar sounds. Strongly reliving, too, the precious objects in the room she once treasured, she will end up shattered—an emotional wreck—on the floor. She will be acutely aware that in the course of the exercise she was momentarily devoid of her normal compulsion to cover up and invent. She will feel exhausted.

A tall, thin young man with small round glasses and curly hair will approach her afterwards in the foyer and observe:

*That was quite a reaction. I'm presently studying psychiatry and one major thing I learned from Freud is that nothing is ever lost. It is all inside you. One day, when you feel strong enough, if you wish, you can find what you believe is missing.*

Agnes will absorb the perceptive remark and then feel compelled to ask him whether, to be a method actor, a person inevitably had to be screwed up.

He will smile at her sympathetically and tell her that every development of the person and the personality is fraught with misunderstanding and suffering. He will tell her that the plays they put on reflect life. And that life is unavoidable.

After three months, Agnes is feeling comfortable in her new job. She enjoys working the switchboard and, after a few initial minor mishaps, learns exactly what plug goes where. What she has absorbed of switchboard lingo from films has been enhanced by listening to Doreen and Brenda—the two straight-talking, unsentimental girls who alternate as the voice of the firm and who are always up for a laugh.

What will change everything at this happier time in Agnes's life is a call from Grandma. As Agnes has never spoken to her grandmother, or to anyone else for that matter, on the boarding house phone, she had not recognised her voice:

*How are you, dear?*

*Oh Grandma, it's you! I'm fine thank you. I got myself a job at an import/export company in York Street.*

She has deliberately left out her start as a tea-lady. That would seem far too common. She has already started to stumble over her words. As she hears her grandmother's steady breathing on the line, once again she feels like a small, insignificant child:

*I hope you are going to Mass on Sundays.*

*Oh… yes, Grandma… of course, Grandma!*

She has lied clumsily, having lost sight of her religion months ago.

*Good. Well, I just want to let you know—you have been offered a place to train as a nurse at St Vincent's Hospital. Your Aunt Sill trained there if you recall. You'll be receiving a letter with detailed instructions in the next few days. Goodbye for now, dear, and make sure you adhere to the sacraments.*

Grandma's voice had been as neutral as a cloudy day—so lacking in highs and lows, it might have been a recorded message. She still ran everyone and everything. Certainly, such interventions had been synonymous with punctuating cataclysmic change throughout Agnes's life. Now she racks her brains in a flat-spin panic. Wildly enthusiastic about Hayes Gordon and his method acting classes, she had blurted out her new passion for the stage to all and sundry, including Mrs Forsythe, who was probably the route to Grandma. Had it got back to 'Rosemont'? There, in those hallowed halls of rigid Catholicism, the mere word, 'theatre' would have alerted The Matriarch that one of her 'souls for heaven' was in mortal danger.

It also occurs to Agnes that having her reside in a nurses' home would save on the boarding house fees that Grandma was doubtless providing. Yet, as much as life had altered for the better, as much as her self-confidence had increased, it was still beyond Agnes to challenge the ruler at 'Rosemont'.

Decades later, Agnes will know that, could she live her early life again, this would have been the point when she might have turned her back on the lot of them—grandmother, parents, aunts, uncles—and go her own way. But, broken inside, unaware of alternatives, the drive to redeem herself in their eyes had outweighed everything else.

A further pull towards her serious consideration of a nursing career has been that Maria Kelly was on the point of departing, with her aunt, on an ocean liner. A world trip, apparently. Agnes has shared her friend's burning ambition to be an actress but feels she could only achieve it with Maria's support. With Maria's friendship fading away on the beckoning horizon, she has convinced herself that the rawness of the emotional memory experience at the theatre has left her so deeply unsettled that she cannot ever risk repeating it. By eschewing the theatre and tending the sick, she reasons, she would be doing God's work. And taking this path would relieve her of all other supplementary acts of charity to stay alive.

Strangely, to have been 'selected' to train at St Vincent's has planted an intriguing seed. She waits for the invitation letter from the hospital with mounting curiosity. This sudden turn of events is beginning to cause Agnes to feel as if she belongs. She, too, could finally become a secure and trustworthy part of the family—the dynasty of polo, of educating boys at St Joseph's and girls at Rose Bay, of expensive brand labels, of Royal Doulton tableware, of crested silver-plated cutlery and sedate Regency-striped dining room chairs.

\* \* \*

Although part of the New South Wales state public health system, St Vincent's Hospital has remained under the auspices of the Catholic Church since its founding by five Irish Sisters of Charity in 1857. Its mission? To give quality care to the poor. Today, one hundred years later, the spirit of compassion and dedication is still alive in the Women's Accident Ward on the second floor where Agnes has been posted after her initial three months' training.

Agnes has never seen anyone pass away, nonetheless it had been instantly clear to her that a death has just occurred on the Accident ward where she is currently training. Fluid from a drip in the patient's nose has bubbled out of her mouth and the chest has just expelled a rattle like an old exhaust pipe. The poor old lady wasn't an accident patient but had been brought to the ward for lack of space elsewhere.

Agnes rallies sufficiently to call Sister Teresa, who swiftly pulls a curtain around the bed, closes the patient's eyes, and disconnects the drip. Then a senior nurse arrives to lay out the body. To her horror, Agnes is instructed to assist in this task while the nun in charge goes to phone the patient's relatives. Then, to add to her turmoil, she finds herself landed with the job of taking the corpse to the mortuary. Sister Teresa pinches Agnes's cheek:

*It's the living you've got to worry about, not the dead. Sorry to send you down on your own, but we can't leave her here a minute longer and I have to attend an emergency. Don't look like a stunned mullet! Just go!*

A body completely covered by a sheet on a trolley was a scene straight out of the cinema and it hasn't occurred to Agnes it would be a frequent occurrence in a big hospital. She has difficulty manoeuvring the castor wheels of the heavy trolley out of the ward door. They wanted to go every other way but straight ahead.

Within seconds of knocking on the mortuary doors both sides are flung wide open and a short, stout man in a dust-coat scurries sideways across the white lino floor:

*Hello. I'm Mortuary Mick. You've come to the right place. I don't need to ask what's under the sheet!*

He helps her guide the trolley to the front of a stainless-steel fridge with many doors, flings open one door. Agnes gasps out loud. Through the gap, she can see naked bodies.

*What did you expect Blue Eyes? Frozen peas? Nothing exclusive here! All stiffs together in the same cooler. Lawyers, politicians, dunny-men, street sweepers. Death is real democracy. We don't ask if they like the company. This is where all divisions end. No protests for equal rights and no changing fridges. Our inmates don't need sheets or blankets because their winters and summers are over. Now what's the name of this one?*

*I... I don't know...*

Mick winks at her:

*Name will be on the tag around the foot or the right big toe. And what's more, there's no need to whisper. This ain't a church.*

He writes the dead woman's name in a book beside a number and then slips a card with the same number into a plastic slot on the front of the fridge tray:

*Okay, gorgeous. Now we got her registered, just slide her onto the slab.*

She is doubly horrified at this lack of reverence and that she is obviously expected to tip the body onto the slab herself. There is a huge cheer from the football crowd on a blaring corner TV.

*I'll give you a demo, shall I? Okay—here comes the slide...*

Agnes watches in amazement as Mick lifts the sheet to reveal the naked form—already unrecognisable as its former self. With a flip action of the trolley, the body sails through the air, landing on the slab outside the fridge like a small plane making a smooth landing. The remains are then shunted unceremoniously into the chilly depths.

But there will be little time for further contemplation on the bleak nature of death as Agnes will shortly find herself posted to the ground floor section of the private hospital, which is situated in another building at the far end of the hospital garden. Here, her life will falter once again. In fact, face down is how Agnes has landed in St Vincent's 'Ground Floor Private' having tripped on the last step at the main entrance.

Her fate is sealed when she feels the iron grip of a strong hand hauling her to her feet by the collar and a snarling voice close to her ear:

*Don't you know junior trainees should use the side entrance? What do you mean crashing in here and making such a spectacle? What's your name, nurse?*

*Agnes Keen.*

The owner of the voice sizes her up:

*Ah. You're the new one. The last one was hopeless and now they've sent an even sillier version. And why are you covered in make-up like a common tart? This is a hospital, not a stage set. And loosen that belt before you die of asphyxiation.*

Agnes has always admired the neat hospital belt that attractively cinches her 22-inch waist. There is no time to reply as Sister Scruggs takes off at speed, whilst ordering her to follow. She dutifully traipses after her over plush red carpet—more indicative of an upmarket hotel than a hospital. Abruptly, they turn off into a narrow, brightly lit, white-walled passageway which opens into the working area of the hospital. In the bright light of the sterilising room, Agnes observes that the Head Sister's double-sized veil is matched by a shelf of a bosom large enough for a cat to curl up on comfortably, and with room to spare. The bulging king prawn eyes that are now focusing on Agnes slant with malice:

*You will have learned in your initial training about Joseph Lister— pioneer of antiseptics. So, you understand why we sterilise. Here, we strive for exceptionally high standards—from the smallest to the most complicated procedures. Do you understand?*

*Yes, absolutely, Sister.*

Agnes has replied politely but finds herself struggling to control an urge to mimic her superior's owlish blink.

*Very well, close your mouth and try and look intelligent. Your job this morning will be to kill off microorganisms by putting everything you see on the left of the sink through the steriliser. By which I mean all these stainless-steel bedpans, bottles, jugs, kidney dishes and sundry objects. The machine is programmed to maintain boiling temperature for half an hour. Twenty minutes is sufficient, but we give it that bit extra to be sure. Any questions?*

*No, I understand the procedure. I've done it stacks of times in the main hospital.*

After this slightly flip remark, Agnes braces for the inevitable backlash:

*The public hospital is not the private hospital, nurse. We expect the very best here and will not tolerate the shoddy attitudes so many of you young girls bring here.*

Sister Scruggs stands up from her chair, and the bosomy shelf rises to point at Agnes accusingly:

*Find me when you finish, so I can inspect the job.*

She turns swiftly and marches off briskly, like a military officer after a drill.

It takes Agnes an hour to complete the task. Unable, after an extensive search, to find her superior as ordered, she returns to the sterilising room feeling dejected. Her back to the door, Sister Scruggs's unexpected lightning entrance makes her jump. After a cursory glance at the pile of steaming hot sterilised objects, the sister yells at her:

*DO THEM AGAIN!*

Agnes presumes she is being punished for not reporting back as ordered, and so tries to explain herself. But her efforts fall on deaf ears:

*You will always locate me via the staffroom just inside the main entrance. Now do what I've told you to do and REPEAT THE JOB.*

After the command to re-sterilise is issued for a third time, Agnes knows she is being tortured by a sadist. It's February. The temperature outside is warm, but it must be a hundred degrees in the sterilising room, and she is soaked through with steam and perspiration. Too scared to ask to leave for lunch, she goes without. When Sister Scruggs finally dismisses her Agnes is on the point of physical collapse. Slinking out of the side entrance, she hears her name being called:

*Nurse Keen! I'll expect you tomorrow at 8am! And don't come in looking like a sideshow!*

Since being made up by an attendant at a cosmetic counter in 'David Jones' Agnes has continued to cover her freckles with a light coat of pancake foundation. She also slightly darkens her fair eyelashes with a touch of mascara. As she stares into her mirror, she is starting to see a person she likes, and now feels naked without the usual added extras.

This morning, as she debates whether to put on make-up or not, she feels the beginnings of a cold dread. She does not want to go back to the private hospital—isolated from the good-natured public wards, the cheerful morning sunlight, the sound of patients' radios, the antics, the stories, the laughter, the camaraderie between the nursing staff. The private hospital, by comparison, is a tomb. But, at 8am sharp, she duly returns.

Down on her knees, scrubbing the floor of the staff bathroom, she manages to hold her tongue, but with each unreasonable task, she is beginning to nurture a deep hatred of Sister Midge Scruggs, fervently wishing the obnoxious woman would disappear off the face of the earth.

Her wish will be answered when, after a week of persecution, the Head Sister leaves to attend a nursing conference in Brisbane and is replaced by a temporary sister. This woman will be as easy-going and jovial as Scruggs is strict and unyielding and Agnes will happily accompany the pleasant Sonia Williams on her rounds to take the patients' temperatures and blood pressure.

All the private rooms have ensuite bathrooms—the most luxurious enjoying the added benefit of a balcony overlooking the courtyard garden—and Sonia will put Agnes in charge of changing the water in the copious vases of flowers in the patients' rooms. Agnes will love arranging the beautiful blooms in fresh water and will make great efforts to vary the display in the vases each day. She will even receive several compliments on her artistic creations from visiting friends and relatives.

One patient, the recipient of particularly extravagant floral displays, is a wealthy brewer called Mr Green. He, according to rumour, has a sizable bequest in his will in favour of the hospital. Although never openly alluded to, the permanent staff are conscious of having to humour the old man and his visitors.

Mr Green's faded brown eyes become particularly bright whenever Agnes brings an elaborately wrapped new bunch of flowers to his bedside for his inspection. Sniffing the perfume of the lovely roses and carnations sends him into an ecstasy of vocal delight and he has taken to clapping his hands like a child whenever she walks in.

But, one day, any trace of Mr Green's supposed senility will disappear when Agnes helps Sonia, the temporary sister, wash him and then dress him in a fresh pair of smart paisley-patterned silk pyjamas. Treating him like a baby, smiling and exclaiming how good he looks when she finishes combing his wiry grey hair, Sonia will not realise what a Pandora's Box she has opened as she and Agnes minister to him on either side of his bed. For, when Agnes leans over him from her side, Mr Green will shoot his hand up under her pinafore and start squeezing her breast. It isn't until Sonia gives his hand a gentle tap and tells him playfully that he's 'a naughty boy' that he will retract his fingers with a cheeky smirk. Inexperienced Agnes will be shaken, but Sonia will make light of it as she explains gently that these 'old boys' sometimes do naughty things of which they are hardly aware.

After the Brisbane conference, having spent a long weekend at Surfers Paradise with the other nursing sisters on the trip, Midge Scruggs will return with the golden glow of a slight suntan and the dark circles expunged from under her eyes. In fact, she will look to Agnes as if she has finally joined the human race. Because of these outward signs, Agnes will hope the holiday has transformed her persecutor's mood and will be further encouraged when she catches sight of Sister Scruggs fawning over several grateful, elderly patients on the red carpet at the hospital entrance. She will be relieved, too, to hear that Sonia is staying a further week while Scruggs writes up her conference report.

In the absence of her nemesis, Agnes has been applying a tiny dab of pancake, and painting her lips with the palest possible lipstick. As Sonia hasn't objected to this hardly noticeable facial improvement, Agnes has felt vindicated. But a catastrophe worse than a make-up transgression will happen. And it will happen unexpectedly.

Mr Green will have his head down and will pretend not to see Agnes when she enters with a lovely bunch of long-stemmed red roses that have arrived for him at the front office. As she presents them to him, he will suddenly grab one of her arms in a surprisingly tight grip and, with the other, tear the buttons off the front of her uniform, grab one of her breasts and start squeezing it like a pump. She will be so shocked she will freeze like an animal in a bright light. He will jump up from his bed and force his tongue in her mouth, his body gyrating frantically up and down. When Agnes eventually manages to push him away, he will become enraged and scream obscenities at her.

Stunned by his strength and vile language, she will be even more horrified by her inability to scream and defend herself. It will be beyond unfortunate that it is Sister Scruggs and not Sonia who rushes into the room. Had it been Sonia, Agnes's whole future would have unfurled differently.

She will find herself staring down at the bed—now a tangled mess of cellophane and rose petals. And she will notice, with horror, her pink lipstick is smeared on the old lecher's lips. She will struggle to smooth down her hair, for not only did he tear off her cap, but has yanked her tresses loose, free now to fall wildly over her face.

Sister Scruggs will rush into the room and take in the scene in front of her. She will push the buzzer to summon Sonia who arrives speedily:

*Nurse Keen has provoked a disturbance. Bring a sedative for Mr Green and get someone in to clean up this mess. No, don't pick the roses up! Throw them out! Better he doesn't remember them!*

Then Agnes will feel the steel fingers close around her arm as Scruggs pulls her away as if she is a thief she has just apprehended. She will be dragged into the sterilising room and lambasted:

*Straighten yourself, you minx! What do you mean by provoking that poor old man?'*

*But I didn't provoke him! You're blowing the whole incident out of proportion. It is Mr Green who assaulted ME!*

*How dare you talk to me like that you insolent, insignificant girl! That man has your lipstick on his mouth! Didn't I tell you NOT to wear make-up! You were flirting! You provoked him!*

Aggrieved at the injustice, Agnes will strike back in her own defence:

*Everything went perfectly last week when you were away. Ask the temporary sister! She'll tell you what a good job I did!*

But Scruggs is not to be swayed:

*It is my job to sort the wheat from the chaff. And you in my opinion are chaff of the worst kind! You are DISMISSED and don't you dare to come back here! Get out of my SIGHT!*

Within minutes, news of Agnes's dismissal will reverberate around the private floor and cross the garden to the public hospital. She will tuck her hair inside her nurse's cap, straighten her uniform as best she can and slink back to the nurses' home. Her companions will be sympathetic and will recount infamous stories of other junior nurses who's careers reached an abrupt end after a run-in with the draconian Scruggs. Then a secretary will find her at lunch with friends in the canteen and will tell her to go to the matron's office at 4pm. Everyone will know what this means.

At the interview with the matron, Agnes will be asked if she has a vocation for nursing. As she has never asked herself if she wanted to be a nurse she will stare back in silent amazement. They will both sit quietly, with the unanswered question hanging in the air for what seems like an eternity:

*Well, child, your reticence indicates to me that nursing isn't for you. A girl chosen by God to nurse the sick wouldn't hesitate to affirm her devotion. I have read Sister Scruggs's report. She considers further training to be neither beneficial to you, nor to the hospital. Would you like to read what she has said?*

Agnes will decline. Desperate to get out of the place as quickly as possible, she wants to run a mile from this condescending woman who, nevertheless, provides the coup de grace:

*I will contact your grandmother personally and let her know our decision. Here is the pay that is due to you, plus an extra week in compensation for the abrupt departure. Sign this form and you can leave tomorrow. I wish you every success in finding a suitable future career.*

Agnes will sign where indicated and, when she returns to the Ground Floor Private to collect her bag from the sterilising room, she will overhear one of the senior nurses—someone she has never known or met—describe her as provocative and flirtatious. Although this is a description she doesn't recognise or understand, she will be instantly plagued with the old shame.

When she eventually summons up the courage to ring Grandma in an attempt to explain her side of the story, she will be tersely told by Lieutenant Aunt Sill that they have already heard from the hospital and that her grandmother has nothing further to say to her.

Agnes has failed to fit in again.

## CHAPTER 18

# ROSARY VILLA

Agnes has been allotted a small room on the second floor of Rosary Villa. Her bed is under a large window looking out over the front entrance. The hostel is run by the nuns of the St Joseph religious order of California and can accommodate up to 80 girls. The high ornate plaster ceilings, oak-panelled entrance hall and monumentally grand staircase hark back to its origins as a palatial home—once known as Hopewell House. Positioned like a palace on the shore of the Eastern Harbour, ferries, yachts, and flurries of boats can be seen from every corner of the sweeping grounds. High stone pillars either side of the entrance support wrought-iron gates in decorative panels. The imposing gates are rusted at the edges and have been open for so long, they look as if they will never close again.

The hostel is staffed by a hard-working band of five nuns who struggle to run it alone as a way of keeping their charges low. But low prices do not mean low standards. An enticing aroma of bacon and eggs mingles with that of percolating coffee, to permeate the double-height wood-panelled dining room at breakfast time. Here, Agnes find herself in heaven, piling her plate with what is on offer: sausages, mushrooms, grilled tomatoes, baked beans, toast with marmalade and giant mugs of tea. The slow disappearance of the mouth ulcers with which she has been afflicted since starting work in the private hospital heralds the happy fact that she is on the mend.

Breakfast is the only meal on offer and Agnes duly fills up for the day, slipping sausages, bread rolls, biscuits, and fruit into her bag as the other girls do. She eats this secret hoard on a bench in the garden during the long and muddled days ahead. On Friday evenings she watches as the place pulses with shouts and laughter, for girls are lining up to pay their weekly board to a hook-nosed old nun in a back room who barely looks at them. Haunted by her mother's bad debts, Agnes is always scrupulous about paying what she owes, but her savings are perilously low.

After a few days spent in the sanctuary of the hostel, Pamela Thomson, the friend who has found her a temporary room there, returns to Rosary Villa from a visit to her family. She is beaming when she spots Agnes at breakfast. The sunshine in the young woman's smile reassures Agnes of a sincerity that will never wane over the years:

*Hope you've recovered, Agnes! Did I tell you my sister was so shattered after her own ordeal with Scruggs, my father gave her a week's holiday at Hayman Island! Listen, I thought of the perfect job for you while I was away! Registration Clerk!*

Agnes has not got a clue what this means and pushes for more details. It is the same work Pam does as a law student. The job entails the filing of documents at various public offices around the city. Agnes admits that it sounds appealing and agrees with Pam's shrewd observation that it would alleviate the scrutiny she loathes as she would be mostly out and about—away from prying eyes.

Puffing on a cigarette, and between sips of black coffee, Pam continues to map out Agnes's future as if it is the most natural thing in the world:

*I'll ask in my office and put the word out on the network. We'll talk tonight. Chin up! Get ready for something new! Arrivederci, bambino!*

And, with that, she blows Agnes a kiss and whirls out of the door.

Agnes is punch-drunk with astonishment. In a curious way, she has Scruggs's brutality to thank for Pam's empathy. She might become a Registration Clerk for a legal firm! She might yet show that bunch at 'Rosemont' that she is a *person of substance!*

In a clever move, Pam asks the girl leaving a clerk's post in Pitt Street to recommend Agnes for the job, and, as a reward for protecting him from being caught snoozing, or with his head in a pin-up magazine, John from the import/export firm will compensate Agnes with a glowing testimonial. She is all set for the next big step in her future.

Wandering the Sydney streets like a stray dog for months has meant that Agnes knows her way around the city, but Pam helps her to pinpoint the location of the Law Courts in Macquarie Street, the Probate Office in St James Street, and the Registrar General's offices opposite St Mary's Cathedral. Agnes is in awe of how Pam simplifies the seemingly complicated, and still manages to look her magnificent self, though staying up half the night studying. More importantly, Pam has unwittingly offered Agnes an image of herself she can finally agree with, and so she stops apologising for herself to others.

On her first day at the Pitt Street office, Agnes will be relieved to be allotted an isolated desk in a nook near the strong room, with no one looking over her shoulder and where she can easily hide her poor writing skills by secretly using a dictionary concealed under the desk. She will start at 9am prompt, sort out the written instructions from the solicitors, and set out to be ahead of the queues at the Public Offices that open at 10am. She will soon be greeting familiar faces on the beat, added to which Pam will introduce her to the few other women studying law. Agnes will greatly enjoy listening in to their lively chat in the Ladies Common Room at the Law School in Elizabeth Street.

Her favourite part of the job—searching the property titles at the Registrar General's offices—will soon diminish, however, as the Pitt Street firm opts to abandon property conveyancing in favour of more divorce litigation. Divorce has been something Agnes is only familiar with from the publicity given to Hollywood film stars, many of whom she is aware remarry multiple times. The very idea of anyone divorcing at 'Rosemont' would be tantamount to everlasting shame, yet it is clearly a lucrative business. She will discover that divorce on the grounds of adultery is the quickest way to untie the knot. Thus, although it might not be the actual cause for the marriage breakdown, many Pitt Street clients will follow that route to a swift 'decree absolute'.

Imbued with a new sense of purpose, she decides to continue her acting classes. In time she will be offered a part in a Victorian melodrama called *The Drunkard*. Her few lines will be hardly more than an extension of the scenery, but she will delude herself into believing it is a good beginning.

As it is impossible to finish late in the theatre each night and still be on time for work the next day, Agnes will apply for—and secure—a job in a bigger solicitors' office where there is a variety of work and which, crucially, starts an hour later in the mornings. However, the joy of having a friend like Pam in her life will be abruptly swept away due to the pressure of her new friend's preparation for exams. It means that Pam will no longer be able to seek Agnes out for walks in Centennial Park on Sundays after Mass or to enjoy their regular meal together in the evening in Rushcutters Bay. And then Pam will meet Paul at a university college party and fall in love. Six weeks into the romance, Paul will graduate as a veterinary surgeon and propose—their small, happy, rushed wedding is precipitated by the fact that he has accepted a job in a veterinary clinic in Victoria and wants Pam to accompany him.

*I always knew you were special, Agnes.*

These will be Pam's final words to Agnes as she walks out of her life on Paul's arm.

There will be lengthy intervals when the friends do not see each other, but they are destined to remain close until Pam's tragically early death.

## CHAPTER 19

# CHARLES BURGESS

Agnes could have continued juggling the job at the solicitors' office with her small acting part at night if Charles Burgess hadn't crashed into her life. She can't remember how, or where, she met him. Given her childhood conditioning, it seemed he had been shadowing her all her life. But she does recall that there were no flowers, no hand-in-hand strolls along the beach, no running together through soft meadows, no dazzling smiles or stars in the eyes over candlelit dinners. Charles Burgess seemed to spring out of nowhere, like a noxious weed, and cause her to disappear into a labyrinth she could not find her way out of.

She finds much of what he says in his put-on English accent incomprehensible, but never questions its validity. He flaunts a superiority based on some half-cocked English aristocratic pedigree: a family tree that connects him back to a Hampshire Earl on his father's side. Or it might have been Norfolk—or possibly Suffolk. These are names that mean nothing to Agnes. Never has it occurred to her to look at a map of the world, let alone England, to locate countries and places she hears about.

Charles struts along, his nose in the air. He is swinging a black umbrella and is on his way from Wynyard Station to work in a stockbrokers' office in Hunter Street. He is dressed in one of the bespoke suits he buys at Hunts Menswear shop in George Street. He also favours their sports jackets and handmade shoes. Nothing adorns his noble person that isn't imported from the land of his ancestors. He concedes the wool might have been shorn off an Australian sheep but says it transcends its lowly origins by being fashioned in the mills of Yorkshire. He complains of being persecuted by crude, uncouth fellow Australians whom he sees as inferior. Just like Agnes.

The overblown 'old country' history is tacked onto a middle-class childhood. Charles has an older brother, Ronald. They both reside in a Tudor revival house in Killara on the Upper North Shore. Ronald has assumed the responsibility of caring for a grieving mother and problematic brother after his father's sudden death.

Not only has Ronald's training in the law allowed him to take over his father's legal practice, but he has been able to advise Charles on a charge of manslaughter after his girlfriend, Sally-Ann, was killed in a car accident. Agnes learns that the British racing-green Morgan sports car Charles had been driving had skidded and hit a tree on a stretch of the Pittwater Road. Ronald had briefed an eminent Sydney QC, who had meticulously stage-managed Charles's defence appearances in court, and successfully got him off.

It is not long after his liberation from a potential jail sentence that Charles appears outside the theatre at the end of the evening performance of *The Drunkard* and offers to drive Agnes home. Being claimed by someone fills the great emptiness she feels after Pam's departure. Maria, her only other friend, has moved in with an Italian boyfriend and is no longer in touch.

Agnes has never expected the lift home to become a regular event, but there Charles constantly is, waiting outside the theatre every night, a pair of thick-rimmed tortoiseshell glasses enlarging his restless, hawk-like hazel eyes. Eyes which, for some reason, alarm her. The lifts are convenient, but what she just cannot comprehend is why Charles drives so fast, having initiated an accident that killed his girlfriend.

They have started kissing in the car whenever he drops her off at Rosary Villa. Relief, rather than desire, prompts her submission to this intimacy; relief that the car hasn't smashed into a girder on the

Harbour Bridge or spun off the Cahill Expressway into the harbour. She sometimes imagines Mortuary Mike telling her estranged family—when they come to identify the body—that he once knew her. The outburst from the back seat of her father's car that fateful night on the road to The Farm would be silenced forever in their minds. Loss would stir the sympathy of the beloved polo group. Indeed, Agnes's early death might well prove to be the perfect gift.

But she no longer *wants* to die. And Charles, it would appear, is not about to co-operate with her efforts to remain alive. Her requests to him to slow down only make him drive even faster. She gradually learns to humour him in the way she humoured her father when he got drunk. She already knows intuitively that, like Eric Keen, Charles never forgets a real—or imagined—slight. Behind a seeming silent passivity lurks, she has come to recognise, the self-same whirlwind of inner rage that never goes off the boil.

She has started rehearsing a speech in her head to get rid of Charles but, when the moment arrives to deliver it, she crumbles. To her own disgust, she goes on tolerating the fear of mutilation or extinction by road accident for a few more days but, after a particularly hair-raising journey, finally manages to summon up her courage:

*I don't want you to come and pick me up from the theatre anymore Charles.*

Having delivered this with as much gravitas as she could muster, she enters the gates of Rosary Villa in Darling Point, an Eastern Suburb; The Ensemble Theatre being near Milson's Point station, a Northern Suburb.

A fortnight passes with no sign of Charles at the Stage Door and, feeling confident that he has gone for good, she stops sneaking out of a side entrance and scurrying like a rat up a dark parallel street to the station in case he happens to be parked nearby.

She will still be able to summon up this sense of deep relief years down the line. And she is now able to recall, in detail, how briefly it lasted:

*The show is over. Then I see him. Waiting at the Stage Door.*

*At first, I don't recognise him because he is wearing what he describes as a Harris Tweed cap. It is pulled down over his eyes. Standing guard by the open door of his car, in a light drizzling rain, he looks more like a chauffeur than the potential heir to a so-called grand estate. The impact of his appearance is further diminished by the fact he is wearing gumboots. No ordinary gumboots, he informs me, but Wellingtons—lined in cashmere wool from Hunts.*

*Don't worry, he says. I've no intention of picking you up regularly like before. Jump in the car. I've got a surprise for you. He sounds quite breezy for Charles. Even carefree. Something about the way I had woken up that rainy morning makes me hesitate by the open door of the car. I am not sure what to do. I don't want to ride with him, but I am the last one out of the theatre. Come on, he says. Don't be afraid. I'm not going to bite you. He never refers to me by name. I follow suit by never using his. Christian names are too intimate for whatever is between us.*

*Standing near him again makes my skin crawl. My heart thumps in my chest so hard I think it might come out of my mouth and I consider dashing back into the theatre but then remember the click of the caretaker's key behind me. It is very dark. There is no one around to help me.*

*Lacking a better plan, I take off down the street at a run. I am a good runner. A fast runner. Pumped with adrenalin, I know I can outpace him. But I trip over a raised paving brick and land flat on my face. Charles is suddenly on top of me—pulling me up. I glance down and see I have torn holes in my stockings. The grazed skin on my knees starts to sting in the cold night air. Charles yanks my arm tightly behind my back, picks up my handbag, and frogmarches me back to the car.*

*I can't speak. He reeks of silent anger. He shoves my head down and pushes me roughly into the passenger seat and, in what seems like the blink of an eye, he's in the driver's seat. I see him press a button on the dashboard that locks the car doors.*

*We eventually turn right off the highway at Pymble Shopping Centre and he twists the Volvo down tree-lined streets past winding rows of houses. Then we are on a dirt track in the bush. The high beam of the headlight picks out thick shrubs that scrape the sides of the car. The windscreen wipers sound like a drumbeat. He pulls up abruptly in the centre of a small clearing. I can glimpse a patch of thick gravel surrounded by low spindly shrubs. When he turns off the headlights for a few minutes it is so dark I can see nothing.*

*He laboriously removes his gloves, folds them into the Harris Tweed cap and places the cap on the dashboard. The sound of the rain on the roof is deafening. He has not said a word to me since he told me to get in the car. I am more afraid of his silence than of the endless monologues that I have never understood. He reaches down and, with a flick of a lever, my seat tips back. A further flick and he is at the same horizontal level. I am trapped. His perspiring skin has a sweet smell I can't identify. I do get a little excited when he starts kissing me and putting his tongue in my mouth, but soon he wants more and snarls at me like a ferocious dog when I try to move his hand away from under my dress. Then he pushes his finger deep up inside me. My head starts to spin and I feel sick. I don't want this to happen and tell him I am a virgin and ask him would he please stop. He doesn't stop and I wrestle away and shout for him to get off me. But I know he is determined when I feel the elastic of my underpants bruise the side of my hip as he wrenches them off. Then he shoves my skirt into my mouth. I shout no, I beg no, I cry no, but he prises my legs apart and thrusts himself inside me. He moves frantically, hurting me, then cries out like a wounded animal and sinks on top of me. So, this is sex. After what seems like an eternity, he lifts himself up, grazing my shin with the toe of his boot.*

*He turns on the inside light of the car, checks himself, and says: 'Where's the blood, you whore? I just slid in like butter! I suppose you put on this virgin act with all the boys!'*

*I tell him I didn't want him to do it. That he forced me. That I'd never really seen sex or known how it was done. I tell him that my mother said girls had to be careful as they can break their hymen riding horses and that this must be what had happened to me.*

*He laughs mirthlessly and says: 'Well now, if you really did lose your virginity to a horse, you've just lost it to a man. I have made you a woman.' It was as if he had given me a gift, instead of stealing what was never on offer.*

*He drives me home to Rosary Villa in silence. We pull up under the hanging trees on the gravel entrance way in the early hours of the morning. He grabs my wrist tightly as I attempt to slide out of the car. He says: 'You belong to me. You know that don't you? Never, ever run away from me like that again. And if you tell anyone about what happened tonight—I'll kill you.'*

That night, Agnes will lie motionless in bed until exhaustion swamps her churning thoughts. Conditioned when attacked to retreat inside herself and to try and expunge it from her mind, Agnes will be unaware that she has just been raped. The accident with the girlfriend had left Charles with deep scars across his forehead and she will wonder if he had left his sanity in the mangled wreck on the Pittwater Road. He could be an escapee from a mental asylum for all she knew. But because she knows nobody he knows, there will be no one to ask.

Charles will now exercise a ruthless hold over her and refuse to answer any of her questions about his past. Instead, he will go on monotonously recounting the fanciful tale of his illustrious British heritage. Increasingly fearful of his violent temper, Agnes will meekly submit to his constant sexual demands in the back seat of the Volvo. That first brutal night in the rain will be repeated in other parking sites all over Sydney, and Agnes won't be able to shake the possibility that Charles might have captured poor, dead Sally-Ann and held her as a psychological prisoner before bringing about her demise, and that perhaps he is now doing the same with her.

By the time they are spending 'social' weekends in the house of Charles's middle-aged colleague from the stockbrokers' office, Agnes will have left the Ensemble Theatre and will be on the verge of losing her job for arriving late to work once too often. Devoid of sleep and proper nourishment, she will find it increasingly hard to function.

She has lost her way. Charles has perforated her will, and she will gradually forget that she ever had an ambition to be an actress—or anything else.

Whilst out on a delivery of legal papers across town, Agnes will collapse on the pavement in Pitt Street and know no more.

When she opens her eyes again, she will find herself in bed at— The Farm. The room will be spinning, and she will be completely unable to focus or hold her head up. She will hear a male voice she does not recognise:

*There is no time to grow a culture. Her condition is critical. I'll be back as quickly as possible with a broad-spectrum antibiotic. It will hopefully kill the infection.*

Agnes will hover between life and death in a raging fever. The doctor will come every day and give her an injection, and Uncle Ben and his children will visit her at the weekends and stand at the bedroom door. Their voices will sound like the buzzing of a distant beehive.

After two weeks, when she is finally able to sit up, she will discover it was Charles who drove her to her parents, a journey of which she will have no memory. Charles. Shadowing her still.

\* \* \*

During her slow recovery Agnes reflects for hours on end upon the subject of madness. Could Charles's absolute assurance that she will be in his life, *must* be in his life, be a sign of an unhinged mind? She plucks up the courage to mention her fear of him to her mother:

*I'm scared he's going to kill me in a road accident, Mummy. The way he killed his former girlfriend!*

The retort from her mother is rapid and vicious:

*Well, if he is off his rocker, you make a good pair. Expect he'll be coming to pick you up soon.*

Agnes is aware that her father's return from a business trip looms when her mother shows these old familiar signs of wanting to get rid of her. On the day of the expulsion, Madge tries to soften the blow by calling her Darling and Possum and sharing bits of family gossip. She even gives Agnes one of her sixth-floor frocks as compensation for her betrayal. It is pink linen with raised embroidered white flowers bordered in a darker pink with flecks of olive green. It is left on the bed for her when Agnes gets out of the bath:

*Thank you, but I don't want it. Pink's your colour, not mine.*

*Don't talk back to me Agnes! The clothes you arrived in were worn out and, given the nature of your illness, I threw them away!*

All Agnes will be left with of her own possessions is a handbag and a pair of shoes. As a result, she has no choice but to accept what is on offer from her mother, right down to underwear and stockings. But she does try to assert herself one last time:

*Why don't you want me to see Daddy?*

*It's got nothing to do with me. Your father has his mind made up. He still hasn't got over that episode in the car.*

*But that was nearly two years ago!*

*You dug your own hole, Agnes, and now you must lie in it.*

The departure hour is imminent. She is hurt and angry, but the truth is that Agnes is not safe at The Farm. And never will be. And, although the air is wonderfully fresh and the roses that line the sides of the path to the front door are in full fragrant radiance, all Agnes will think of as she gazes out on the garden is climbing into the beating heart of a giant open rose, travelling down its stem, and burrowing down through the soft earth to find a peaceful place.

The way Agnes's mother flirts with Charles when he arrives to pick her up will shock her, but she will know full well that her mother, in her predictably perverse way, is displaying to her daughter how attractive she is to her own man. It is a competition. It always has been.

# Part Four

I am not accustomed to telling myself what happens to me, so I find it hard to remember the exact succession of events—and I can't make out what is important.
—*Nausea* by John-Paul Sartre

## CHAPTER 20
# A CHILD FOR GOD

It has dawned on Agnes that she has missed a period. She never keeps a check, but it seems ages since the last one. After feeling sick all morning, she makes an appointment to see a gynaecologist in Macquarie Street. As soon as she steps out of the lift, she knows she has made a mistake in choosing a lavishly decorated place such as this, frequented as it obviously is by the wealthy and well connected. But, lost in her usual muddle, it was the first port in a storm that sprang to mind.

The gynaecologist confirms her worst fears. She is just over two months gone, and the baby is due on 30$^{th}$ September. He tells her that she has a big surprise to impart to her husband that night. Surely the man has seen that she has no wedding ring on her finger. She does not respond. Disoriented, she trips over the chair as she stands up, bracing herself to leave:

*Are you all right, Mrs Keen?*

*Yes... yes... thank you...*

He tells her to make an appointment with the nurse to come back in two months when she will be kitted out with a book on how to look after herself. He tells her there is absolutely no reason, at her age, not to expect to have a perfectly normal pregnancy.

With that, the white panel door gently shuts behind her and she is thrust into a new world of confusion. She finds it hard to accept that Charles's perverse enslavement could result in a baby. The idea of marrying him is inconceivable. She could try and arrange an abortion, but she has no money and, after all, having an abortion is a mortal sin. The only person she can think of turning to is a priest in the confessional. And so, she wanders down Martin Place in the general direction of St Patrick's Church. It is where her mother claimed to attend Mass when Agnes sought Monsignor Harrington's help to save her soul. Now she must save her own.

It is just after five and still stifling hot. Red, sweaty-faced office workers are heading for trains and buses to take them home. After the din of cars accelerating up Grosvenor Street, the silence inside the big doors of the church is bewildering. The click-clacks of her high heels echo sharply as she stumbles down the central aisle and slides into a pew. There is a short queue outside the confessional box. She notices a coffin on a brass stand inside the altar area with a woman's straw hat on top, its brim adorned with colourful dried flowers. Mourners in black are sitting in the pews directly in front of her. She wonders if, when Grandma dies, they will put her red hat with the feathers on top of the coffin.

Suddenly, it is her turn for the sacrament, and she is kneeling inside the confessional box. When the shutter opens, her mouth goes dry and, predictably, she can't find her voice. The priest speaks softly:

*Go on, my child, don't be afraid. You are safe in the house of God.*

*Bless me, Father, for I have sinned. It is fourteen months since my last confession.*

She has plucked the number of months out of the air as she cannot count back past all the dark parking spots with Charles. As she finds the words she needs, she is astonished by the priest's calm reactions to all the backseat, out-of-marriage sex, the eating meat on Fridays, the missing of regular Sunday Mass, and the persistent suicidal thoughts.

The latter had haunted her as little as 15 minutes ago, when the possibility of a watery grave in the harbour had, once again, crossed her mind. Murder—and it isn't as if she hasn't contemplated it before—is now the only mortal sin she still has in reserve. Had she died from the recent ugly throat infection, she would have been bound to go straight to hell. She prays she has come back to the Church in the nick of time. The penance the priest hands out—chanting a few rosaries—seems insignificant compensation for the utter relief of unburdening her soul.

After the absolution, the priest invites her to the annexe at the side of the church to discuss the pregnancy. The man she imagines from the voice turns out to look completely different to the man she had pictured in her head. Father O'Donnell's freckled face and red hair makes Agnes feel she is in the safe hands of someone from her own tribe. The apprehension that foreshadowed the unexpected interview vanishes with the compassion shining from the priest's autumnal eyes. When she explains how she would like to go it alone and not tell her parents, or anyone else, he smiles reassuringly:

*You'll be safe with Sister Wilfred at St Anthony's Home. Your privacy will be absolute.*

His next words are a wondrous revelation, and one that she interprets as a sacred prophecy:

*This is a new beginning. You will have a child for God. The seed in you is sanctified.*

The priest walks her to the door of the sacristy and shakes her hand warmly, apologising for the abbreviated proceedings because he is due shortly to officiate at a funeral service. Agnes looks into the man's kindly eyes and thinks of the Virgin Mary after the annunciation.

She has been born for this moment. *A child for God. A child for God.* She keeps repeating the phrase to herself, marvelling at how much joy could suddenly enter her life in such a short space of time.

\* \* \*

It is nearly the end of March, but the muggy summer weather

persists. Agnes's top priority is to nourish the child inside her. She pays attention to her diet and tries to regain a regular sleep pattern. After work, where she is now extra careful to be both industrious and prompt, she visits a delicatessen to buy egg and salad sandwiches, bananas, apples, and yogurt. Then she catches a bus uptown to have a picnic on the grass at the Domain opposite the Sydney Art Gallery. It is all part of her plan to avoid Charles, as he would never think to look for her there.

Charles has no idea about the pregnancy. The drive back from her parents was stiffly polite, neither of them speaking much. She needed time to recuperate, she told him. She hopes this might buy her some precious respite from his attentions. She must, at some point, of course, find the strength to rebuff him completely. All her life on standby to serve others, she now feels strange in these attempts to carve out a tiny space for herself. Nonetheless, her all-consuming desire for a little peace is still tempered by a haunting self-consciousness—a mad preoccupation about what others will think of her eating on the grass, there, in solitude. She must follow the priest's instructions. The next stage of her life is approaching.

The short time Agnes is told to wait in the white lace-curtained parlour at St Anthony's Home is an agony. A picture of the Sacred Heart bears down on her from the wall opposite, as if it is about to crash-land on her head. She doesn't feel she can move to another chair because the brisk nun who answered the door pointed to this specific one—as if it was the approved spot for all girls in her predicament.

The door swings open in front of Sister Wilfred's office with the force of a Southerly Buster. A short, dumpy nun, with cheeks like newly polished apples, greets Agnes like an old friend:

*Well, well, Agnes, here you are! Sorry to have kept you. Good to see you!*

The nun looks Agnes up and down as if assessing her reproductive potential. She beckons Agnes inside her office and directs her to be seated on the other side of a large untidy desk. The pale-yellow walls in the office smell of fresh paint and are bare—except for a large photo, in a splendid frame, of a gigantic red bull. The magnificent beast sports a purple ribbon trimmed in gold around its neck, upon which is written 'First Prize':

*I see you're looking at Sam—our prize Santa Gertrudos. Isn't he something! He looks dangerous with that great head and shoulders but he's as docile as an old tabby. I'm about to reinstate shots of all our other stud favourites now the walls are dry. They're all Gerts. They resist disease, you know—and changes of temperature.*

Sister Wilfred stops abruptly and rummages in a drawer of her desk, before leaning across it and, with an almost parental pride, spreading six photos of similar equally adorned beasts in front of Agnes:

*These are our other winners. Aren't they beautiful? Such smooth, silky coats! Wonderful mothers! They calve easily and have plenty of milk. I'm back on the Mildura farm every time I look at them.*

*Well, Sister, if I'm ever in the market for a handsome beast, I'll know where to come.*

The little nun smiles, clearly picking up the intended irony.

Looking closely at her face, Agnes suspects the deep frown lines across her brow are probably the result of years of working out in the hot sun on a country ranch without a hat.

*So how many months are you?*

*Just over two—I think. Sister, please, I don't want my parents to know, nor be forced to marry the father. He would make my life a misery.*

*I see. Well, if you remain healthy, there's no reason why we can't arrange a good cover story while you're here. My sister June lives on the Mildura property. If you give family and friends her address, she'll forward on their mail to us here. You send the letters you write home to her, and she'll post them on to your parents with a Mildura post mark. The Gerts should provide a good sentence or two! Oh, and you'll have a false name here to protect your identity.*

Agnes can't quite believe it. All this clever subterfuge willingly laid on for her convenience! She has always wanted to be someone else, so the prospect of a change of name is thrilling. She considers this for a few seconds:

*I'll call myself Katherine. Katherine Lea De Winter.*

Experiencing huge relief beyond her dreams, she now relishes the fact of becoming a *Rebecca* character. It is the icing on the cake! Also, this Mildura ranch cover story is an absolute godsend. No one need know a thing! She feels a surge of renewed confidence. She has only ever been a conversation piece and now she will be directing the dialogue:

*I know, Sister! I'll tell my mother I got a job in Mildura as a governess! She loves anything to do with country properties!*

Sister Wilfred smiles at her kindly, then fills in an admission card. Agnes is expected to arrive back at St Anthony's home when she starts to show around four or five months. She likes Sister Wilfred immensely. The woman's slow drawl clearly has been nowhere near an elocution lesson. It is such a relief to deal with someone so down to earth. Everything is crystal clear. There is no hidden agenda. She is beginning to feel secure. Agnes might be an outcast from her family, but she knows she belongs to the Catholic Church and is having a child for God.

On the train back to Sydney her mind races with plans for her future. She will have to secure a second job and start saving up for the extra money needed for the months spent at St Anthony's till the birth. But the major obstacle, of course, is how to handle Charles. She has managed to avoid him for a couple of weeks, but fears a showdown is looming.

Her stomach lurches when she reaches the rusting entrance gate of Rosary Villa for, like a metallic portent from hell, she can see his Volvo parked on the gravel in front of the front door. Perhaps he hasn't seen her in the rear-view mirror. Her first instinct is to slip into the gardens and hide in the thick foliage until he leaves. But there is no time. He has looked up and already spotted her.

Springing out of the car, he runs to where she stands, frozen. She can see the simmering fury in his cold hawk eyes. It *must* be now or never:

*Go away, Charles! I can't see you anymore! I beg you! You MUST find it in your heart to leave me alone! I need to work and save up money to prepare for my confinement! Yes, that's right! I'm pregnant!*

There is a long pause as he computes this bombshell information:

*Why in hell's name didn't you tell me?! You've made me look like an idiot!*

*Charles. Listen to me. I will kill myself if you don't leave me alone!*

His raptor eyes are heavy with fatigue, and he seems almost desperate:

*Look here. I can marry you and we can have the baby together. I promise I'll change. If you give me another chance, everything will be different!*

She has never heard him speak in this conciliatory manner before. She stares in disbelief. It is so important that she muster up all her dwindling inner strength now, in the face of this pathetic and exhausted man. He takes a step towards her:

*Please. Let's just drive to the Botanical Gardens where we can walk together and calm down. Only for a bit, all right? You owe me that at least.*

Something—she will never know what—some misplaced sense of fairness perhaps, will prompt her to make this concession and she will climb, once again, into the Volvo death seat. Charles will drive in the usual reckless fashion along New South Head Road, through King's Cross and down William Street. He will park the car at Lady Macquarie's Chair, and they will walk along the pathway by the edge of the harbour and talk. It will be a civil exchange, with no heightened emotion. She will speak with him calmly as she does not want to ruin one of her favourite places—a place where she usually finds beauty and peace.

It will already be dark when they arrive back at Lady Macquarie's Chair and where Agnes will announce that she is not getting in the car and will be catching a bus instead. He will look at her sharply: *At least let me drive you to the bus stop.*

Again, she will go against her instinct, get back in the car, and will end up in a dark corner under the Harbour Bridge—with Charles on top of her.

In the confessional box the next evening, Father O'Donnell at St Patrick's will advise her to go to the police. He will give what happened to Agnes under the bridge the name it deserves. He will call it 'rape'. It is a police matter. But she is fearful, she tells him, that the police will want to arrest her assailant and will also want to contact her parents. All she wants in the world, she says, is to quietly move on. To have her Child for God.

Father O'Donnell will advise her to avoid Charles completely. To keep to public places. To hold her nerve. If she only had enough money to move out of Rosary Villa, then she could probably manage to do all this. But how?

Shortly after the discussion with the priest, two minor miracles will occur. Ever persistent, she will land a second job as a cleaner in a language school where she starts at 4am each morning, finishes cleaning at 7am, then returns to a tiny studio flat housed within the school that she has convinced her new boss to rent out to her for three months. Here she will shower and get ready for her current registration job. It is hard going, and makes for a very long day, but those three extra early hours will make her good money. She will love having a little kitchen all to herself and will, every morning, cook up hearty egg and bacon breakfasts and be sure to include a large glass of milk for baby. She will start talking to her Child for God and will feel certain she is having a girl.

She will be catapulted up from simple contentment to seventh heaven when she returns briefly to collect her mail from Rosary Villa and finds a letter from Charles's brother Ronald. It informs her that Charles has been placed into temporary custody with his business partner—pending an appearance in court. Insider trading and fraud.

Able to breathe deeply again, and all prayers answered, she will no longer have to look over her shoulder—at least for a while. She feels completely justified in not responding to Ronald's letter—jail being precisely the right place for rapists, abusers, and embezzlers.

As predicted, Agnes's mother will lap up the news of the bogus governess post at the Victoria ranch with unimaginable delight. Within a few minutes of Agnes hanging up the phone, she will ring her back, hungry for yet more details. The inspired fabrication will reinstate Agnes into the family fold, albeit temporarily. Madge may know the names of all the wealthy property owners in New South Wales but, fortunately for Agnes, is unfamiliar with those in Victoria. This means Agnes can now happily provide her own fictitious input, which saves her mother the bother of making it up.

When the time comes to go to St Anthony's, she will terminate her two jobs, pack up her few possessions, and pay the nuns to leave the moving boxes in the storage room at Rosary Villa. Then she will splurge on a taxi and stroll into the main hall of Central Station where, purely for appearances' sake, she will wait on the platform beside the Melbourne train until it pulls out without her.

Swinging her suitcase, handbag slung over her arm, she will descend the stairs from the main hall to the suburban lines below. As the train passes station after station heading west out of Sydney to Croydon, Agnes will congratulate herself that another future is beginning—a future for her Child for God.

\* \* \*

Agnes's arrival at St Anthony's is an anticlimax. The home comprises three buildings. The unwed girl mothers sleep in a long, narrow two-storey building that borders the back of the block. It is accessed by a road, big enough for a car, that traverses in a straight line from the tall iron gates at the street frontage. The caramel rectangular brick building—The Archbishop Kelly Wing—that lies to the left of the huge iron gates is where the nuns reside and where Agnes first met Sister Wilfred. A small brick chapel nestles opposite on the other side of the road.

She unpacks her suitcase but leaves the special fine full-length blue wool dressing gown with its satin piping edges in the bottom of the case—ready to wear to the hospital when the time comes. The dressing gown is a purchase she has splurged out on. It has cut into her savings but, she reasons, a girl needs something special for such an important event. She sees it like a going-away outfit after a wedding for, after all, the ultimate trip to St Margaret's hospital will be the beginning of the end of the story.

Agnes soon learns that it is the unwed girl inmates who run the home. Everyone works at chores and duties. While the rest of Croydon sleeps, lights go on in the dormitories at 5.30am. Work starts for Agnes in the nursery at 6am—alongside Sister Bernadette. This occupation evokes memories of the sterilising room in Ground Floor Private, although the young nun's sarcasm is a mere irritant compared to the relentless cruelty of the heavy-breasted Scruggs. Yet the same hostility towards her, it seems, has been carried over:

*Didn't you go to school? Haven't you got eyes? Didn't you listen to what I said?*

Such acerbic comments hover constantly in the background as Agnes cleans, makes beds, and bathes and dresses the sweet little orphans whom the home also houses. She decides not to let the stiff-necked nursery nun get to her. Whenever she sees an opportunity, she steps in to help. She often asks Sister Bernadette's opinion and dutifully turns the other cheek to her insults until they stop coming.

Lunch and dinner are delicious and plentiful. There is a baked dinner on Saturday night instead of Sunday lunch because most of the girls go out with their families on Sunday. Wednesday is rissoles with thick gravy, mashed potatoes and beans or peas, and Friday, of course, is fish and chips. Agnes can recognise the day of the week by what is on the menu. A matchstick when she first arrived, within a few weeks she has put on weight, and the bump she has so carefully guarded from view pops out in solidarity with her pregnant companions.

The dining room in the Archbishop Kelly Wing doubles as an assembly room and is where Agnes discovers, to her delight, that she is to receive a weekly payment from the Social Security Department. This means that, after the splurge on the blue dressing gown, her savings balance is as before, and is set to increase every week. The social security, she discovers, will also pay for the ambulance to the hospital, and the return ride to the home with baby in a taxi, together with a small amount after the birth to help get started again.

Nobody talks about the past, although vivid individual stories of suspect truth circulate the corridors.

After a month of pulling herself out of bed in the dark, Agnes starts dreaming of improving her lot at the home. Work in the office is undoubtedly the top job—the handful of unwed girls who work there enjoy the privilege of starting at the later hour of seven, when they attend morning Mass alongside the nuns, then enjoy a leisurely breakfast, and still have time to return to the dormitory before getting started at nine—like any Sydney office worker. Agnes determines to break into this inner circle, for laundry, kitchen, and cleaning duties smack of her past enslavement.

One evening, before lights out, she will sneak downstairs and boldly confront Sister Wilfred on her way to the chapel:

*If working with us would interest you, Agnes, I'll keep you in mind. One of our office girls is due any day now so, when she leaves, I'll give you a try.*

Even at this desired distance, Agnes's relationship with her mother will traverse the extremes. One minute she will be insulting Madge under her breath for a remembered attack, and the next she will be labouring over heartfelt letters to impress her. There will be flowery missives of events related to her by Sister Wilfred— as arranged between them—winging their way North. Long paragraphs will describe horseback-riding the boundaries of the huge property where Agnes supposedly works as a treasured family governess. She will describe watching a man on a tractor winch one of the giant Santa Gertruda cattle out of a patch of quicksand. She will describe helping the flying doctor—who has just landed on the property in a light aircraft having been guided by the name 'DUNROVEN' emblazoned on the roof of the homestead. Madge will learn how the doctor plans to airlift an injured farm worker to hospital. To add further authenticity to her audacious cover story, Agnes will forward a newspaper article, supplied by Sister Wilfred's sister, which is headlined:

MILDURA—THE MEDITERRANEAN IN THE OUTBACK.

She will also enclose a couple of extra photos of the prize bull featured on Sister Wilfred's office wall.

Madge's effusive replies will confirm Agnes's achievement as a temporary member of her elevated polo circle. Thus, Agnes's country life inventions will grow even more elaborate. Many of the activities she invents on the property will not match the seasons but, fully aware she isn't corresponding with an enquiring mind, she will steam ahead regardless.

Life, under the circumstances, couldn't be going better but, exactly like a character in a Greek drama accused of dangerous hubris, Agnes will be struck down.

She has always associated bad weather with Charles. And, true to premonition, she is woken by a violent storm in the early hours of Sunday morning. The wind howls around the building, smashing against the windows like the fist of someone desperate to be let in. Agnes hovers for the rest of the night on the edge of sleep and wakes exhausted. Between morning downpours, she will keep nodding off during Mass. Her stomach will be so churned up she will even forego Sunday's frankfurter sausages.

She will spot him from the window of her cubicle, parking his silver Volvo. Had the charges against him been dropped? Had he wriggled out of them with brother Ronald's help?

## Chapter 20  A Child for God

The branches of the jacaranda tree at the entrance to the dormitory block, which had swirled all night like the tentacles of an enraged octopus, will hang limp. She will smell his irritation as he struggles to navigate the tight parking space. She will flinch inside as he kicks the gate that resists his effort to open it. She will hate intensely his self-assured stride as she watches him carrying what looks like a cellophane-wrapped bunch of white arum lilies mixed with carnations, doubtless intended for Sister Wilfred, to further smooth his way. She had never received flowers, or anything more than dull conversation, forced sex and dangerous driving from him.

There he is—striding up to the convent door with the usual pugnacious assurance of being the one in control. Agnes will observe Sister Bernadette open the door to him and see him and his bouquet swallowed up inside. What will Sister Wilfred do? Has she told Sister Bernadette the score? *Will* these nuns be able to protect her, as Sister Wilfred had once promised! The street and the home deserted, the atmosphere to Agnes will feel like the running of the Melbourne Cup when, on one day in November at precisely 3pm, everyone abandons what they are doing to listen to the horse race. But she will continue to wait. It is all she can do.

What happens next will be beyond analysis or prediction. The front door of the convent will burst open. Crouching down by the open window, she will be astonished to hear Sister Wilfred raise her voice to cattle-herding levels:

*I am warning you again, Mr Burgess! The police are on their way! Now kindly stop shouting and behave yourself!*

Agnes will risk a glimpse through the window. She will see Sister Wilfred wielding a five-iron golf club, and Charles now firmly backed up against a wall. Sure enough, she will detect the whine of approaching sirens and, as their noise increases with proximity, and the police car enters the gate, Charles will seem to shrink into nothing. He will never return.

## CHAPTER 21

# REBECCA LEA

After Charles's arrest, Sister Wilfred accompanies Agnes to the Infirmary where they run her a warm, relaxing bath. A short time later, the feisty nun personally serves her a hot mug of tea. As Agnes sips at it, Sister Wilfred addresses her formally:

*Now, my dear girl, it's over. I've asked you if you wish to press charges against Mr Burgess and you have declined. But I'll ask you again. Are you sure this man should be allowed to have inflicted such a crime as rape upon you without a reckoning?*

*I don't want that, Sister. I just want to forget him—and everything about him.*

*So be it. I'll be guided by you. Now then. Tall in the saddle, yes? We've got work to do. I want you to help me in the office.*

Yes. Agnes has been promoted. The wiry nun with the five-iron could not eradicate the effects of a lifetime of abuse, but having someone defend her willingly, and respect her wishes, will forever be a pivotal turning point in her life. Yet self-recrimination, regardless of the support, will continue to haunt her, and she will seek out Father Dominic to hear her confession in the chapel. Why, she will ask him, in contrast to the shy, deferential girl she believes herself to be, is she haunted by being perceived as a temptress? Does she act in ways she isn't aware of? The priest's kind and wise assurances of her unsullied innocence having propelled her into a new state of religious devotion, she is now first in the chapel for morning Mass. She has established her spot at the end of the front pew, as close as possible to the presence in the tabernacle. Her sin-stained soul has been washed clean. She walks up to the altar rails to take Holy Communion freely with the others and vows to herself to prove her worth.

Sister Ambrosia, who manages the office, is Sister Wilfred's antithesis. She is tall, with a soft, rounded figure. Agnes imagines that the billowing pleats of her brown habit must consume a whole roll of fabric. Patient and softly spoken, she glides around the office like an ocean liner in a calm sea. Her milk-white skin is as smooth as silk, and her large watery grey eyes radiate a pious religious fervour that Agnes has learned to mistrust. Sister Ambrosia appears to be particularly fond of Teresa—a green-eyed beauty from Melbourne who works alongside her.

There is a third member of the office team—Nola. With her broad shoulders and big hands, she looks more like a man than a woman. Long hair might have softened her appearance but, as if in defiance of femininity, she wears it cut short like an army soldier. She prefers to walk around in a loose brown dustcoat like a warehouse worker, so it is hard to see that she is pregnant at all.

Having all but ignored Agnes during her first days in the office, today Nola has elected to sit with her at breakfast and is focusing fiery nut-brown eyes on her with an unnerving intensity:

*Do you mind if I sit here and talk to you Katherine?*

*No, not at all—go right ahead.*

Agnes is getting used to her alias, though it has taken a while. Surprised by the feminine quality of Nola's voice, she smiles at her encouragingly and the nervy young woman seems to relax a little:

*I'm starting to hate this sanctimonious place. They just ignore the sad facts—it's like we acquired these bellies by divine intervention! I look at little Annie over there and hate the hypocrisy of the Catholic Church. Giving birth to her own father's baby! How barbaric is that! Doesn't this place seem like a baby factory to you? We're all making a product for someone else! I keep asking myself—is this what I want? I regurgitate that question obsessively!*

Eventually, Agnes will discover that Nola is the eldest of five children from an Irish Catholic family who eke out a living on a small, freezing farm in the Snowy Mountains. To bring in extra cash, her father, a bad-tempered boozer who beats his wife, works in a local tanning factory. Nola will tell Agnes that there wasn't a day she didn't yearn to leave home. Fortunately, exceptional exam results landed her a scholarship to a good high school in Melbourne, where she stayed with an aunt who worked for the government. But, after an almighty row with the aunt—over what, Agnes was never sure—Nola moved to Western Australia to do her Master's degree.

Over the next few days, Nola will declare that she belongs to a left-wing group at the university and is interested in the ideas of Marx and Engels, both of whom Agnes will be ashamed to admit she has never heard of:

*Crikey, Katherine! Surely you've heard of the Russian Revolution!'*

Agnes will reply apologetically, exposing her limited historical knowledge outside the modern newspaper headlines in her mother's knitting bag. She will wonder if Nola might be a Communist. But what did *that* matter? She will learn about the 10 days that shook the world and will be given a copy of the Communist Manifesto as a farewell present. She will continue to be dazzled by her new friend's ability to articulate her thoughts but, more than anything else, she will love Nola's ability to laugh at herself. On Sundays, the two friends will fall into the habit of strolling together to Croydon to have a milkshake. Their first stop will be the newsagency, where Agnes will buy a sketchbook and the *Women's Weekly*, while Nola will be keen to read in a newspaper the latest on the Eichmann Trial in Israel:

*It's phenomenal, Katherine, how they tracked the bastard down in Argentina!*

Agnes finds herself confiding in Nola more and more about the unfathomable behaviour of her mother. Nola advises that perhaps she thinks too much about her mother and not enough about herself. But Agnes will still try to make excuses for Madge. It is second nature to her.

Nola will put her arm round Agnes's shoulder and speak very gently:

*My dear Katherine, you don't have to be Einstein to understand it. By brutally abandoning you, neither parent gave you a chance to abandon them. Do you see? When conditions in a country become intolerably unjust, a revolution erupts that topples the old order and creates something new. It's the same with families. One day, the foundation cracks, and no amount of paint or wallpaper can prop up the crumbling edifice. Banishing a Machiavellian mother from your life is an affirmation of your self-worth. Life is change and change is life. You have great chances ahead of you! Reach out beyond your family and embrace your own future!*

Agnes will trust the genuine warmth in Nola's eyes. She has loved listening to her over the days. She has marvelled at how bravely Nola has stood up for her rights at university. With what fortitude she has overcome the difficulties she has encountered in the man's world of academia. But, in this instance, Nola will be talking about a place Agnes doesn't inhabit. The guidance Nola has just imparted will frighten her. She will feel ashamed of bad-mouthing her parents. She cannot imagine walking away. Because of her grandmother's pervasive influence, she carries the sanctity of the family in her very bones. Yes, Nola might have given eloquent expression to the pain residing deep inside her, but she cannot let the relief she feels settle and take root. It is impossible to accept.

But Agnes and Nola are set to go in different directions. Gossip will reach Agnes's ears that Nola is becoming increasingly fearful that her baby might be taken away at the hospital against her will. Thus, her aunt will be flying into Sydney to collect her and take her home so that Nola can give birth in Melbourne. Nola is to keep her baby.

Standing outside the home with the other girls as they wave goodbye to Nola and her aunt, Agnes will feel a surge of warmth for her courageous friend. Interestingly, although she has pushed Nola's guidance to the very back of her mind, she will stop writing to her mother as further fiction seems meaningless.

\* \* \*

A week after Nola's departure, Agnes wakes with a strange cramp in her stomach that seems to run into her back, and she tries to remember what she ate the night before. It is 6am and she has much to do. As well as laying out the priest's vestments she will have to change the water in the vases and rearrange the flowers on the altar in the chapel. Nonetheless, she suspects that by the end of the day she will probably find herself packed off to hospital.

The truth is, that unlike Nola, Agnes doesn't want to leave. She is attached to the home because it's the first time she has felt safe since leaving the house on the corner of Rose and Edmond Street at sixteen. Another spasm takes her breath away. It dawns on her that she is, assuredly, in labour. Her girl is on her way. Like Nola, she is convinced she is having a daughter. She will call her Rebecca.

The second contraction will arrive conveniently—exactly an hour after the first one—just as she finishes preparing the vestments. She will be doubled over in pain when she hears Father Dominic's motorbike pull up outside, but she will make it through Mass, seated in her usual spot, beseeching God to guide her through the hours ahead.

When she feels another contraction coming, it will be easier than she thought to walk out of the office and away from her duties. Soon, very soon, someone will take over her desk. She will go to the laundry to steam-iron her blue wool dressing gown and, when the contractions are five minutes apart, she will shower and walk back to the office to ask Sister Ambrosia to ring the ambulance. She considers it demeaning the way the St Anthony's girls have to arrive at the hospital dressed for bed, but this will be no time for rebellion.

The sun will be setting as she waits in the garden outside the tower for the ambulance. Shafts of golden rays will illuminate the textures and imperfections in the cement surface of the path, a halo will surround the reaching arms of the jacaranda tree, and a shimmering light will glance off the raised hair on the back of a glossy black cat which, frightened by a barking dog outside the gate, will speed to safety up a gum tree. Streamers of thick clouds will be increasingly tinted pink and violet.

Elated by the beauty of the sunset, an imaginary *Hallelujah!* will fill her ears as darkness descends. She will walk hand in hand to the ambulance with poor little Annie, who all the girls have followed Sister Wilfred's lead in nurturing. She will hand the driver her brown suitcase and then ease herself onto the front seat.

*At the hospital I am upturned onto a trolley and buffeted from one nurse to another in preparation for the birth. The blurred rush of faces and bright lights feels like being back on the busy Parramatta Road on route to the hospital. Someone shaves my pubic hair, there is an enema, a stint on the toilet, a soapy all-over sponge and then they all disappear. I focus on the familiar smell of a bar of Palmolive soap a nurse gives me to hold and forgets to take back. It looks like amber. I am alone in a windowless white tiled room. The only light seeps in from the glass panel above the door. I panic in enclosed spaces. I can't see. The room swirls around me. I sink my nails into the soap and press it against my cheek. I hear myself praying aloud:*

*Lord—I feel forsaken—like you did in the Garden of Gethsemane. Please hear my prayer and comfort me.*

*An Italian woman is screaming 'Mama Mia!' at the top of her lungs as she struggles to give birth. The pain in my back is intense. I want to scream too, but when I open my mouth, nothing comes out. I feel like I'm drifting away, locked in a silent straitjacket. I feel myself sink into a restless daze. I'm back in Lennox Street, a day or two after the electrocution, shaken by the bloodcurdling cries of Paul's mother outside our house. 'Madge Keen should be in jail! Her negligence killed my son! You're to blame, Madge Keen! I know you're in there—come out you bloody coward!'*

*They drag her away from our door, but she keeps coming back.*
*The judge in the nightmare prepares to pass judgement.*
*The impertinent girl's silence is proof of guilt.*
*I'm locked in a struggle for a voice that never comes.*

*The next contraction shakes my whole body. My insides are on fire, yet outside I feel cold. I see a nurse beside me through the haze. They keep coming and checking between my legs with a bright light. I hear someone speak: 'She's only nineteen... never utters a sound... lovely face and beautiful hair... she's a saint... no trouble... wish we had a few more like that in here.'*

*More blurred faces pop their heads in to catch a glimpse of the modern miracle—the silent angel smiling in her distress. I don't know if I should be proud or ashamed. I long to cry out like the others, but my throat is clamped shut.*

*I'm blinded by a powerful light. I close my eyes and hear my father slurring in my ear. He smells of whisky. I feel his dribbles on my back, but I never wake up. I stay asleep. The face that hovers over me breaks into tiny pieces like an exploding jigsaw puzzle. Uncle Parry smirks as he holds up the stump of his missing finger, squeezing a sultana eye in a lurid wink. Posturing Charles has joined the parade. A voice inside me whispers—they're all the same man... they're all the same man. I'm lost in a labyrinth of stained bathrooms. My mother and aunt are throwing children into a furnace. I'm afraid I will be next.*

*A crowd of gowned bodies with surgical-masked faces burst into the room. The sour smell of whisky on my father's breath is drowned in an all-pervasive wave of antiseptic. A mask is put over my nose. My legs are yanked into straps. I am overtaken by a powerful contraction which tears through me. A female voice says: 'Not yet... resist pushing, dear.'*

*Obediently, I clamp my muscles against the urge. There is a volcano erupting in my guts. I am being split down the middle. The voice is louder: 'Now push!'*

*I tell her I can't do it—finding my voice at last. She is holding my hand.*

*Let's do it together—one, two, three. Now, push.*
*I push with all my might.*
*And again, child, push again.*
*This time I feel the baby's body slide out. A little later I hear a distinctive cry. The soft voice tells me it is a little girl. I feel my eyes fill with tears. I ask if I can see her but am told not till tomorrow. I object but am told to sleep by a hypnotic voice that hovers behind me.*
*I give up.*

\* \* \*

Agnes wakes with an incredible thirst. She finds herself in a bed parked in a corridor with people walking backwards and forwards— as if she has been left at the side of a footpath.

She is terrified she will be recognised by someone and all her efforts at concealment will be for nought. A middle-aged nun is looking at her from under thick eyebrows that resemble tiny hedges. The nun slides a metal extension out from a contraption at the side of the bed on to which she places a little tray with a glass and jug of water:

*Take these tablets. They will dry up your milk.*
*I don't want to take them! I'll give the milk to my baby!*

The nun instructs her that this is not allowed. Agnes watches the muscles around the nun's small, mean mouth tighten:

*You seem to have forgotten your position. These are the rules. Unless you take the medication, you will never see your baby.*

Stunned, Agnes watches the woman's white habit swish like a breaking wave around her legs as she disappears at a brisk pace down the hall. The euphoria of giving birth instantly tips into dejection. There is no buzzer or bell. No ways or means to contact anyone. She sinks down in the bed, pulls the sheet over her head, and weeps soft tears.

When she emerges, the shrewd eyes lurking under the little

hedges are back. The voice is as brusque as ever:

*Well? What do you want to do? Do you want to see your baby or not?*

Agnes meekly swallows the pills in one gulp and drinks the whole jug of water.

But, when she finally holds Rebecca Lea in her arms, all resentment disappears. She kisses her and calls her by her name. She loves the smell of her. She examines her arms, fingers, legs, feet and toes. She is perfect. She is relieved to see she doesn't have her mother's red hair and thus the inevitable freckles the sun will bring—a hopeless colouring for the harsh Australian climate. She sings to Rebecca as she feeds her with a bottle. Then a young, jolly nurse comes to spirit the baby away just before the visiting hour. Fearful of being recognised as the throng of visitors surge past her in the corridor, Agnes, once again, pulls the sheet over her head.

She wakes the following morning, her head still under the sheet, to find she has been wheeled into an airy room. The sound of the advancing food trolley is heaven to her ears, and she gets up to intercept it. She is starving, for when she was parked in the corridor, it had passed her by several times without stopping because, fearful of being recognised by anyone who might know her family, she had kept the sheet over her head.

Scrambled eggs on toast have never tasted so good and she sips a cup of strong, hot tea with delight. She spots the officious nun whisking her way past the doorway:

*Sister—if I must stay in bed, could you bring my baby to me?*

The vicious response floors her:

*I give the orders here, not you! Stew in your sin, you little floozy! Deprivation is the only way the likes of you will ever learn self-control!*

\* \* \*

*I haven't prepared myself for the strong attachment I feel for my daughter. With each passing day it becomes harder and harder to think of parting from her. My duties at St Anthony's over, I go to the nursery at my leisure to bathe her, feed her and carry her around. I love watching her little legs bounce when I put her on a rug in the sun. I take endless photos of her and get the girls in the nursery to take photos of us both, so I will always remember these moments spent together. I try to think of ways I might keep her. But I have hostile, unpredictable parents, no home, no job, no career like Nola. I have no money and my absence has been spliced to a fictional story. How can I be a fit mother when I don't even feel like a fit person? If I give her up, little Rebecca will be loved and cherished by a mother who can't have her own baby. I shall be complying with the prophesy in the sacristy at St Patrick's Church. It is a tale foretold.*

*But regardless of my reasoning, my attachment to Rebecca only strengthens. I find myself haunting her crib at night. I love the way she sinks her head into my neck and snuffles when I squeeze her tight. I put off leaving her. I spend as much time as I can with her. I can't think of anything but her. My life has changed. Yet I am gently being edged towards the signing away. I know I am not unique. I have seen Sister Wilfred steer many a conflicted girl towards the adoption papers. She never forces anyone.*

*When she invites me to her office, I hear myself agree with her that it is for the best. The prevarication is becoming intolerable and so, as if in a waking dream, I comply. I sign the papers with a broken heart. I feel like death.*

*The day arrives. I can see my baby's new parents pull up in a white Ford. It is midday. I watch them from the same balcony from which I watched Charles arrive that fateful Sunday. From that distance, I can't distinguish their features. They are, perhaps, in their mid-twenties, the rest I don't remember. Perhaps the new mother is wearing a blue hat.*

*Earlier that morning, before dressing my baby for the last time, I had carried her in a pink blanket to the little church where I mounted the red carpeted steps to the altar. Her tiny eyelids were heavy with sleep as she snuggled in my arms. I laid her down. Down in front of the tabernacle. Cradled between vases of sweet pea blooms. I begged the Sacred Presence to guide my darling girl through the years I would never know her.*

*I watch them carry Rebecca Lea out of my life forever. I know that I'm walking away from the one thing that is meaningful and valuable. That I am passing back into a shallow world. But, as usual, the forces are assembled against me, and I am vanquished.*

CHAPTER 22

# THE HOMECOMING

It is a lovely, bright spring morning without a cloud in the sky, and Agnes's footsteps have reverberated in her ears as she drags her sluggish feet to Croydon railway station—hardly noticing the weight of her suitcase. She purchases a one-way ticket to Central Station and boards the train in a dream.

As Agnes glances at her watch, she realises that when the Western City train pulls into Central Station, she will have to rush if she is to meet her mother on time. The platform looks unfamiliar, and she takes the stairs two at a time—arriving at a crossroad of unfamiliar underground directions. She can't find her way. She runs past platform entrances and down a labyrinth of corridors, dashing blindly, having to backtrack, panicking that not giving herself enough time will expose the months of careful deception.

Nerves at the prospect of seeing her mother affect her ability to listen to directions from a station guard. She finds herself swept along a crowded enclosed walkway. She is waiting for an exit that never comes and then, at the very end, like Alice through the looking glass, she bursts into the vault-roofed concourse of the main station. A brass clock, encased in a pagoda-shaped adornment, stands at the pinnacle. Twisted spherical plaster heads on either side resemble faceless bulls, infusing strength into frivolity. Drenched in overhead light from the vast glass roof, the three-storey stone structure of Central Station never fails to impress with its grandeur.

She stands in front of the huge railway indicator board, where she has arranged to meet her mother. The wooden slats with their printed destinations and station stops are rotating, along with the departure times and platform numbers. Agnes counts the 22 vertical slats in the frame to try and stay calm. She remains, despite herself, plagued with such a crippling responsibility for her mother's well-being that, until she can find a way of making her happy, she knows she will never be free of her.

The Roman numerals on the great clock are showing five minutes to the proposed meeting time. The arrival of the Melbourne train is announced on the loudspeaker. Still no sign of her mother. It occurs to her that her cover will be blown if her mother finds her waiting under the arrivals board before the train gets in and so she rushes down the concourse in search of the correct platform. Luckily there is no ticket collector at the gate.

Nearing the last carriages, with passengers already flooding off the stationary train onto the platform, she turns and tries to walk sedately to the exit gate—as if she has just alighted. The timing is perfect and, for once, she is glad her mother is always late. Then she spots her. Madge is striding into the enormous space from the George Street entrance.

Crushed as she is in the tightly packed crowd, Agnes remains invisible to Madge. As her mother draws closer, Agnes is struck by how plastic and unnatural she looks—the horns of her bouffant echoing the plucked curve of her arched eyebrows. This odd effect makes her look slightly demented, and her briskly determined stride only diminishes the allure of the stylish pink linen dress she wears. To Agnes, her mother's face appears to be contracting and stretching into the ugly image of a painted witch as she walks. She stares in horrified amazement, longing for the apparition to disappear.

And then, like magic, her mother's beauty is suddenly resurrected. Agnes fleetingly wonders whether what she was just glimpsing was the hidden inner psyche that Nola had described? Hadn't her friend insisted that Agnes should try to analyse what she sees and hears? But then how could Nola know that analytical thought was as alien to Agnes as the whereabouts of Upper Mongolia.

*Hey Mummy! I'm over here.*
*I see my mother swing her head in line with my voice. Her recognition evokes a look of annoyance in my direction that makes me shrink. I feel instantly diminished. We don't run into one another's arms, as many new arrivals from the Melbourne train are doing. My mother stops short to survey my appearance. All my superlatives, all my 'missing yous', the legions of kiss crosses running off the pages of my fabricated letters, are for nothing. I might not have expected a hero's welcome but, at the very least, I had hoped for an affectionate one. Although nothing I imagine ever happens, I still carry on like the ripe idiot I am—hoping for change.*

*Her first utterance proves she is a long way from showing me an even basic level of civility: 'What have you done to your hair?' I reply: 'Nothing, I just haven't cut it. I'm going to grow it long. Not a crime, is it?'*

*It is when her critical eyes start boring into my body that I lose composure. I hate the silly, childish petulance simply being in her presence provokes in me. Then she says: 'You've got very thick around the middle and very bosomy while you've been away.'*

*I feel myself blanche. I hadn't anticipated the change in my body. Signing the adoption papers and losing Rebecca Lea have consumed me completely. My mother metamorphoses into the old familiar monster with the burning coal eyes. Why did I bother to protect this mean, slothful bitch from any gossip? What does it matter if they all know I got pregnant out of wedlock? My father is illegitimate, and no one died of shame! How important is all this reputation stuff? Perhaps it's a Catholic Church tactic to swell their ranks? Perhaps Nola had a point!*

*A turmoil of truth and fury rises in me, exactly like the day I expelled my uncensored feelings onto my father: 'Oh, God – you, stupid, ridiculous woman!'*

*I have exploded. I have taken the lid off, and I no longer care.*

*She is staring at me, her face frozen.*

*I am shouting at the top of my voice:* 'There WAS no governess job! I've just come from St Anthony's! A home for unwed mothers! I had a baby!'

*I am screaming and sobbing and am aware that everyone can hear me, but I don't care. I want to strangle the cold, heartless bitch right there on the concourse. Normally, there's no way I can shut her up, but this time I appear to have succeeded. For once, the surprise exhibited in the arched eyebrows has turned into eye-popping shock. I feel gratified. I want to shock her into her grave. The truth spills out of me in torrents. I tell her I invented everything. Invented it all so she could impress her vapid friends. I tell her that Sister Wilfred's sister redirected the mail between us. I tell her my beautiful little girl was taken away from me that very morning. I scream it in her face.*

*I am aware that people are stopping to look at me, but I am so overcome with emotion I don't care. A man with a handlebar moustache asks the uncaring woman who is my mother if I am alright. She puts on her best tragic look and tells him that I have received some bad news and will feel better in a minute. Then she grabs my arm and pulls me away from the crowd. Her fierce expression warns those who remain concerned to keep their distance. Her fingers are pinching into my arm. She grabs my suitcase, dragging me to a bench under one of the sandstone arches on the opposite side of the concourse where we can be alone and safe from prying eyes.*

*She hisses into my face:* 'Stop this nonsense immediately! You sound like a raving maniac! STOP making such a scene! Someone should cut that loose tongue out of your throat! I never SAW such a performance!'

*I can only stare at her. It's crazy to think how long I went on expecting from her what was beyond her nature. Assailed by inconsolable disappointment, I slump over the bench with my head in my hands and sob my heart out. I have protected her for nothing. All the attention to detail in the letters, the enthusiasm with which I imagined her telling her friends, my huge outpouring of love and energy towards her, would bear no fruit. I had battled to preserve what didn't exist. It was all pie in the sky. Stupid dreams and silly fantasies. All imagined. None of it real.*

*I can't really read the expression in her eyes when she says:* 'You never fail to get me churned up and it's hurtful, Agnes. Especially after the preparations I've made for you. I've put nice fresh sheets on your bed, bought sirloin steak, beans and baby carrots for you. I've even made your favourite chocolate blancmange—and this is the way you treat me. At least let's attempt to have a pleasant drive home, shall we?'

*She sounds like a temperamental girl who has just been stood up on a date. And then it comes. The inevitable threat:* 'Just as well your father is away in Adelaide. It's better he doesn't know ANY of this. Don't push me into having to tell him how you've dishonoured us. Be warned Agnes—this is one matter that is to remain a secret forever.'

\* \* \*

Agnes jumps out of the car to open The Farm gate, infected by Madge's anxious haste to rush home to do nothing. She notices the gate is still pivoted on the upturned champagne bottle Uncle Parry sank into the ground during the first flush of building work. It must have rained the day before, as murky puddles are dotted along the dirt road. A new metal-tubed bridge has been erected in the lowest dip of the road, where cars used to get bogged down in heavy rain. Although the sun is shining, the place feels to Agnes as if it is submerged under a cloud.

While the front of the old timber cottage remains the same, the back has been transformed into an American ranch-style house. Intrigued, Agnes opens a further gate in a sturdy fence that encloses Madge's new garden. A golden Labrador runs across the lawn, barking and wagging its tail frantically:

*Don't let him jump up on you, Agnes! His paws are all dirty!*

Madge is scrutinising her daughter's every movement like a policeman with a suspect under surveillance. The dog, having initially run back to his kennel, has now returned with a ball in his mouth and is snorting and pushing it into her skirt. Agnes pulls it out of his jaws and throws it. His unexpected friendly, boisterous presence has cheered her considerably:

*When did you get him? What's his name?*

Madge sighs as if bored to tears already.

*His name's Sunny. Don't you remember? He sat by your bed when you were sick. He used to come in every morning and look up at you and wag his tail. You were delirious. The doctor blamed us for letting you get run down, but I told him you wouldn't let us help you out. You could have come here any time, Agnes. No one was stopping you. But, instead, you preferred gallivanting around with that boyfriend.*

*But you told me Daddy didn't want to see me and I was warned by Parry not to ring you!*

Madge's eyes narrow:

*Listen to me and listen carefully. I don't need any more of your smart talk. You were always welcome here. I don't know where or why you dream up these silly stories. Now come through to your old room.*

Resistance being futile, Agnes follows in her wake. She pauses to pick up the small vase of rose blooms on the bedside table and closes her eyes to savour their delicate scent. When she turns around, she is astonished to see her mother has opened her suitcase. She can tell from Madge's demeanour that everything pales into insignificance beside the allure of the contents.

Madge's eyes are riveted on the evidence behind the Mildura fiction. She is in the act of plunging her hands deep into the case's contents and has already pulled out the two maternity smocks, now ragged after intensive use. Impatient, she upturns the case and tips the entire contents onto the towel on the bed. The cherished photographs of baby Rebecca Lea are flicked through without comment, and Agnes imagines that this is how a humble housemaid might feel as she shares something of a personal nature with her employer. This house, new as it is, remains devoid of any photos of family because—in the true sense of the word—they are *not* one.

Tears suddenly sting in Agnes's eyes. It's all so terribly recent, but here, watching this woman gleefully invade her privacy, it already seems so dreamlike and dreadful.

Madge is now busy flicking through Agnes's sketchbook. Then Agnes sees her eyes dart towards the diary Agnes has been keeping:

*Don't read that, please. It's personal. Put it down!*

Agnes has spun across the room to reclaim it. Like a spoilt, recalcitrant child, her mother pouts, and puts it behind her back.

*Give it back to me at once!*

Agnes wrenches it out of her mother's hand with an uncharacteristic fierceness. Her mother smiles up at her:

*Oh Agnes. How nice to be together again, isn't it? Just the two of us. I've missed you.*

Madge's sudden ingratiation is an echo from the past. This phony ameliorative manner after a spat used to have a hypnotic effect on her. But now, both wary and weary, Agnes will snap out of the old, transitory delusion of abiding maternal love and be desperate to escape her presence. Obeying her mother's suggestion, she will go for a walk while Madge prepares lunch. She will put on a pair of her father's overalls, a pair of clean socks she finds in the laundry and will slip her feet into an old pair of her father's elastic-side riding boots. She will stride down to the stables, past the old barbecue where the extended family once cooked sausages in the happy stable-building days, past the row of poplar trees which are now taller than the stable roof. At the far border fence to the polo field, she will see glimpses of water through the walls of dense gums—the creek that runs along the full width of the property, creating a natural boundary—and she will reflect that a bandit could hide out there and never be seen.

*I bang the ground with a stick to alert inquisitive snakes to keep their distance. I'm on the old path to the creek. On the right, I pass the overgrown track to a glade of stringy bark gums. They are covered in parasites and tangled vines. As a child, I imagined the glade inhabited by strange creatures. No longer a child, I still run past, feeling the old fear.*

*I am entering a tunnel of strangely shaped trees, covered in lichen, and where the sun never penetrates. My heart is beating so fast, I think it might jump out of my chest. Abruptly, I arrive at the clearing in the furthest corner of the block, where the creek forms a natural boundary. I have always imagined fairies dancing here—dancing under the tall trees that encircle the clearing, as if in 'A Midsummer Night's Dream.'*

*This is the only place with easy access to the water. As I sit on the enormous fallen tree trunk, long embedded in the earth, and which acts as a retaining wall, a memory returns... before the inquisition at 'Rosemont'... before jumping out of the moving car... before the forced rehabilitation in Maroubra.*

*I am fishing alongside my father. I see his line in the water before my eyes. I see myself wearing a swimming costume, leaning back on the trunk of the same tall gum. I have struck a pin-up, film-star pose. I have a flimsy notion of once being photographed like that. I can see my white sandal falling off the back of my heel. I am clutching at the dreamlike image of fishing in this creek with my father. I am trying to hold on to it because it is proof that I was living at the farm that summer. Was it summer? After I left school? My poor head rebels when I try and put such patchy memories together. Something is edging closer to me. An unseen presence. Whenever the hot air cools at dusk and the birds call to each other, I have felt shadowed. Shadowed all my life. Shadowed by a presence in a bushland just like this.*

*I jump up. I am panicking. I cannot catch my breath. I run. And I keep running till I reach the gate. The late sun is hiding behind a cloud as I stride up the dirt road beside the polo field. Now I am on the slope leading to the stables and I can see my mother in the distance. She is bending over the old barbecue. My stomach sinks as I get closer.*

*My suitcase is lying open on the ground with a petrol can beside it. I recognise the maternity smocks I made. They are bunched up amongst the weeds in the old fireplace. I hear myself scream as I run towards her:*

'No! No! Don't do it!'

She knows I am shouting but does not raise her head. She strikes a match and, before I can reach her, throws it. As petrol and flame unite, she staggers backwards and falls. I run to her and lift her up. Her hair and eyebrows are heavily singed.

'What do you think you're doing, throwing petrol on a fire!? You might have killed yourself!'

She does not look at me. Perhaps she cannot look at me. I turn away from her and rush towards the fire to see what else she has destroyed. I see my diary pages twist and curl. My sketchbook, too, is now glowing red. She has scattered the photos of my baby randomly and I watch helplessly as bits of my child burn—a foot, a hand, the shawl, my smile, our faces close together—all disintegrating into silvery flakes.

I think of the newsreels of the Gestapo in Germany. The burning of books. Like my mother, they destroyed what they could not understand. And there are Rebecca's little yellow woollen booties—consumed in a gulp. And there is the edge of the envelope that contained a snippet of her hair.

A rainbow of flames rises into the air. I can't save anything. The whole contents of the suitcase are incinerated. It's all gone. The ugly smell of destruction comes from deep in the earth. Comes from deep within my mother. She has eradicated all evidence of my crime against her warped family pride.

I scream my rage into her blackened face:
You bitch! You bloody, bloody BITCH!

# Part Five

A wrong that cannot be repaired must be transcended.
—Willy Brandt (at the Warsaw Memorial)

## CHAPTER 23

# AUNT MARNIE REVISITED

Words have come to Agnes's rescue. Words that once turned their nose up at her. Words whose absence once relegated her to the dunce's corner. Words, the lack of which, had her occupying the lowest rung of existence. They have come back to her like manna from heaven. She has been scribbling in the Sydney apartment for weeks, fearful that, should she stop, her rekindled literacy will evaporate.

She stabs the returning words onto the page. She writes them in big bold letters. She inscribes them in a huge notepad because she fears to use her laptop in case of a technical hitch. The least distraction, after years of resistance, could sabotage her. Her hand flies over the notebook pages. Scrambled events start to unravel and take form. The biro she uses has wings and can barely keep up with her thoughts. It writes of many things. Puzzling things. Dreamlike things. Distressing things. Things she has run away from all her life. All spills onto the page. Barely punctuated. Few indications of speech or of who is speaking or to whom. The outpouring throws up questions, but answers are few. And so, as she pauses to take stock of all she has written, it becomes suddenly urgent to see those who are still alive—who once bore witness to the events she is attempting to describe.

The rhythm at the Grantham Apartments rotates around her small space on the sixth floor. She feels sandwiched between check-ins and checkouts. She is thoroughly enjoying her stay. She suspects there isn't a better vantage point in the whole of Sydney from which to gaze upon the city's famous iconography. She thrills to overhear the gasps of delight when any new arrival flings open the balcony doors to view the wonders stretched out before them. But the busy writer is conscious of resisting getting too chummy with anyone. She knows now that the least hint of rejection, or sudden change of mood, could detrimentally influence the urgent project upstairs. Her inner world requires her complete concentration. She walks on eggshells around herself. Be as temperamental as you like, she tells this newly emerging entity that is her. This moment is *yours* and you don't need to explain anything. And you don't need to apologise to anyone.

Intriguingly, her powers of observation of the outside world remain acute. King's Cross never goes to sleep. It is open around the clock. There is always a restaurant or corner shop where Agnes can find a snack. She is glad of an atmosphere where anything goes. Streets full of tourists in costumes from other lands, office workers on a night out, heavily made-up transvestites—all false boobs and eyelashes—strutting their stuff. And the discreet—and not so discreet—sex-workers on street corners and down the side alleys.

In the evenings she is often gifted with a 'second wind'—a surge of energy that has her scribbling with an even greater urgency, sometimes well into the early hours of the morning. There are desperate moments, too, but the solid sight of the brazenly lit Harry's Café down at street level below remains a reliable comfort.

Her brother Jim will arrive in a week. She decides that she must brace herself to see Aunt Marnie before he comes. After 40 years, she wants to look her in the eye. This time she will not be ignored. But, at the mere thought of Marnie, the pain of the past resurges in waves, and Agnes wanders around the apartment like a caged animal, procrastinating about making the call.

Then, abruptly, as if some outside force has compelled her, she picks up the mobile and dials the number.

\* \* \*

Agnes walks down a steep drive and past an impeccably well-cut lawn. As she proceeds, she disperses a flock of tiny birds who are splashing around in an ornate stucco bird bath. As if scoffing at their frivolity, a kookaburra on a nearby overhead wire laughs his head off as she arrives at the entrance to Marnie's nursing home.

There are no gasps of joy when their eyes meet. She watches Marnie search her aging face for the girl she once was and immediately senses the old tension. With half her face frozen, Marnie seems even more inscrutable than ever. In her mind's eye, Agnes again sees her aunt let the newspaper disdainfully drop onto the green carpet on the day she first arrived to stay in the Maroubra house. She struggles to gain control of her thoughts. The woman marooned in the wheelchair seems frail. Marnie may be a former enemy, but it's still regrettable to see her in this state. Her aunt's speech is laboured:

*Shall I ring for some tea?*

*Yes. Let's have tea.*

Marnie stretches for the phone on a side table and orders whoever is on the other end to oblige. Then she reaches out to retrieve a silver-framed picture of a man:

*Remember him?*

Her aunt has pronounced the question sharply—in a tone that smacks of accusation.

*Yes. Of course. It's Uncle Parry...*

She is instantly revolted by the sight of her uncle's beady raisin eyes and the familiar sly smile. Marnie nods slowly:

*He struggled with a horrible illness. We went to America for a cure, but nothing prolonged the years. He ended up in a wheelchair. And a pitiless deterioration to the end.*

*I'm so sorry to hear that.*

*You'll never know how fond he was of YOU.*

Marnie has made this statement with slurred intensity. The word 'you' is emphasised. It is like a scene in a film when an older woman grudgingly forgives a younger one for a clandestine affair with her husband. And it further reminds her of the way her mother used to say: 'Your father loves you,' as if she would like to alter it.

Agnes hands the photograph back.

A knock at the door presages the arrival of tea. As Agnes ministers to her aunt, she can feel the woman staring at her. Marnie accepts her cup from Agnes and lifts it to the good side of her mouth with an unsteady hand, quickly dabbing at stray drops with a lace handkerchief. The diamond on her wedding finger sparkles as it catches an overhead light. She turns her head to address her niece:

*I suppose you know… I haven't had anything to do with your mother for years.*

*Well, that makes two of us!*

*After your father died, we used to go to the races together, but you know her. Always looking for a better offer. Snubbed me completely. She never cared about anyone but your father.*

Agnes stares at her aunt. An overwhelming need to speak of her pain takes her over. She *must* find the words. Words are the tools she must summon to come to her aid. Words, like the manna from heaven that has flown onto the pages of the notebooks back at the Grantham Apartment.

*Yes. I arrived at Liverpool hospital a short time after he died. She stopped me going to see his body. You don't want to see him, she said. He's all blue. Remember him the way he was. She cornered me outside the entrance to the hospital, raving about Ben. We have got to get home instantly, she said. Ben will be snooping around the farm. He's probably already there going through your father's papers. I've got to get back now, she insisted, dragging me to her car! That can't be the reaction of a loving wife, Aunt Marnie, can it!? Her husband not an hour dead and all she can think of is outfoxing her brother!*

Marnie fixes her with a shrewd look:

*Well—she and Ben are both tarred with the same brush, Agnes.*

Her aunt is paying attention. It is a good start:

*I know you don't like Ben, Aunt Marnie, but in his own clumsy way he* cared about my father and mourned his loss. Insensitive to his backbone, true, but he would have been shocked to hear the things my father said about him behind his back.

Agnes relates the circumstances. That Eric Keen had died of a *Staphylococci* infection. How, having ignored a sore throat, he had pushed himself to go to a factory party at the Automobile Club, staying the night there, before driving to the farm the next day. How, on the way to the Club he had stopped off to see a doctor who advised him to take his badly inflamed throat home to bed. How, later that afternoon, her mother had brought him a cup of tea and that the hot liquid caused an abscess in his throat to burst and block his windpipe. How he had managed to stagger to the car but had collapsed in the back seat. How her brother Jim tried to give him mouth-to-mouth resuscitation. How only a tracheotomy would have saved him.

Marnie listens with obvious concentration as Agnes reaches the climax of her story:

*Children aren't responsible for the blind love they have for their parents—no matter how diabolical those parents are. Did you know I paid for his funeral and catering for the wake? Being financially successful didn't liberate me from being Madge's slave.*

Is it her imagination, or is Marnie now leaning forward as if to better catch every word?

*A few days later, Madge knocks on the door of my Paddington terrace house, wild-eyed with his same fever. Imagine! But I took care of her willingly, even though I'd been desperately ill with it myself. And, then she wangled her way into working in my real estate office! She just appeared! After six phenomenally successful years, my mad mother shows up out of the blue and expects to be given a job! I put her on the reception desk. It felt like the business had been taken over by an alien invader. Her ridiculous behaviour—giving orders, showing-off, name-dropping—lasted just over a week. On the day she started telling my clients that she owned the business, I received an ultimatum from my staff—either she goes, or we go! It wasn't* hard to persuade her that an office job was beneath her and so she wafted back to the skittish spending spree she'd been on since Daddy died.

She notices that Marnie's eyes are glittering with curiosity:

*What did your mother do with the inheritance, Agnes?*

*She squandered it, of course! When the solicitor neglected to file for probate within the stipulated time, the estate reverted to us three children. Bert and Jim came to my Paddington terrace to discuss the matter. I told them I was signing it back to her. That it was a technical hitch—not my father's intention. I said I made my own living and wanted to be free of any connection with my mother. Jim signed as he felt the same. Bert, of course, who knew how to manipulate her, was keen to keep the money. But it was two against one, so he lost. Oh—and I almost forgot! A life insurance policy from the factory left her phenomenally well off.*

As the unflattering tales of her arch enemy unfurl, Marnie's cheeks turn bright pink with outrage:

*My God! How unjust that someone who did nothing for anyone should have it all handed to her on a plate! Typical Madge!*

Encouraged by the comment, Agnes finds herself on a roll. Words flow out like a river in full flood:

*Then she asked me to invest her money in property. I should have refused, but like Scheherazade warding off execution with another story, solving my mother's endless problems was how I survived childhood. So, her money went into a block of 12 flats in Paddington—with views of the harbour. It included a block of land she could build a house on. There was also a beautifully renovated terrace house in Union Street. Both rental investments were managed by an agent. Honourable. One to be trusted. You don't have to do anything I told her. Just put the cheque in the bank at the end of the month and you can live the life of Riley. I thought I'd sorted her out. And myself, for that matter. But I underestimated how much my father's death had affected me. After he died, I lost interest in my business. I could hardly drag myself out of bed to go to the office. All that hard work—day and night, seven days a week, was about winning his approval. His love. I may have bought myself a wonderful house and* amassed investments, but once I achieved it, nothing had any meaning. And do you know, Aunt Marnie. He didn't even thank me for the two horses I bought him and had sent to the farm! Yet, back then, how could I criticise someone I had spent my whole young life trying to save!'

This outpouring of the sad facts is wonderfully liberating. She believes she can still detect her aunt weighing up whether her recalcitrant niece is right in the head, but she just can't seem to stop talking. This woman—this uncaring, unkind woman—has to be the person who hears it all. All the pent-up hurt and distress. All the unfairness and desperation.

As she pauses for breath, she detects that Marnie is looking fatigued. She has talked the woman's head off. And, as she didn't come all the way back to Sydney to endlessly re-hash Madge's sins, she decides to ask the one burning question that has spurred her to visit Marnie in the first place:

*But what I really don't understand, Aunt Marnie, is why I was sent to live with you against my will?*

Her aunt sits back in the wheelchair, adjusting her weight. A few seconds pass. Is her silence indecision? Reluctance? Perhaps she cannot even remember? But then Marnie speaks:

*Your parents sent you to us with no money Agnes. They didn't pay us a penny towards your keep. Can you imagine being put in a situation like that?*

This is no answer. Agnes must try again:

*Then why did you allow it? Why did two people who had taken no interest in my life, suddenly decide to interfere in it? It's my parents you should have punished, not an innocent girl in need of kindness! And, if you feel I still owe you money, do let me know and I'll pay you back right now!*

Marnie pinions Agnes with a steely look:

*I didn't mean to infer you owe me anything Agnes.*

Her aunt has responded defensively. This is no time to waver:

*Tell me—please. Why, in Christ's name, if you really didn't want me, why was I kidnapped by Parry and brought to your house?! Torn from everything I knew, only to be tortured by the two of you! Tell me!*

Marnie seems startled now. Her hand is hovering near the internal phone.

*I'm sorry Aunt Marnie. I didn't mean to frighten you.*

But she isn't sorry. Not really. She doesn't care if she has alarmed this woman. She can tell she is on the edge of something. That having pushed Marnie in this way could be about to yield fruit. She waits. She is trying to project the impression she is going nowhere until she gets what she wants.

It pays off. Marnie sighs deeply. It is as if she is drawing up water from a deep well:

*Tortured? Really, Agnes, your dramatics! Your grandmother gave all the orders, as you know. She had a subtle way of punishing the least insubordination. You're not the only victim where she's concerned. Once, when I wouldn't comply with her wishes, she waited till Parry was away and sent a worker to take away my company car. Leaving me stranded in Maroubra—with three small children. What do you think of that? She was a cruel woman. We were all scared stiff of her. Nobody dared disobey her. She was behind it. She told Parry to bring you to stay with us and try to make you see some sense.*

Agnes's heart is pounding in her chest:

*Because I was off my head, I suppose? Around the bend? Stark staring mad? Well, if I wasn't crazy when I arrived at your house, I certainly was when I left!*

Another sigh from Marnie. But she must keep on at her. She *must* pile on the pressure, for there will never be another chance. She can hear her own voice rising in anger. *Why,* she demands of her aunt, was she blamed for the fire in Marnie's kitchen?

*There WAS no fire, Agnes! You imagined it! Just as you have imagined so much else that is supposed to have happened to you!*

There was no fire. As Agnes absorbs this massive blow to her sanity, her thoughts are obliterated by the ringing of Marnie's mobile in the pocket of her dress. Marnie fumbles to retrieve it:

*Yes... yes... I'm having tea with a friend... yes... just a moment... it's my mother!*

Marnie is acting like a girl who has been caught not doing her homework. She is holding the phone away from her ear. Marnie's mother. Pushing 90 and still going strong, apparently.

Agnes, her breath coming fast, her heart bursting in her chest with adrenaline, pulls back the curtain and steps onto the balcony to give her aunt privacy. She turns and stares back at her. She seems happy talking to the handsome woman, Parry's mother-in-law, whom Agnes remembers playing the piano in the sumptuous back room behind the bar. This unexpected memory of Parry and their visits to the White Horse Hotel makes her stomach turn over.

Out on the balcony she will slowly regain control of her breathing. She will become aware her aunt has no intention of cutting the call short on her account. She will intuitively know this woman has absolutely no regrets about the despicable treatment meted out to her in the past and, if anything, remains tacitly hostile.

Knowing there is no more to be gained here, she will walk back into the room where she will catch her aunt's eye briefly, cross the floor, and pick up the silver-framed photo of Parry.

Then she will walk rapidly out of the door, without looking back. A final delinquent act for Marnie to remember her by.

CHAPTER 24

# THE REUNION AT ROSEMONT

Agnes wakes with a start, feeling as if she's been drugged. The confrontation with Marnie has utterly drained her. She looks at her watch. God, it is already 10! But there was still plenty of time to get ready.

She drinks down a glass of cool water before leaving for 'Rosemont' and remembers with a tangle of pleasure and shame the photo she stole from her aunt. She fishes it out of her bag and puts it centre stage on the narrow kitchen worktop. She stares hard at the long-dead uncle who, as usual, isn't giving anything away. She hears herself intoning: *Fire... fire... fire...* But Marnie had been adamant that there was *never* any fire. So why does her brain keep telling her the opposite?

Today, the keeper of family secrets, aging Aunt Sill—whom Aunts Charlotte, Tina and Jean take turns to care for in Melbourne—will be looked after by a neighbour. Thus, the three younger sisters are getting together today to celebrate Jean's new home as Jean is now the doyenne of the old 'Rosemont' flat. And, it seems, they are also taking this opportunity to meet up with Agnes. Unlike Madge, big sister Sill has been prudent with her money, amassing healthy investments—generous portions of which will eventually go to each of the three caring aunts on her passing.

As revelations of past events in Agnes's early life start to emerge, she has realised her longing to be part of the Aunt Club has diminished. They might as well be strangers. Bereaved of sweet childhood memories, she had clung for years to the brief happiness around the farm barbecue with Jean and her artist husband Richard. Richard's drawing of the guardian angel above her bed had been a soothing talisman. Now, as she saunters along familiar streets towards the celebration, she realises the futility of seeking retrospective gratitude from Jean. Agnes, years ago, had fought hard to find Jean a cheap house in Double Bay in which to rehouse her large family. It would have been unthinkable to charge a commission for this favour, as she had felt so honoured and privileged to help a family member.

The building itself feels both familiar and menacing, right down to the ghostly pale grout that cements the solid, stubborn bricks of the façade. Once equivalent in her imagination to the great fictional residences at the movies, 'Rosemont' strikes her now as an undistinguished block in an identical row of red-brick apartments. The late midday glare is intense as she scans the front of the building and wonders from exactly which third-floor window, all those decades ago, Grandma attempted to fly like a bird. Was it even true, this tale of Grandma's transitory madness? She still finds it hard to believe that the Grand Matriarch, the ruling despot of 'Rosemont', could have ever been plunged into such a state of mental debility.

She enters and ascends in the lift. As she stands, rooted to the spot, outside the entrance to the 'Rosemont' flat, Parry's words, uttered outside the same door on that long-ago Christmas Day, creep back into her head:

*You haven't told anyone, have you?*

Now, here, in this same space, decades later, she can feel the rough edge of the stump of his half finger running down her bare arm.

Agnes bangs hard on the knocker on what is now Jean's door as if landing a punch on Parry's broken nose.

Jean flings the door open and blinks at her in disbelief:

*Oh, Agnes, it's you! Why did you knock so hard? I thought something terrible had happened!*

*So sorry, Jean. Sometimes I don't know my own strength.*

This is the kind of flippant quip she is famous for. This is the trusty sense of humour that has propped her up and dulled the pain for years. She hears voices coming from the living room and is glad she isn't the first to arrive. She hands Jean the magnum of champagne she has bought on the way. Jean takes the bottle and puts it on the hall table with little enthusiasm:

*Go into the living room. I'll put your coat away.*

Agnes watches the mink coat she wore to impress the aunts disappear along the corridor. To avoid the intimidating prospect of walking into a room full of people, she slips through the dining room to have a look at the old kitchen.

A tap on the shoulder makes her jump. She turns to see Beth, the only aunt, apart from the long-deceased Carmen the Kind, whom she remembers with any warmth. Aunt Beth and Uncle Ben have been divorced for years. He sent the cotton factory broke, married his secretary, and moved to a suburb out in the country that Agnes has never heard of. She's not sure in what order these events happened, but it was already ancient history:

*Hello, darling girl! I heard your voice and came to find you!*

*Wow, you look wonderful, Beth! You've hardly changed a bit!*

Agnes gazes into the attractive woman's smoky grey eyes, whilst savouring hearing again the sweet coquettish laugh she had once found so endearing.

*And you've still got that lovely red hair! Jean tells me you've been studying at Oxford since your marriage break-up in London.*

Agnes informs her that the studies in Oxford were undertaken in a small way. That she attended a few summer schools at one of the colleges. She reminds her that classrooms were never for her. She is strictly an autodidact, she tells Beth, and adds that she lives alone with a Persian cat and sleeps in a bedroom full of books. She hears herself laughing nervously at the admission. Despite the pleasure of seeing her aunt, she feels distinctly out of place.

Beth takes a small step closer to her:

*If there is anything that I can tell you about the past, Agnes. Anything that might help your investigations, ring me. We can meet for coffee. I know from my own children how undiagnosed traumas can affect adult life. My son revealed that he was abused by a priest at school and it's only now, years later, he can talk about it.*

Agnes is aghast. Such a revelation! And so unexpected! But she wonders if the promised private meeting would ever manifest. Family interference could put paid to it in a heartbeat and so she decides to push her luck in the moment:

*Could we catch up a little now, Beth? Please.*

Beth considers for a moment or two, then shepherds her into an adjoining room:

*I'm not sure how much you know, but after your parents moved to the farm, your mother became terribly possessive about the house. She was so hostile to Ben and me that instead of stopping off to see her, we would go straight to the stables. Before the factory went broke, Ben poured thousands into financing players, including your brothers. I was lucky to get a little cottage not far from here and enough to live on in the divorce settlement before it all turned sour. My only problem is my children keep coming back to live with me! I just get rid of one and another one moves back in!*

Agnes is looking quizzically at the pleasant, anxious woman standing awkwardly in front of her. Beth needed to toughen up before it was too late. She was always a pushover. Her aunt leans towards her and lowers her voice even further:

*Was it helpful to see Marnie?*

What a question. Had the two women been in touch since her kleptomaniac visit to the care home?

*To tell you the truth, Beth, I'm not sure. Please. This is so important to me. I have a memory of a fire. A fire for which I was blamed. Aunt Marnie denied to my face it ever happened.*

Beth looks at her intently:

*She rang me last night. She's very upset that, after all these years, you're still fixated on something that never occurred. Do you think you might have muddled it up with some other event? Or accident? Memory plays funny tricks.*

*No! When I close my eyes, I see flames in that Maroubra house! It's the one thing I am sure of in the loveless mess that was my early life!*

Agnes is aware she has raised her voice and sees Beth shrink away from her. She searches her face for truth and sincerity and sees the woman's expression remains sympathetic:

*My darling girl. You're preaching to the converted. Yes. I saw how badly they treated you.*

Her aunt has reached out and is now squeezing her hand. Agnes is suffused with a sudden flood of tenderness for this kindly woman:

*Oh, Beth—thank you for saying that!*

A rush of secret, long unspoken words suffuse her brain like a sudden gush of water into a pool. She can't keep them from spilling forth:

*I have no memory of the move to The Farm, you know. The summer spent there. Nothing. Nothing until I entered this very building one day to hear I had failed my leaving certificate. Everything that lies behind that event is blank. Freud says nothing is lost and that it's all inside you. It's just a matter of getting access. But try as I might, I can't seem to do it!*

She is aware of hot tears burning in her eyes and she swallows hard to keep them at bay. Beth takes both of her hands in her own:

*You were a sweet, innocent girl, Agnes. Your mother made you out to be a delinquent. The family, well, they poured lies into your grandmother's ear too, I'm sorry to say. And Parry joined the chorus. I have never understood why they behaved like that towards you.*

*Oh, this family, Beth! This so-called bloody family!*

But she has stepped on dangerous ground now, for Beth is looking at her oddly. After all, her aunt is from a pious Catholic family and unused to such straight talk. Aware her outburst could be construed by Beth as tantamount to committing the sin of calumny and detraction, she backtracks:

*What you told me is very helpful. Thank you so much.*

Beth nods, flashes her a quick smile, but the candid atmosphere has evaporated. Agnes is relieved that Marnie appears not to have mentioned to Beth the stolen photo of Parry.

Beth cups her elbow, and Agnes finds herself guided firmly away to greet the other guests. She is swept into a whirl of cousins she recognises but knows nothing about. As they greet her in turn, she momentarily loses sight of who she is and what she is doing there. She finds herself fighting a strong impulse to dash from the room.

The hurly-burly subsides when Jean rings a little silver bell, inviting guests to help themselves to a smorgasbord lunch which has been laid out on a long trestle table, under the windows at the end of the dining room. Jean is now decidedly convivial on her second glass of champagne, and obligingly chatty, and Tina, the youngest aunt, who is seated opposite, appears equally merry:

*Look! Agnes has got my hands!*

Agnes embraces the domestic comedy instigated by Tina. It comes as a relief.

*Yes, and I've got Grandma's legs, and my mother's bottom!*

She hears herself laughing aloud as all eyes fall on her ink-stained fingers with their bitten nails. The sight of her hands alongside Tina's magnificent, long-red-nailed manicure makes her feel awkward, but the shape is, indeed, identical. In fact, it is impossible not to admire how attractive and well preserved these three women are. All possess bright, dark eyes set in small, regular features, and have beautifully unlined skin. Alongside decades of applications of Elizabeth Arden night cream, their lustrous appearance has obviously benefited from religiously staying out of the sun. Hats in summer, gloves to drive in, and gloves also to be worn when hanging washing out on the line. Just like their mother before them.

Charlotte decides to add a comment into the mix from across the table:

*It must have been very hard for you to manage such an unpredictable mother.*

Agnes can only nod at this massive understatement. But the women clearly mean well. In fact, here, today, in this room, she believes all three sisters are trying hard to be supportive of her, even if it does not come naturally. They all appear to want to make some attempt at amends. To show, at the very least, some form of last-minute solidarity with her predicament.

Charlotte has paused, as if waiting for something. Agnes holds her breath. Will the next statement, or question, be what she thinks it will be?

*Jean told us you had a baby. That it was adopted out.*

*Yes. I did. She was.*

Charlotte says nothing.

This unexpected reminder of Rebecca Lea, and the cruel loss of her, galvanises Agnes to turn her back on this gathering. To leave all these people behind once and for all.

The three aunts are now bunched together like an alien species of birds at the end of the table. They drink their coffee and do not notice her observing them. They are survivors—all widows or divorcees— just like her mother and Aunt Marnie. Perhaps, by pampering her sons, Grandma only weakened them for, with the sole exception of Ben, they have all joined her in heaven while her long-suffering daughters stoically remain.

Agnes is slipping into her fur coat and is about to exit when her brother Bert—with whom she has long ago severed relations— sweeps through the front door. He is too absorbed in whirling from aunt to aunt, titillating them with his caustic one-liners, to notice her. The girlish giggles that greet his glib asides only confirm her innate awareness that she is a duck in the wrong pond. But, before she can escape unseen, he turns and recognises her:

*And what wondrous visiting angel have we here draped in mink? Don't ring us, we'll ring you and let you know if you've got the part!*

He is gushing theatrically, obviously piqued by an antagonistic presence amidst his adoring fans. She knows he has quickly assumed his responsibility as the only creditable example of their parents' union and that he will happily rise to the challenge of putting her down on their behalf. He turns from her, instantly focusing his charm assault on Charlotte, keen to expunge any admiration for Agnes, who is now attracting some pleasant general attention in her mink. It crosses her mind that he is the living image of their mother at the polo—chasing away any family member whom she construed as an intruder on her territory. She cannot, *will* not, let this man have the last word:

*Your entrance is a signal for my departure!*

She launches this remark at his retreating back as he walks away through the crowd. It is a version of the George Sanders' time-honoured line from *All About Eve* and really fits the occasion.

He has heard her. Never a man to be gainsaid, she sees him turn on his heel:

*If wit were shit, we'd all be dead!*

She might have guessed he would jibe back. And crudely too. She closes the apartment door behind her.

## CHAPTER 25

# HER BROTHER BERT

Always one for the last word herself, she reckons she had still beaten Bert at his own sardonic game. His cold, blue eyes had always unnerved her. Seated in the snug café across from the Grantham Apartments, memories of her younger brother from decades ago resurface as she sips her coffee.

Eager to forge an alliance with him, she had been excited at the prospect of reuniting permanently with a sibling. Watching him stride up Manning Road towards her had been the cause for a surge of optimism. Everything there appeared washed clean after the rain. A canopy of high branches from a central line of trees shaded both sides of the street. She and Bert had paused together in a tiny patch of sunlight, in front of a single-storeyed pitch-roofed house. Potted pines stood to attention either side of the front door.

A pretty, auburn-haired young woman in a purple gingham dress had answered their knock and greeted them like long-lost relatives. She had grasped Agnes's hand and Agnes had watched her gaze moving from her brother's face to hers. She seemed to be picking up a resemblance many swore by, but which Agnes could never see:

*You must be brother and sister!*

*Yes, you're right.*

*The resemblance is uncanny. Don't you think so, John?*

The woman had turned bright eyes on a man, probably her husband, who grunted some response without looking up from his newspaper. He was seated in an enormous wood-framed lounge chair that looked capable of floating across the harbour. His feet were crossed on the chair opposite as if directing the trajectory of travel.

After her recent years in the wilderness, Agnes had been thrilled that Mrs Vickers had made a visual connection with herself and Bert. They had followed her down the narrow passageway at the side of the house, Bert trailing sulkily behind, patently embarrassed by his older sister's exuberance. To Agnes's delight, they had been greeted by an intimate garden surrounded by a semicircle of tall trees, like a secret clearing in a sylvan wood. A green ping-pong table stood in the centre of a spacious patio. Her practiced eye had already taken in the interior décor, which was uncluttered and adequate, although the two bedrooms at the back had no direct light. Her disappointment over the dark bedrooms had been swept away, however, by the enchantment of the garden.

They had moved in one misty Saturday morning. She first, Bert sauntering along later with his small suitcase, intent on disguising his obvious pleasure in being delivered from the old shufflers on the downbeat corner Agnes had rescued him from. Having invested the sum of money she had given him in obtaining a haircut and some new clothes, he had barely been recognisable as the bedraggled down-at-heel young man she had bumped into less than a week earlier.

Gazing at his altered appearance, she was aware in that moment that she hardly knew him. He had never made connection with her, never confided in her, as Jim had done. When a child, he had shown contempt for the few possessions his younger brother and sister treasured, regularly breaking apart Agnes's painted shoeboxes to steal the sweets she saved for Lent, and gleefully messing up the meticulous arrangement of Jim's small cars on the bedroom floor. How he had relished their plaintive cries on discovering the destruction.

Watching him taking stock of his new bedroom, she realised she had no idea what he really felt or thought. Instinctively, she didn't trust him with knowledge of her dark past, for he used gossip to score points—like her mother—and she sensed he had internalised the same antipathy to his siblings as Madge had to hers. While she and Jim would laugh about the sacred cows at the polo their parents venerated, Bert would have none of it. So compelling had been his elevation of everything Eric and Madge admired, he might have been their only child.

She had landed in a perfect location to be self-employed. Bondi Junction was already a busy Sydney satellite and just a short walk up the hill from where she lived. She had approached three recently established small legal practices, all of whom appointed her as their registration clerk—on an agency basis. Soon she was earning so much money that, having paid out for rent and food, she had still saved enough to put a deposit on a second-hand car.

Agnes's sense of being a ghost around her brother—the same feeling elicited by her parents—still prevailed, especially when he was with his girlfriend Mary. Bert had continued sharing nothing of his life with his only sister. Eavesdropping on his conversations with Mary was how Agnes learned that her taciturn brother, like her, had reading difficulties. She discovered, too, that Bert's boarding school once made the same fatal mistake of consulting their mother over the issue and had achieved the same disastrous result—for no child of Madge's could possibly be deemed word-blind and the accuser expect to get away with it.

In fact, Bert's dyslexia served to establish a deeper bond between him and Mary. Mary had sought professional advice and accompanied him to group sessions with others similarly afflicted. Future girlfriends would do the same, for Bert would master the art of evoking female sympathy and would manage to turn his dyslexia into an irresistible attraction. Comfortable in relationships he could control, he would settle into letting female partners read to him like a blind man. Informed that dyslexics are often highly intelligent, Bert, in his own eyes, would become a wounded and misunderstood genius.

*Chapter 25   Her Brother Bert*

Agnes had remained silent when Bert's condition was first revealed, unsure if she was also a sufferer. There was a time in her young life when she had read voraciously, with no noticeable difficulty—that was, until the mysterious shattering of her concentration had taken its toll. Only two years between brother and sister, yet she had felt *so* much older.

Eventually Bert will buckle down to show the world was wrong to judge him and will land a job in a city finance company. The scrawny fugitive rescued by his sister will go off to work looking dapper and handsome in a smart business suit. Today, seated in the café, Agnes can still see herself standing on that hot pavement, watching him depart. Handsome in his smart new suit. Confident in his stride. She had felt a glimmer of pride. The resentment always came later.

And that poor old car of hers, that Bert would co-opt as if it was his own. Abandoning it in the street, often broken and without petrol. Agnes can still recall a particular car repair incident in detail. She takes another sip of her cooling coffee and remembers a short mechanic with a beer gut. The one who had helped the tow truck driver lower her car to a thudding stop on the cement floor of a garage:

*Looks like we've got some serious work here, Bluey!*

But before he had a chance to depress her further, they were interrupted. A smartly dressed, middle-aged man, with a sharp nose and a thin scar on one cheek had appeared as if just parachuting in from the roof of the Rose Bay Catholic church next door. He had taken a long searching look at Agnes:

*You've got it! You've got the look I've been searching for! You'd be perfect for what I want!*

*And what would that happen to be, Sunshine?*

She recalls how the squat mechanic had grabbed the sleeve of the stranger's tailored white shirt, how secretly elated she had been to hear the mechanic gallantly intervene on her behalf. How, stopped in his tracks, the Englishman's face had flushed pink beneath his greying fair hair, the white scar standing out like a brand. Angry, he had pulled away from the mechanic's grip. She felt implicated, as if she had—somehow—provoked the altercation.

The three had looked awkwardly at one another until the Englishman apologised to Agnes, saying he meant no insult. That they were not to take what he said as a provocation. He introduced himself as Roger Johnson. Out from England to do a series of television commercials for Senior Service cigarettes. He had, he told them, spent most of yesterday auditioning young women and was starting to despair he would ever find his Senior Service girl. Then, lo and behold, he stops for petrol and sees Agnes. 'The stunning redhead' he has been searching for.

The mechanic may have been smirking in disbelief, but any mutual suspicion evaporated when the owner of the garage walked over to greet the interloper deferentially by name:

*Hello Roger! No further problems with the chariot, I hope!*

*No—she's purring like a contented tabby, thanks Ross. Couldn't be happier. Grateful for your help, old pal.*

Agnes had followed the owner's gaze to a shiny red Jaguar sedan parked at the pumps, where a young man in overalls was meticulously cleaning the windscreen. She had noticed Roger's eyes travelling over her body and felt tangled in his gaze, like an insect on flypaper. Out of the blue, he had offered her a lift. The damsel in distress, devoid of transport till her broken axle was fixed.

She had settled into the cushioned passenger seat with her briefcase on her lap. And, as the Jaguar cruised slowly through Double Bay, she had found herself hoping someone she knew might see her in this splendour. Roger had been so persuasive that, by the time he dropped her off, she had agreed to a screen test. And, by the end of the following week, she had become the 'Senior Service Girl'.

Professional photos printed, Agnes will register with the Gloria Patten Casting Agency in King Street and sign a contract for more money than she has ever earned in her life in one hit. But a natural pragmatism will still rule her actions. She will deem it advisable to keep her current employment going and get someone to cover for her. Better safe than sorry. You never knew.

She will wash and dry her hair the night before the first day's shooting and set her alarm for 8am, giving her plenty of time to arrive at the Cruising Yacht Club of Australia where filming is due to begin.

To gain heavenly protection, she will pledge 10% of her earnings to the starving black babies but, fearing she might have undercut the Almighty, will drag herself back into the prayer position and double her offer. Secure in the celestial deal, she will hit the pillow and sink into a deep sleep.

*I consider it a miracle that I have managed to get through all three commercials—all shot in sea locations—without a major hitch: a yacht in Rushcutters Bay, a fishing trawler in Cairns and a catamaran at Pittwater. Smiling at men dressed in nautical gear as I puff on a cigarette has not exactly been challenging. Certainly not method acting. I have problems on the first day, as the filter-less cigarette keeps sticking to my lips when I pull it out of my mouth. I must have swallowed a whole packet of tobacco! This problem means extra shots. But, in the end, I get through.*

*I have rejected all Roger's overtures for off-set activities. I so wish I could just giggle and fluff off these inevitable male passes as I see other girls do. Instead, unable to speak, I can only turn to ice and stare at the ground. Even though I reject him, I still feel guilty when his wife arrives on set. As if I have somehow provoked his amorous advances behind her back.*

*With the proceeds from the commercials, I buy a new white VW Beetle that I categorically refuse to lend Bert. I am cast through Gloria Patten in other commercials, and this means I must travel to different locations around Sydney and interstate. I am increasingly sick of paying for everything in the flat and am also disillusioned with my attempts to infuse retrospective sunshine into a relationship with my brother. A relationship that never existed.*

*Living under the same roof ends abruptly after I take Bert up on his offer to drive me in my new VW Beetle to the airport to catch a flight to Canberra for a Range Rover commercial. It becomes clear he is deliberately procrastinating in setting out to the airport. Tears of frustration and panic stream down my cheeks as we crawl through heavy traffic, and I pray the flight might be delayed. But I arrive to find I have missed it and that the next flight isn't for another hour. But that flight is also delayed because of fog. And so, landing very late, I miss out on the laid-on transport from Canberra to the snowfields set. There are no taxis, and I have to resort to hitchhiking, which fails to get me there till late afternoon—by which time the production company have flown up another girl by helicopter.*

*The agent drops me. My new career is over. Why did Bert deliberately sabotage me? Was it revenge for not lending him my new car? Or was it simply the pleasure of seeing me suffer? Confronting him is useless, as he will feign innocence. I am devastated. I give up the flat and move into a house with some girlfriends in Double Bay. I have no idea where Bert ends up.*

\* \* \*

Not long after the move, Agnes will bump into an acquaintance in a street near her new house. In the process of establishing his own architectural practice, he is exploring ways of attracting work and she will accompany him to see a development site, set on a steep hill in Woollahra high above the old flat in Russell Street. He is thinking of taking out an option, designing a block of units, and selling the approved project to a developer.

*What do you think, Agnes?*

She will scent an opportunity:

*You can't go wrong. Apartments looking over the harbour and the whole of the Eastern Suburbs. Can't fail to attract buyers.*

And it will all come together. Brien will obtain the loan for the 10% deposit, take out the option and start work on the plans. For Agnes, entering his world of design and colour will be like entering a hitherto unknown magical world. She will fall in love with everything she sees—from his brilliant office decor to the glorious paintings by Australian artists hanging on the walls. Particularly captivating is a series of primary block-coloured primitive pictures in the manner of Gauguin. They are by Ray Crooke. She will dream of learning more about the local art scene and imagines herself—one day—buying similar pictures.

Plans for the building on the steep hill finished and approved by the local council, she will accompany Brien, dressed in her best, to dine in fancy restaurants with developers who profess interest in investing in his project.

It is on one of these evenings that a short, red-faced man with a nose like Pinocchio will stride over to her table and offer her a job in his real estate office. His chest puffed out like a turkey, he has been circling the restaurant like a celebrity, calling the waiters by name, and greeting the property fraternity who are dining there. When Agnes recoils from the proposal, Brien will nudge her and, under his breath, tell her it is a great chance.

Mr Bill—alone, and with partners—buys up rows of tenanted Paddington terrace houses, pays out the tenants and, after a quick coat of paint, sells them on individually via the front office. His business partners include suave pinstriped solicitors and high-rolling bankers who choose to ignore the uncouth behaviour of their loud-mouthed partner as he fills their pockets with cash.

The horror of being powerless, penniless, and hungry when a teenager still haunting her, Agnes will vow to take full advantage of this present opportunity. Dedicating herself to the job, she will build up a good sales record and Mr Bill will let her keep the office open all weekend so she can continue to work. One day she will pluck up the courage to ask him a big favour:

*Will you put up the money and go half shares with me if I find a good property deal?*

*You'd better get to the bank, Agnes! I just went past and saw the window open!*

Apart from managing this kind of constant teasing, she will be sharply aware she has to be careful of Mr Bill, as she has seen him literally throw people out of his office. She was with him one day when he threatened an obstinate tenant like a gangster out of *The Untouchables*. Yet, for all his loud-mouthed posturing, she will have him to thank for the £1000 profit she earns from the deal she successfully pulls off with his capital.

In the following years, she will build on that £1000, buying and selling property herself. She will lie in bed counting her money and calculating the next return. Financial security will buffet her through the emotional rollercoaster ride that lies ahead.

She will fall in love with Paddington and come to know the area so intimately that, wherever she is in the world, she can lie in bed and walk the streets in her head. Friendships with local artists will lead to her involvement in converting several old corner shops into galleries and restaurants displaying art. Although she will have amassed a portfolio of rental property, will have helped friends onto the property ladder, will constantly have come up with solutions to difficult transactional problems, deep inside, she will feel as disconnected from the world as ever.

Her success will bring brother Bert back into her life yet again. When he saunters into her office, he will ignore her as usual, instead focusing his charm on her female employees. But her impulse to help him will, yet again, continue to override caution, as the sacred, inviolable nature of the family, infused in her from Grandma, will remain strong. She will applaud the way her staff and friends take him to their hearts but, to her, he will remain as inscrutable as ever. Money can't buy love and that was a certainty.

The same chasm of misunderstanding will apply to Bert who— by denying his sister any gratitude for lifting him up, for making him part of her world, for establishing a foundation for his future by buying him his first house at auction—will succeed not only in harming her, but also in ultimately denying himself all that is worthwhile in life. Given their seriously dysfunctional childhood, Agnes will arrive at the conclusion that, perhaps, Bert is only able to feel anything by pulling the scabs from the wounds of others and watching them bleed. She will accept that, when she is well, Bert's hatred could be dangerous but, when feeling at her weakest, it could prove fatal.

Many years later, following her discharge from a London hospital after a serious illness, he will visit her, accompanied by his wife, and she will realise she has made a mistake in permitting it. Their dismissive, insulting behaviour towards her does no more than reinforce her second husband's abuse.

It will remain a final, unforgettable, and unforgivable audacity.

## CHAPTER 26

# HER BROTHER JIM

The announcement that Jim's flight has landed blares over the loudspeaker and Agnes dashes through the airport to the arrival lounge, where passengers from the flight are already trickling through. She is intent on searching each face. After 10 years or more, she no longer has a clear picture of the man she is looking for.

She feels a tap on the shoulder and spins around to see a barrel-shaped man with a bull neck and swollen red face. He is staring at her. The shock of the sight of him is enhanced by the scent of alcohol-impregnated sweat which swirls around him like an invisible halo:

*Agnes, it's me—Jim. Good to see you after all these years.*

His lack of verbal intonation throws her every time. A colourless monotone. Exactly the voice in which he had once told her by phone that her father had been brought to Liverpool Hospital dead on arrival:

*Well—here we are! It's good to see you. I can smell you've had a relaxing flight.*

She feels instantly bad being so direct. The snipe burst out of her because she is fearful of being driven miles into the countryside by a drunk. He shoots her a look:

*Yeah, I sank a few on the flight to help me relax. The beers were included in the ticket you so generously paid for.*

He gives her a tight-lipped smirk. Unlike Agnes and Bert, Jim has never taken much interest in his appearance and doesn't realise what an impact it has on others. Wearing a stained grey T-shirt, worn jeans and a faded brown jacket that even a charity shop would reject, he looks like a tramp. She persists:

*Okay, well, I'll be relying on you to abstain while you're at the wheel, as I'm no longer able to drive with confidence on what, for me, is the wrong side of the road.*

*No worries. You can rely on me. Like Qantas—never had an accident!*

He is grinning now, exposing a mouth full of broken teeth that look like the aftermath of a bomb explosion. Yet, through the ravaged features, she sees he is still the only one of the three siblings who looks like Madge. What distresses Agnes more than the broken teeth, puffed face and worn clothes, however, is how the colour has faded from his dark eyes. She doesn't want this depleted man to be her brother. For months she has listened on the phone, in silent disbelief, to accounts of various disasters on a failing farm she will never see. All she can think of at this moment is that no financial institution will take him seriously:

*Jim, you can't possibly see a bank manager looking this way. Never go to a bank looking like you need money!*

Again, she feels bad, being so blunt. In line, waiting for a taxi, a voice inside her is telling her to hug him, and she finally does so clumsily—feeling even more awkward when her arms won't fit around his waist. He drops the old canvas bag on his shoulder and hugs her back. The awkward embrace seems to break the ice, and they relax together in the back of the taxi on the way to the Grantham Apartments.

Earlier that day, while at a loose end awaiting Jim's arrival, she had wandered around King's Cross looking for a gift for him and was pleased to find a book called *The Horse Whisperers*, which she had hoped would please her horse-breeder brother.

When they enter the apartment, the first thing he sees is the billowing red bow on the gift-wrapped parcel on the pillow of his sofa bed which had been prepared that morning for him:

*Open it, Jim. It's for you.*

She watches him rip off the paper with shocking ferocity. He holds the book in his rough hands, staring at the title. She smiles at him reassuringly:

*It's to celebrate your new start.*

*Thanks. I've heard of it. Marline will like it.*

It is as if he is merely an agent through which things pass to his wife, and Agnes feels instant anger at the way Marline has dissipated his retirement money. Compensation for years of work had been lost in months on her hare-brained schemes. She shudders to think of the last time she saw Marline—it was at the farm she and Jim developed in Queensland after selling up in New South Wales. Jim had landed another job and was commuting to a Brisbane office. He had still looked good back then, but everything had fallen apart when he left the well-paid Personnel Manager position and joined Marline as a full-time horse breeder.

Agnes knows all this because she lent them a bridging loan to buy a cheaper house while they waited for a buyer for the lovely place that they were forced to sell to cover their debts. She had feared the worst when she realised that Marline not only had more tickets on herself than the National Lottery but had Jim firmly under her thumb. Presumably feeling threatened by Agnes, she had used the presence of a ferocious white Italian sheepdog to make sure she never returned. Agnes can still see the enormous creature throwing itself against the glass door of their courtyard in a frenzy. She had made no effort to say goodbye to her hostile sister-in-law.

After settling in at their table, Agnes suggests to Jim that, perhaps, they have ordered enough, as she watches him add more and more dishes to their order at a Thai restaurant in Macleay Street. Henceforth, she will watch her brother with a mixture of disgust and concern, as he devours copious quantities of food at her expense. As if reading her mind, he pauses from shovelling food into his mouth:

*I promise I'll only drink when the day's driving is behind me.*

She crosses her fingers under the table.

## Chapter 26  Her Brother Jim

\* \* \*

When Jim arrives back at the apartment, he is looking as much like a new man as is possible. He has shaved and put on a clean shirt. The smell of talcum powder, mixed with the minty aroma of the aftershave from the Ginseng Korean Bathhouse session Agnes has paid for, has expunged the stale alcohol that so panicked her at the airport.

Compared to their father's long pilgrimage from the cotton factory back to The Farm with the sun setting in his eyes, the westbound drive of Eric Keen's children is a silken affair. In under an hour, they have reached the Camden Valley Way. They are going to visit their father's grave.

Arriving at Forest Lawn Memorial Park at Leppington, Jim parks the car and leads Agnes off a side path and down to an elevated mound under tall gum trees. And there it is:

**Eric David Keen 1919 to 1968.**
**Beloved husband of Madge Keen**
**And cherished father to children Agnes, Bert and Jim.**

The metal plaque is cracked through, as if struck by lightning. Once again, Agnes is hit forcibly by the fact that her father was only 49 when he died. But what surprises her more is the sight of her name inscribed alongside those of her brothers:

*Look Jim! My name's right there!*

*Of course it is! What did you expect?*

He is giving her an odd look. But no tangible evidence can alleviate the profound depth of the alienation she has felt most of her life:

*Remember how Madge wanted to have the horses at the funeral?*

She has ventured this remark because she is keen to change the subject. Jim responds:

*Do I ever! She turned the whole thing into a three-ringed circus. Lucky he wasn't there to see it. Enough. Let's get out of here. Why don't we drive to Mittagong and take a look at my old house? We don't have to be at Madge's till six.*

Agnes readily agrees. This graveyard is a creepy, phoney place that smacks of advance funeral plans and false sentimentality. As they drive, she questions Jim as much as she dares, culminating with:

*Have you any good memories of our father?*

But she didn't need to worry about reticence on his part:

*Let's put it this way. He didn't give a shit about his kids. He never came to see me play football. Never visited me at boarding school or, for that matter, bothered to come and see me during my months in hospital. Once he even forgot to pick me up for the school holidays. Another time he stopped at the Crossroads Hotel on the way for the inevitable quick one and then drove on to The Farm without me. I'd got out of the scorching car to wait under a tree. I watched him dash out and drive off! He didn't even remember I'd been with him until Madge asked where I was. Too eaten up with himself to take an interest in anyone else. You're right about the horses though. They didn't answer back.*

She looks at her brother, finding it strange that, after growing up together, this is the first time they have ever spoken frankly about their parents.

As they reach Jim's old house they pull up at the side of the road in silence. When he speaks, his voice is slow and measured and she can detect a hint of sadness:

*What I can see of it looks the same—although the garden's turned into a jungle.*

Further contemplation is cut short when a woman in a red dress suddenly swings in front of the entrance in a white BMW. She gets out of the car to open the gate. Jim seems to take her appearance as a sign he is no longer wanted. Looking uncomfortable, he sets his shoulders and points the car in the direction of the main street of Mittagong. He tells Agnes he is heading for the restaurant where he and Marline used to order Marline's favourite—Chicken in the Basket:

*There's the place, Agnes! On that corner. But it's called something else.*

He seems disappointed. The trendy decor, with vegetarian gluten-free alternatives exhibited on the window menu, certainly isn't what they are looking for, and so they drive on out of town, settling for a cosy roadside café. Suddenly Jim bows his head over his plate, like a tired plough horse:

*You know, Agnes, you're the only person I could ever turn to for help. You were always kind to me—and I want you to know I'm grateful.*

His eyes are watering as he puts his rough hand on hers:

*Well, Jim. Now you're on your way again you won't need any more help from anyone.*

She has responded like this in the hope he would finally see the predatory nature of his wife and make the necessary changes for the better. But honestly, what were the odds of that happening?

## CHAPTER 27

# MADGE AT HOME

Jim has parked the car inches from the double garage doors. They are lingering—neither of them inclined to move. Agnes is the first to rouse herself:

*Right. Let's get it over with.*

Jim collects the bags from the boot. Agnes follows him along a stone path beside a lawn covered in leaves, to a set of cement steps cantilevered off the front wall of the house.

The lady of the house is glaring down at them from the porch above. As soon as Jim sets eyes on her, Agnes sees his body contract in the middle as if he has just been punched in the stomach. He ascends the stairs like someone mounting the scaffold.

Predictably, there is no greeting at the door. Agnes hears her mother hiss over her shoulder:

*Close the door behind you!*

As she steps over the threshold, the old dread returns – utterly undiminished by the passage of time.

She isn't prepared for the toll the years have taken on the old warrior. Her mother literally has the face she deserves. Spite is etched into every sagging muscle. The beauty that thrilled her as a child has left without trace. Standing before her is an overweight woman diminished in height, looking anything but stylish in a pair of beige slacks and a soiled open-necked white blouse. The coiffure has not altered, except there is now an unnatural sheen on the dyed bouffant.

The stiffly lacquered curled horns either side of her forehead make her resemble a deranged bull about to charge. The lustre-soaked pearls are still visible around the wrinkled neck:

*What took you so long? I told you to be here for drinks at five sharp!*

Agnes looks at Jim for support, as he is the one who has made the arrangements. He splutters an apology:

*I'm sorry. I thought you said not to come before 6pm.*

Madge bridles:

*Well, I don't know what I said. I wanted Tammy to meet Agnes. It will have to be on your way back now, as she's going away for the weekend.*

Agnes is genuinely disappointed:

*What a pity. I would have liked to see her.*

Tammy had made her previous visits with her mother half bearable. She lived opposite and came over every evening for a gin and tonic. She worked as a doctor's receptionist in a local practice. It was a gift knowing her mother had a concerned neighbour, as Agnes's greatest fear was being embroiled into looking after Madge in old age. Now that dreaded time had arrived and, thankfully, Tammy was still hanging in there.

It is 12 years since she last visited her mother, bubbling with news of Daniel's romantic marriage proposal on her departure at London Airport. Today, a divorced woman again, she hands her mother a bunch of white carnations mixed with blue clematis together with a bottle of red wine—all that was available at a supermarket on the way:

*I hope you like this one. It's Brown Brothers. I often drink it in London.*

Madge puts the bottle on the desktop next to her and dumps the flowers beside it in her usual uncouth fashion. There are no thanks. She skewers Agnes with a look:

*What have you done to your hair?*

Agnes explains that she has had it cut short. That it's easier for travelling. That she just washes it under the shower and flicks it into place with her fingers. She can tell from the shadow of a question mark in the old eyes that Madge senses a change in her daughter. It is an animal thing. As a result, Agnes is no longer on the defensive, even in the face of the familiar petulance. But, nonetheless, here it comes:

*I don't know what it is, but you children always get me churned up. If you only came at the right time everything would be different.*

Agnes exercises her new resilience:

*Well, Jim admitted he made a mistake, and now we're here, so let's make the best of it shall we?*

Her comment brings a well-worn response:

*None of your smart tongue, Agnes. You know where it got you. A first, now a second marriage on the rocks. The trouble with you is you don't know how to keep a man.*

Agnes sees red. She is not going to be upset by this woman. Not any longer:

*What rubbish! Why on God's earth would I want to hang on to avaricious predators who steal my money and treat me badly? If holding onto your man means manipulating the shit out of him, like you did to Daddy, then you're dead right about me!*

Madge rises to the occasion as of old:

*How dare you speak to me like that, you wretched girl. I was so looking forward to seeing you, and now it's made me sick. You've provoked a turn, and you haven't been here five minutes. Where are my pills? Hand me those!*

Madge is swaying on her feet for effect and pointing at a side table:

*Yes—yes, that's them. Unscrew the top... hurry, hurry!*

Agnes obeys the tyrannical command. With an air of resignation hanging over him like a fog, Jim goes to fetch a glass of water. He places it down on a small table beside the lounge chair into which his mother has slumped. The sister and brother watch as their mother swallows two tiny pills, after which she lies back in the chair and closes her eyes. She really does look her age.

A sudden pang of all-too-familiar guilt has Agnes kneeling on the floor, with her hand on her mother's arm. In the house barely two minutes and they are at one another's throats. The lifelong patterns are indelible. Printed on the walls of their lives like hieroglyphs. But

Madge refuses to speak.

Agnes looks at Jim, who shrugs, and glances at the ceiling in tired exasperation. Their mother waves them both away with her hand, her eyes still tightly shut. Agnes attempts amelioration:

*Are you all right, Mummy? Do you want us to call anyone?*

*Just leave me alone. I'll come around in a minute. I don't need outside help.*

Jim walks back into the kitchen and puts on the kettle where Agnes joins him. They sip their tea thoughtfully, leaning on the kitchen counter. The colour starts to come back into Jim's face:

*Why does she behave like that? What does she get out of it?*

*Don't ask me. She's a monster. Jean told me that when they were growing up, she'd scream till she got what she wanted and that it's been the same ever since. It's got her nowhere. Everyone loathes her. Except good old Tammy.*

*I'll have some tea...!*

It is a plaintive cry from the sick woman on the lounge chair and it curtails further chat.

Agnes had planned to take them all out to dinner, but no. Apparently Madge has the dinner planned. They were to have rump steak, potatoes in their jackets with sour cream and chives, along with mushrooms and peas. The English girls had done the prerequisite shopping yesterday.

This offer of hospitality surprises Agnes, as her mother tended to jump at any invitation to go to a restaurant, where she ordered the most expensive thing on the menu—usually lobster.

Agnes persists with her invitation, as she would far prefer to dine around a table in a neutral setting. She decides to wave a proverbial carrot:

*I enquired at a place in town. They have lobster.*

But the ploy fails.

*I've already told you! I've got it all planned. Come, darling and I'll show you—it's all in the fridge.*

Teacup in hand, her mother is sounding suddenly carefree, as if she is sashaying along the red carpet on the sixth floor of 'David Jones'. This typical mercurial mood change is another reminder of times past, and Agnes starts to feel as if the walls are closing in. She controls this unwelcome upsurge of anxiety by concentrating on the decor of Madge's home.

The interior mirrors the exterior's absurdity. A narrow double-sided fitted kitchen, with no natural light, sits in the centre as if a railway carriage has come crashing in from the side. The living room rotates around it, merry-go-round style. It is more like the layout of a community centre than a home. Further exploration reveals a desk below a set of shelves—containing the now tarnished polo trophies. Several clumsy floral loose-covered lounge chairs are scattered around, and a dining table and chairs inhabit a narrow nook at the far end of the room.

Seated at the dining table after dinner, prepared by Agnes under the close direction of her mother, and the usual mindless chit-chat having been exhausted, Agnes decides that enquiries about the past can't wait a moment longer. Unable to stomach the underlying tension, Jim gets up to wander into the backyard and have a smoke. Now is the time. There will never be another opportunity.

Agnes stares at her mother's tight, wrinkled mouth:

*Mummy. I'd like you to explain a few things I never understood.*

*Well, make it quick, Agnes. I'm tired and don't want to stay up much longer.*

*How did I end up at seventeen in a godforsaken boarding house for old people all alone and with no money?*

Her mother dabs at her mouth with a linen napkin and sighs deeply, as if someone has told her that the next train is going to be late. She doesn't look at her daughter:

*Why on earth are you bringing this up after all these years?*

*Because, to me, it remains a painful, unsolved mystery.*

Madge shoots a shrewd glance at her daughter. It occurs to Agnes she is weighing up the impact of what may be coming next:

*Well, if you must know, you were sent there because you were cavorting with your uncle and your aunt was jealous.*

Her mother has dropped this bombshell in such a matter-of-fact way that it is as if the rationale should have been obvious to all but the most stupid.

*What on earth do you mean?!*

Madge's facial expression borders on the incredulous:

*Flirting! You were always a dreadful flirt, Agnes. Everyone said so. You were a classifiable delinquent. Everyone thought so—your school, your grandmother, all the family! Your father and I cared about you deeply, but we couldn't handle you.*

Here it was. The showdown. Let it rip.

*Cared about me! Nobody tried harder to annihilate me than you did! Those other people—that so-called family—belonged to you, not me! They only heard the pack of lies you fabricated. Even Marnie said you sent me to them with no money. Gave them no money for my upkeep. How caring was that?!*

*Oh, don't listen to her! She's always got an axe to grind. She's a poor pathetic woman who doesn't know what she's talking about. It's the stroke.*

Agnes feels rage rising like flames in her chest:

*You O'Connor women are such wilting violets! I was no Lolita! If Marnie was jealous, why didn't she hit him over the head and send him packing? As I recall, he was a lazy bastard who did fuck all! You demonised me to get rid of me!*

*We did nothing of the sort. You're exaggerating all this. Grandma was prepared to pay for you to go to an expensive boarding school, but you thumbed your nose at her.*

*I couldn't concentrate! Something went wrong inside me, and I know it had something to do with you and Daddy. Something triggered such extreme anxiety I lost the ability to read properly. I've been extremely handicapped ever since!*

*Well, how would I know any of that Agnes! I'm not a mind reader!*

*Right. Well. Perhaps you can tell me how old you were when your father showed off his penis to YOU?!*

There is a pregnant pause. Her mother's Adam's apple bobs in her fleshy throat against the pearls:

*How dare you even suggest such a thing! My father would never do that!*

*Well, mine did and you know it! You didn't even seem shocked! Instead of sending the pervert packing, you laughed!*

*Oh, that! With Rita Ryder, wasn't that her name? It was just a silly joke!*

*Really? Well, you've got a poor sense of humour! Rita Ryder went straight home to tell her parents! THEY certainly didn't think it was a joke! It forced those I loved most in all the world to cut me out of their life! And while we're on the topic of abusive behaviour, what about Lennox Street and Paul?*

Madge moans dismissively as if now profoundly bored by the proceedings. Agnes half expects her to retreat to her bedroom, but she doesn't move:

*None of that was my fault, Agnes. The boy was a troublemaker.*

Agnes holds back her rising disgust with difficulty:

*Paul was intelligent and curious and kind. And he'd still be with us today if you had acted differently. Why didn't you report the live cable spewed over the street to the authorities?*

*We didn't have a phone, so what was I supposed to do?*

*How about running down the road to the bloody phone box! Or asking a neighbour? Or just screaming your fucking head off until someone alerted the police? How could you knowingly let little children play around a live cable with thousands of volts running through it? If I had kept holding his hand, I would have died too!*

Madge purses her lips:

*I made sure you were wearing gumboots.*

*Dear Christ! What kind of twisted logic is THAT?!*

In these seminal moments, these moments of pure, unadulterated truth-telling and its consequences, Agnes has it irrevocably confirmed that she has been protecting this idiotic woman most of her life, and what a phenomenal waste of heartbeats it has been.

Madge stirs in her chair, preparing to stand up:

*Enough of this childish nonsense. You've worn me out.*

Once Madge finally closes her bedroom door behind her Agnes and her brother, standing side by side, systematically wash and dry the pots and plates used for dinner. Agnes is the one who breaks the silence between them:

*I had to confront her, Jim.*

*I know.*

She tells him how she went to Lennox Street recently and how it all came back to her. *Years* of feeling responsible for Paul's death. She declares to Jim that she believes it is a miracle they both survived what passed as their upbringing. That it hit her tonight that she was always the mother and Madge always the child. That it was all arse about from the start.

Jim hears her out. He is looking towards the door of Madge's bedroom:

*That woman in there, Agnes. Snoring her lazy head off. That woman used to beat me so badly sometimes I couldn't go to school because of the bruises on my legs. She'd do it when there was no one around. She'd get this crazed look in her eye and attack me with a belt. That's why I ran away. I thought she'd kill me, so I took 10 pounds out of her purse and caught a train to Hornsby. When I tried to change the big bill for cash the woman in the shop rang the police. The policeman saw the bruises on my legs, then someone else came in and asked about them. Social workers probably. I said I had a fight at school. They kept fishing for information about my home life. I knew I'd be in for it if I ever complained about her, so I didn't answer.*

Truth-telling. And its consequences. Agnes puts a hand on his arm:

*My God, Jim. I never knew.*

Jim leans in towards her, lowering his voice to a hoarse whisper:

*I should warn you that you've been set up. Madge is out of money. She wants you to buy her house and give her a life tenancy. I should have told you earlier, but I couldn't face it.*

Agnes smiles to herself:

*Is that so? Well. I shall suggest she rings Grandma in heaven.*

\* \* \*

Agnes wakes the next morning from a nightmare, her heart pounding. She is in an unfamiliar bedroom in her mother's home. She tries to shrug off the dream but cannot.

Something... something... about scooping up filth. In a bathroom. Of removing an ugly brown mess of shit with a mop and bucket. Of wiping the wet floor dry with old towels until the white tiles sparkle. But, like an Alfred Hitchcock twist, the toilet lid had sprung open and belched out fresh turds like an oil gush over the floor. She had pumped at the flush handle on the toilet, but the level was rising. She was drowning. Slowly drowning.

She jumps out of bed and runs to the bathroom, throwing herself under the shower, letting the water cascade over her face. She scrubs at her body till her arms and legs ache. She washes her hair so many times that she finishes the shampoo in the Pears bottle—that same amber-coloured brand they used as children. The image on the bottle—of a sweet-faced mother holding out a towel to a wet-headed child—collides with Agnes's own memory of herself as a child proffering a towel in her small hands to her own babied mother.

She covers herself in talcum powder and eau de cologne, then touches her toes and runs on the spot to help contain the thunderstorm reverberating inside her. She knows she is firmly back in the terrorising hold of childhood and must face the woman who is her mother again today. Trying to control her breathing, she dresses herself in white jeans, white cotton jumper and white trainers—top-to-toe whiteness in defiance of the putrid nightmare.

## Chapter 27   Madge at Home

It is Good Friday. As a child she would spend all Easter on her knees with Grandma.

She opens the window. The world outside is drenched in sunlight and the sonorous drone of lawnmowers, and the hint of light laughter from the surrounding gardens fills the air.

She enters the lounge area where her mother and Jim are already having breakfast, seated at the table at the end of the room. Jim has been to the bakery and bought fresh bread and croissants. The sun is bursting into the house through every dark crack to spotlight the dull walls.

She can't stomach bacon and eggs today, nor watch the ugly way her mother is collecting the drips of a boiled egg with her fat tongue. The woman is utterly repulsive to her:

*Agnes...?*

Her mother's tone is a little uncertain, tentative. Jim shifts uncomfortably in his chair.

Madge turns towards her daughter, widening her eyes as if petitioning a reluctant suitor:

*I've got no money, Agnes. I thought you could buy my house cheaply and let me stay here. Stay here for life I mean. I'm already eighty-five and have a bad heart, so you won't have to wait long to get possession and then you can sell the place on at a profit.*

Agnes knows she must face her. Yet she wants to make her suffer:

*Why don't you ask Bert?*

Is it her imagination, or is her mother looking nervous? Madge adopts a wheedling tone:

*I did, but he's got no spare cash because he's expanding his business and Jim can't help me because he's struggling, aren't you, Jim?*

Poor Jim lowers his head over his plate and Agnes can feel his shame. But Madge has no mercy for her youngest son:

*Jim already owes me $5,000 and is hoping, aren't you Jim, that you could take over the debt.*

This latest machination is news to Agnes but doesn't surprise her.

Nothing about this family does:

*What on earth makes you think I should help you?*

But she feels guilty just saying it. Her brother is looking out of the window, avoiding her eyes. Scenting what is at stake, what could disappear over the horizon, Madge hits her stride:

*Because Jim said you sold the huge house you owned with your husband in London and because you're my daughter and I'm your mother and all children look after their parents in old age.*

Agnes takes stock. Why did Jim tell their mother about the London house? Are they *both* colluding against her?

A fresh rage against her mother surges inside her—this selfish, self-regarding woman who has had more money handed to her on a plate than the whole family put together. But what would be the point of further interrogation? She might feel like strangling this excuse for a parent but, at the same time, is struck with a perverse sense of honour in being asked by such an abject failure of a woman for help. The conflict is unbearable. She feels hatred yet is still affected by the old guilt. Why? Will anyone ever be able to explain to her *why* this should be the case?

The sight of the floral carpet under her white shoes is making her dizzy. She feels suddenly claustrophobic. She can't breathe. Afraid of making a detrimental snap decision, she can do nothing but escape. Attempt to flee from the massive turmoil within.

She jumps up, opens the front door, and runs down the steps. She strides down the street past neighbours in their gardens who are larking about in the bright sunshine. Friendly in their domestic security, they wave and smile at her. She thinks of the cool-headed way she took control of the London house once she got Daniel out. How swiftly she put it on the market when the tenant returned to the USA after 9/11. How cleverly she avoided an earful of insults by not consulting Daniel personally but informing him via a solicitor. How competently she had managed what had been one of the most challenging crises of her life. She tells herself firmly now, as she walks along this unfamiliar street—you *did* it! And you did it single-handedly. Give yourself some credit, Agnes! By resisting reverting to histrionics with Daniel, by keeping a cool and calm business head on your shoulders, you managed to sell the house yourself and you *escaped*! SO DO THE SAME WITH THIS WOMAN!

Staring into a full-blown white rose that the least breeze would reduce to a stem, she sees her own fragility in its petals. The truth of her situation hits her. No amount of recrimination can change the past. Her mother could *never* love her because she is incapable of loving anyone. But she, Agnes, could learn to love *herself*.

She takes several deep breaths, lifts her head to feel the warmth of the morning sun on her face, and turns back.

Jim and her mother raise their heads expectantly as she enters:

*Thanks for the offer. I'll have to think about your proposal and get back to you.*

The last time her mother has looked this surprised was when Agnes told her about the adopted baby. But it hasn't robbed her of speech:

*You can have it for $300,000. That's cheap, Agnes. The agent said it's worth $350,000. And I'd like new carpets!*

Madge's eyes are darting gleefully around the room. She clearly believes she may have won a victory over this vexatious daughter. And she isn't finished:

*And as for you, Jim—you can't leave without paying me back the $5000 straight away!*

Seeing yet another look of shame pass over Jim's face will be too much for Agnes to take. She cannot put off the decision and make him suffer, so she will agree to take over his debt. She will scribble out an agreement that is good for one year. Should her mother die and go to hell within that time, the $5000 will be paid back to Agnes out of her estate.

She will write out a cheque for her mother. Jim will sign the agreement. Seated at a bureau desk, she will watch her mother laboriously scrawl the name and details of her solicitor on a piece of paper torn from an address book. Because it is painfully obvious that Madge's eyesight is failing, Agnes will check these written details before she leaves and will be struck by how alike her handwriting is to that of her parent.

The only similarity between mother and daughter. Thank God.

CHAPTER 28

# UNCLE BEN AND THE OPEN ROAD

Jim is turning north back towards Sydney on the Old Hume Highway which is now the magnificent M31 motorway. Huge pylons cut into vistas of rolling hills with pockets of new construction dotted on what had once been open countryside. They are rolling smoothly over the surface of the dual carriageway like a ball down the lane of a bowling green.

Off the motorway, on the way to Uncle Ben's house, they see the sign: St Thomas Moore Catholic Church. This must be Uncle Ben's parish church. Jean had told Agnes he had become religious in his old age, dedicating himself exclusively to church work.

In contrast to their mother's hostile greeting, Ben flies out of the door towards them—grinning like a playful puppy:

*Welcome! Lucky I just got back from buying a few extras for lunch!*

His enthusiasm had always been his most endearing quality. But nothing, it seems, has changed in the cardigan-ogling department. He looks Agnes up and down through thick glasses, like a horse he is thinking of buying. They follow him into a large bare-walled living room that feels uninhabited, as if new owners are still in the process of moving in. A coffee table is set up with glasses and bowls of snacks. Agnes smiles at her uncle:

*Thanks very much for agreeing to see us.*

She settles herself down on a blue sofa. Jim sits opposite her, his gnarled hands folded over an extended belly. Agnes is relieved when he refuses a beer. Aware he is eating his way through a daily alcohol craving she offers him the plate of potato chips and he gratefully grabs a handful. Agnes accepts water, and Ben pours himself and Jim a Fanta orange. Agnes breaks the slightly awkward silence:

*I brought you this…*

She pulls a small parcel out of her bag.

*Oh, my goodness! Let's see what we've got here!*

Ben is tearing at the white tissue paper to reveal a small metal box with an image of St Peter's in Rome on the ceramic top. Then he pulls out a string of white rosary beads with a gold cross. He holds them up to the light:

*Are they blessed?*

He is lifting them higher as if searching for evidence of sanctity.

*Yes, they were blessed by the Pope.*

She is aware her affirmation doubles the enhancement, whilst not caring if it's true or not.

*Thank you, Agnes. I'll keep them close.*

She watches him slip the rosary beads into the pocket of his slacks, and notices that his face now exudes the smarmy goodness expressed on the faces of some priests. With his greying short haircut, dark trousers, and white polo neck, he could fit the role to a 'T'. Straight backed, slim, with clear eyes and skin, at age eighty he appears in remarkable good health.

He turns to her, smiling:

*Tell me—how's dear old Maggie? I hear she's been having trouble with her sight.*

Maggie. His pet name for her mother. He has spoken in a cloying tone that matches the benevolent expression. Agnes decides she will give him the bare details. There is still a family grapevine, that's evident, and she doesn't want to feed it:

*She seems to manage. Carers from the local council do her washing, take her shopping, and to the doctors and hairdresser. Meals on wheels bring food during the week. She doesn't want for anything—except money.*

She knows her sarcasm is lost on him.

*Glad she's managing. Good old Maggie. Could be difficult but you had to know how to handle her.*

The delusions of age. He has repeated her mother's pet name like an aging Romeo extolling the virtues of Juliet.

*Uncle Ben. Don't you feel any resentment about the way she treated you?*

*Oh, our Maggie can be a bit tetchy at times, but can't we all!*

Jim is so amused by this understatement that he splutters in the process of taking a gulp of Fanta. He looks at his sister, eyes running, coughing, before standing up and shaking himself like a dog after a bath. He tries to conceal his mirth—and fails.

Ben glances at them both in turn, then excuses himself to go into the kitchen. When Agnes offers to help, he declines:

*No trouble. I've developed a liking for domestic duties.*

But she follows him anyway, to find him pulling a loaf of bread out of the oven with a floral oven glove. He puts the bread down on a bench in silence, then beckons her to a corner near the fridge—out of earshot of Jim in the dining room:

*I hope you haven't come here to make trouble, Agnes.*

Here it is again. She is the perpetual troublemaker. The shaker of foundations.

*Of course not! What trouble could I—or would I—want to make? I was fond of you when I was young. You taught me things and made me feel special. I'm just trying to get to the bottom of the loss of memory I experienced as a child. It's gone on affecting me all my adult life.*

He shrugs:

*I just don't want my wife to be upset.*

He takes the tinfoil off the hot loaf. She knows this man has every reason to love his second wife. The woman might be the prototype for the song 'Stand by Your Man'. Devoted secretary, clandestine lover, she has remained at his side ever since the cotton factory business collapsed. Estimated as over fifteen years his junior, she still travels each day to Sydney by train to work as a secretary to support them both. A little later, when Agnes pops to the bathroom, she will spot the two towelling bathrobes hanging side by side, together with a heart-shaped card with the legend *LOVE YOU* which leans against the mirror.

Having helpfully shipped the used plates back to the kitchen and stacking them by the sink, she returns to the living room to hear the two men in conversation:

*Boy-oh-boy, Jim, when you lost your temper, you really lost it! After a run-in with her, you were so fired up, there was no one to match you. A real bull in a china shop. No—wait—that's not right. What the heck am I talking about—there was masses of room on the field! Nothing to break but your bloody neck and you came close a few times—especially when Maggie got your goat!*

She sees that Jim is squirming as Ben cruelly underlines the power his mother had over him. The power to urge her youngest son on one minute and cut the ground from under him the next. Very much Madge's style. She decides to rescue Jim by changing the subject, despite the earlier veiled threat in the kitchen:

*And what about my father? Any abiding memories there?*

Ben grins at her:

*Only the good die young, Agnes, and he was a good man. Fantastic player. Made every post a golden mile. He was so proud, you know—when you bought him those two horses. He'd go on about your success. Running your own business and all that. Your father is in heaven now with your grandmother and Parry.*

Hearing this allusion to her father's praise—compliments that had never come her way—pulls her up short. She hears herself speak her thoughts aloud:

*He might have been proud, but he never told me. I'll not be going to heaven because I don't want to see any of them again.*

*That right? Well, I can't tell you anything about that now, can I? And I don't like your comment.*

Ben's voice has increased a few decibels to the authoritarian boom that used to frighten his children and Agnes wonders if a life devoid of sensitivity has kept him looking so young. Nothing stuck. Nothing penetrated. All bounced off him without effect.

She will watch Ben as he leans down to pick up a prayer missal from the coffee table and hold it against his chest like a kind of talisman to ward off incipient fury. She will notice the snowy five o'clock shadow on his cheeks that makes him look like a holy fraud. It seems she has shattered his saintly disposition.

Jim will break the impasse:

*Well. We've got a long drive ahead of us, Agnes. We'd better be on our way.*

Her brother will be standing tall in the room as if he means business, and she will see he has had more than enough. She will wonder if this fraught encounter might cause him to want a proper drink. She will get up obediently, putting her own needs on the backburner, and follow him to the door.

Ben will shuffle after them like an eager shepherd, still clutching the missal to his chest. The last-minute apology Agnes is planning to offer him will be spirited away, however, when a wind blows up and forces her uncle to rush back into the house and close the shaking windows. She and Jim will wait for a few minutes in the car, but he will not re-emerge. Instead, she will give Ben a final feeble wave when she spots him, looking out wistfully from what must be his bedroom window.

As Jim backs the car out of the drive, a storm of dry leaves and dust will cover the windscreen and obliterate her holier-than-thou uncle from her view forever.

\* \* \*

The wind is so powerful, it is buffeting the Toyota from side to side. Jim uses the spray and wipers to clear the glass. Agnes feels a surge of strange hilarity:

*Reckon Ben summoned Poseidon to destroy the heretics maligning the dead!*
*See no evil, speak no evil!*
Jim has added his droll tuppence worth as he peers through the fan-shaped clearing cut by the wipers. Cars move at a snail's pace with their headlights on. Then the appearance of a hearse explains this sluggish progress. A solemn, black-suited man is seated in the front. The hearse contains a honey-coloured coffin with brass handles which is covered in a line of wreaths formed of pink and white gladioli:
*Nothing like a funeral to sober you up, eh Agnes?*
Perhaps Jim is making an inward vow to take better care of himself. She hopes so. As they pick up pace, she feels the grime of recent ugly events fall away. We only live in moments—she contemplates—we can't buy them, organise them, or steal them. She closes her eyes, hoping it will help her to hold onto this transitory perception of joy.

She wakes to the sound of water, realising she must have dozed off. Jim is cleaning the car on a garage forecourt. He catches her eye and nods—common parlance for 'the bill awaits you'. After settling the account and using the restroom, they move onto the motorway, heading south. After an hour or so, Jim exits at the sign to Goulburn and parks the car in a backstreet.

As they join the crowds strolling along the main street, Agnes suddenly recalls the nightmarish visit to the polo tournament in her early teens. A deadly chill pervades her bones, mirroring the despair of that terrible night of abandonment by her parents. Anxious not to cast a shadow over their day, she manages to shake the memory off.

Stepping aside to let a group of people pass, Jim accidentally knocks over a display of riding boots in front of a shoe shop. She takes the opportunity to invest herself with fresh verve:

*Let me buy you a pair of boots, Jim, before you break your neck tripping on that flapping sole!*

Necessity overcomes his initial reluctance, and within fifteen minutes of her suggestion, he is walking out of the store in a new pair of tan elastic-sided riding boots, having left the battered pair they replaced in the shop. The spending spree has begun. At a clothes supermarket across the road, wool socks are thrown into a self-service basket to replace the threadbare excuses he exposed when he removed his old boots. Socks are joined by underwear, belts, jeans, shirts, jumpers, and a tan fleece-lined jacket. Next stop is the chemist for a new washbag, a toothbrush, toothpaste, and shaving gear, all of which her brother accepts in a kind of a haze.

Afterwards, over coffee, her brother surveys the carrier bags that surround him in stunned silence. She suspects the beatings that almost killed him as a child have robbed him of the ability to enjoy such simple pleasures. Just like her, he probably anticipates the worst constantly, and is relieved when it doesn't happen. She is kicking herself for not thinking of buying him new clothes before this. Facing Madge's critical eyes in his shabby rags must have been a torture to him.

Crookwell, where they plan to spend the night, is not only an historical rural town, but a popular tourist destination. There are 'No Vacancy' signs on the front of every motel, but they do eventually find rooms in the bizarre Spud Murphy's Inn. The incongruous exterior of this hostelry is echoed in the interior. Different sets of stairs lead through a labyrinth of corridors with sloping floors. The random bathrooms, scattered illogically, prove hard to find and, once located, the trajectory back to their rooms sets a puzzling challenge. Having showered and changed, and got lost several times in the process, Agnes finds her way back downstairs where she settles in an armchair in the expansive open lounge before an enormous raging log fire.

The warmth makes her drowsy. Bleary-eyed, she hardly recognises Jim in his new clothes as he approaches her. He pulls up a chair beside her:

*Agnes. How did you turn into such a hotshot entrepreneur?*

He has never asked her this before, and she gives him a shorthand version of the twisting and turning events that transpired after Sister

Wilfred's fearless defence of her at St Anthony's home. He seems genuinely impressed:

*God. You're a bloody marvel to have survived all that. I've never been able to sort myself out.*

She tells him he can start the sorting-out process at the dentist and offers to send him the money to have his teeth done. He can pay her back when he starts earning again. Open a separate account in your own name, she tells him, and that way it can't go anywhere else. When he thanks her, she can only hope he has spotted the inference—to guard against his wife and her avarice.

She is feeling an ever-deepening commitment to Jim's wellbeing. It is a pleasant sensation, to have him under her wing again after all these years, but is she deluding herself? Is she foolish in believing he has joined her quest on this trip to understand and eradicate the effects of the past? Is she also foolish in believing that he, too, might finally want to comprehend their mutual attraction to being dominated by the will of others?

The next morning, she watches her brother as he tucks into a hearty cooked breakfast. She is drinking copious cups of coffee after a bad night's sleep. The return of the Goulburn nightmare still haunts the new day. Is it caused by buried memories, or is it simply stress manifesting in symbols? Yet again, in the dream of running away from her father, she is trapped in a suffocating fog. His piercing blue eyes had shone like searchlights as he gained distance behind her. When he had caught her and she had frozen before his wordless stare, she had woken up with a start.

They finish breakfast and hit the road. At an altitude of 887 meters, Agnes has read in the room information, the temperatures can vary by ten to fifteen degrees in a day. Desperate for warmth in the cold morning air, she clutches her coat around her. Behind the wheel, dressed in his new coat, Jim looks like a country squire. But as he perks up, she finds herself sinking lower. She has just informed him that she would prefer to cancel their planned trip to the cemetery to look for ancestors. He has accepted this without question, unaware that the current renewal of turmoil over her relationship with her father has obliterated any interest in his forbears.

The deserted road out of town is lined with clumps of willow trees. Bowed down with seasons of bending to the elements, they seem to be fighting to exist. Now, in this moment, she finds the appearance of the Australian countryside deeply depressing. It has stolen her memory. Every tree, road, fence, house, animal—implicated in the crime. And the further inland they travel, the more she feels trapped.

Jim is slowing the car down. They are nearing the little town in which her father was born. It seems, she can no longer avoid Eric Keen. There is no escape from him, either in her dreams or her conscious thoughts. A shaft of sunlight breaks through the clouds and lights up the spreading arms of a line of low-growing golden pines.

They lose the panorama in a rapid descent to the small town below. She hears Jim insisting she has been there before, but her mind has gone blank. She tries to take in her surroundings. Most of the handful of structures in the main street of the tiny town are crudely built, with one exception—a two-storey Federation-style corner pub. This building is wrapped in an elaborate wrought-iron balcony, neatly cantilevered off the top floor. So here they are. Where the hotbed of intrigue—purported to have been played out during her father's youth—took place.

They take a short walk, then Jim announces for her benefit:
*This is it. Where he came into the world and spent his childhood.*

They are standing in front of a sagging green timber house that occupies a corner close to the road. Several panes of glass are broken in the crudely fitted louvre windows that enclose the front veranda. Twisted guttering, and a front door carelessly repaired with timbers that don't match, make it look decidedly unloved. Green paint for St Patrick is the only hint of the old inhabitants of Irish descent. She finds it hard to string words together:
*This is it? It looks like a dump.*

Jim nods.

*I think it always was. There were a lot of them crammed in here. All up early and out to work on sheep stations in the area, then back home to eat and crash into bed. Next day the same. And the next.*

Agnes shudders a little:

*Perhaps that's why he lived like a bachelor with us? He had no blueprint for a leisurely family life. A pint at the pub after work and home to eat and crash into bed. Old habits die hard.*

The anticlimax of the dishevelled green house in the empty town is underscored by the sudden descent of a swarm of flies. They are both covered in minutes. She begins to panic as she feels them in her eyes and up her nose. Her white cotton knit jumper has turned black. The sleeves are hardly visible for pulsating black dots. Jim's shirt is swarming. The sun is fierce. The glare is blinding. It is unbearable here. In every sense. She bolts for the car and Jim is not far behind. Still waving their arms frantically, they jump in and Jim speeds off, dispersing the winged horrors through the open windows. The long-planned pilgrimage is over in minutes.

Jim drives so fast, Agnes suspects he is escaping more than flies. She wishes she knew what he was thinking. The visit to the sad wreck of a house only confirms her growing awareness that this part of the trip is pointless. Her relationship with her father has nothing to do with his life before she was born. But why did she still carry his pain as if it was her own? The superlatives from her mother about his shame when he discovered his illegitimacy are as fresh as if she heard them yesterday. Was it because Madge had prevented her from seeing his dead body that he never died for her? Remember him the way he *was*—her mother's exact words. But *what* was the *way* he was?

Before she and Jim had commenced their road trip, Agnes had long desired to visit 'Pink Dale', the grand property where her father and Madge had originally met. Dazzled by the place since childhood, she now fears Jim might find the visit intimidating, and so has put off telling him her plan. Until now.

Anxiety evident in his sudden heavy breathing, Jim is scowling. Underneath the grim silence, Agnes senses a volcano smouldering. She remembers his predisposition for tantrums as a child. He has never relished sudden changes or surprises. Her own changes of mood may well be affecting him. Perhaps he is growing bored with their travels? Or is bored with her?

She hears him sigh with resignation, as if reining himself in:

*Okay. If you're sure that's what you want. We'll take a quick look.*

\* \* \*

The car kicks up a stream of dust on the dirt road leading into the property. The surrounding paddocks look as if they are dying of thirst—past grandness having offered no protection against the current drought. Jim stops the car. In the distance, Agnes reassures herself, she might be able to see the goalposts of the polo field where, presumably, their maternal Guinevere met her dashing Lancelot.

A thought then strikes her. How history is crowded with princes, tyrants, kings, and generals, all elevated above their worth on horseback.

She forces herself to rally back to her senses, exits the car, and gazes around her. They are surrounded on three sides by gentle rolling hills—acres and acres of land—as old as time. She hears the driver's door open:

*This is some of the best grazing land in the country. Six thousand acres of perfect pasture for sheep and cattle. The Merinos they breed here yield the finest wool in the land.*

Agnes realizes Jim is claiming his credentials as a country man. Having always imagined the Pink Dale homestead as a grand palace, it is now obvious this is not the case. The sweeping white timber structure that stands before them, shimmering in the late afternoon sun, has serene and beautifully proportioned sloping lines and is elevated above a perfect emerald lawn where sprinklers have evidently defied the drought. The edifice makes her think of a fairytale house made of sugar:

*Look, Jim. It's just like Madge said. There's the pergola with the wisteria! And there's the lake! And the Chinese bridge and the weeping willow trailing in the water! And look beyond—the climbing roses!'*

But Jim is back in the car. He starts the engine. He is staring out at the road as if fighting the urge to simply gun the accelerator pedal and leave her stranded. Marooned in her childhood delusions of grandeur.

Agnes gazes at her stony-faced brother and feels a stab of guilt about dragging him out here, so obviously against his will. She turns her back on 'Pink Dale' and gets into the car.

Worrying she has worn him out, there and then she invites him to visit her in Mallorca, telling him she can easily picture him sitting under the lemon trees in her garden. Can see herself guiding him along ancient stone donkey tracks into the mountains where they will stop for a picnic in an olive grove that has a view of the Mediterranean. She would help him lose his beer belly, she tells him, and get back in shape. If he came in early spring, he would be there in time for the almond blossoms.

He grudgingly acknowledges her:

*Yeah. Suppose it's possible.*

As the engine of the stationary car ticks over, and his hands tap at the steering wheel with impatience, she offers to buy him an open airline ticket. After Mallorca, they could travel together: London, Paris, Rome, Venice. It's all waiting for you, she tells him. She will be fully aware she is gushing. She will want him to be happy because he is patently not. What was it about 'Pink Dale' that he resented so deeply? Was it the thought of his parents being young, happy and with a brilliant future to look forward to in this beautiful environment? Was the bitter reality of their union, their failures, their casual cruelty, their utter indifference to their children simply too much of a contrast to take?

She will try and catch her brother's eye, but he will not engage with her. Her own mood plummets, like a hunting hawk, to ground. Like so much she has looked forward to in her life, everything strange and magical about finally setting eyes on 'Pink Dale' has been ruined in an instant.

Then she sees him. Her father. The great undead. Standing at the main gate. Wearing his gleaming polo helmet, he is staring at her with the same blank gaze he wore on the day he ignored her in public. The day she had assembled with her school friends at the polo.

The old pain returns with such vengeance that she closes her eyes and clutches the door handle of the car to stop from slumping over in her seat.

Back on the main road, brother and sister speed back to Crookwell in silence. Agnes's thoughts now focused on her father's eternal demands for sympathy and his inability to forgive. His raised voice in the car after the trip to 'Rosemont', followed by the fierce blow to her mouth. His hesitation before deciding to reverse to see if she was still alive. His complete indifference to her perilous state and the punishing exile that followed. It had been easy to unmask her mother. But why was it so hard to criticise the shadowy figure who fathered her? Instead of defending his only daughter, he had colluded in defaming her to Grandma. What had happened in those dark, shrouded months that she could barely remember? After the move from Rose and Edmond Street?

The question will continue to reverberate like a drum roll in her head until she takes a sleeping pill and descends into oblivion.

\* \* \*

Over breakfast, back at Spud Murphy's Inn, it is easy to dismiss the original plan to stop once again at their mother's house on the way back to Sydney. No extra visit, nor farewells necessary. They agree, instead, to make a final visit to the old farm before Jim catches his flight back to Brisbane.

After crossing the Razorback Mountain, they circle around Camden on a bypass, arriving at the western end of the Bringelly Road. The trees which Agnes remembers standing sentry along the fence of The Farm—now a five-acre subdivision—have been cut down, allowing a clear view of the land from the main road. The grand homestead Grandma planned for herself on the highest point has finally been realised. It stands, like the Lord of the Manor's residence, towering over the lower houses built on new roads across the block. The stables, and the groom's cottage which their parents converted into a home, remains hidden, as before, by the hill in front.

Initially, none of what Agnes sees has any impact upon her. Not even spotting the site of the fire in the distance where her mother had caused so much terrible destruction. But when Jim, at her request, turns the car to drive back in the direction they came in, she suddenly glimpses a flash of water through the thick foliage. It is the creek.

*Stop the car for a bit, Jim. I need some air.*

\* \* \*

I'll be right back! I have shouted over my shoulder to Jim and am moving ahead with a compulsion beyond my control. I slip through a break in the fence and wrestle through a tangle of bushes to emerge in the corner of the lowest paddock. I stand still for a few seconds to check if there is anyone around. The fields and houses appear deserted. It remains the overgrown and pitted no-man's land I remember as a child, and when I visited my mother here years ago. It must have rained hard overnight, as the ground is saturated with water. My right foot makes a mournful sucking sound as I wrench it out of a muddy hole. I hurriedly wipe the mud off the sides of my shoe on some tufts of grass. I leap carefully from one raised clod of earth to the next. I am relieved to arrive, safely out of sight, behind the greenery along the side of the creek.

I dash along the narrow path that flanks the water's edge of the creek. I feel secure screened off by the thick gums, tall grass and scrub that hug the water's edge. Just as when I visited my mother, I find the surroundings both familiar and frightening. Dead trees, branches and roots have fallen and jack-knifed into the water and are making strange shapes beneath the surface. They are like monsters that might leap out at any moment.

I have arrived at the far side of the old block where the creek flows into the next property, still shielded off by the neighbour's old fence. I am in the clearing beside the water. The sight of his fishing line submerged in the creek flashes into my mind. Someone has hung a rope from a branch of an overhanging tree to swing out over the water.

I recall my visit to my mother at The Farm when I was nineteen— after Rebecca Lea was born. It was forty years ago when my baby was taken from me, yet this place has never been out of my memory. I can hear the whoosh of flame and petrol unite and can see my mother thrown back by the explosion of her own making. The contents of my suitcase still burn in front of my eyes. The carefully written diary of daily life, of the history of the little child I brought into the world, and with whom I fell in love, consigned forever to ashes. Fire has haunted me all my life. Fire and flames and the destruction of things I hold dear.

The memory of my father, quietly fishing, glances through my mind now, as I stare at the creek for what I know will be the very last time. I have a recollection of a photo of me. Posing against a tree.

I follow the path towards the house, my feet sinking in a soft carpet of leaves, but hit an impasse. The way is completely blocked by a jungle of dense growth. I turn and wander back to the clearing to find another route out. As a child, I always loved this place. The way vivid lichens and ferns grew on the trunks of dead trees, shaded by gigantic overhead gums. The way reflections would constantly change in the water with the light. It was a magical corner where I could imagine fairies dancing in the moonlight.

I pass through the trees to the left, and here is the glade. I remember it. But, as I approach it, I start to tremble and am consumed by a strange *and powerful sexual arousal. My stomach wrenches as I finally see the horror of what I have never been able to bear—have never been able to recall.*

*I am naked from the waist down, bent over, my hands balancing on the trunk of one of the trees—as my father thrusts his member into my behind.*

*I throw up a disgusting mess of last night's meal onto the ground. Legs shaking, I sit on a fallen log, like the one where he and I would rest. I dissolve into convulsive sobs. How could he violate his own daughter? Why didn't she, my mother, protect me? This is the reason why I have always felt him inside me. Invading me.*

*She was jealous. My mother was jealous because she knew what he was doing to me. This is what she meant when she said—'Your father loves you.' As if she'd like to change it. I can still see his bloated face. Can still smell his alcohol-drenched body. Feel it pressed up against me. The same act I dreaded in my small bed at fourteen, that had me leave my body and levitate to the Guardian Angel in the drawing above the bed, haunts me now. It is his violation of me that obliterated my ability to read. To think straight. He mortified me to the point that I could not remember. A momentary brute compulsion, so summarily dismissed by him, has led me to a life of self-hatred and further abuse at the hands of others.*

*The one photo of my parents I possess, that I have stupidly and blindly held on to, I now place on the ground and in a feeble ritual of banishment, ignite it with the cigarette lighter I keep in my bag. I watch the flame eat into their faces and, once they became unrecognisable ash, I stamp on them and kick the tiny particles of grey dust into the air. The trees alone will bear witness to what has happened here today.*

\* \* \*

Jim is furious. She has been gone for almost an hour and he is in a real temper with her. He keeps looking at his watch as they speed towards Sydney. She had no idea of how long she had kept him waiting. Torrential rain is falling, as if washing away the travesties of her life. She recalls how the early female Catholic Martyrs chose death over physical violation, but with no heavenly aid of any kind, how was she supposed to have protected herself against the father who was supposed to protect her?

She struggles to bring herself back into the moment:
*Ring me Jim and let me know you got home safely.*

The good wishes toward her brother seem redundant. Jim has dropped her off outside the Grantham Apartments. Although he has occasionally shown her some vague form of filial affection on their road trip, she knows in her heart that her intense feelings for him are not reciprocated. His limp and lifeless demeanour upon parting has left her feeling that, for him, the experience has been not much more than a free holiday he might have won in a raffle.

*Better alone than in the wrong company.* The mantra comes back to reassure her.

One needs a full stomach to philosophise, she thinks, fully aware that Jim's financial struggles must have made her present quest seem trivial to him. Apart from the voiced criticism levelled at their violent mother, she has gained no real insight into his true feelings about their parents. He seems, now, to be retreating back into the mechanical man she had met at the airport. She waves him off in the hire car, he will leave at the airport, unsure if she will ever see him again.

Alone in the Grantham apartment, she strips off and stands for a long time under the shower with the water as hot as she can stand. She soaps both feet and watches the mud from the paddock at The Farm disappear down the drain. She shampoos her hair several times, scrubbing her scalp—once again trying to purge a guilt that is no longer hers. She knows she can never wash the stain away, but she *can* learn to forgive herself. The event at the creek was not her fault. Not her guilt. She covers the scratches from the brambles on her hands and face with an antiseptic cream, dries her hair, and gets dressed.

Unscrewing the top of a bottle of red wine, she pours the contents into a fine-stemmed glass, swirling the liquid around the bowl. The streaks that cling to the glass confirm the wine has legs. Good. It needed to be special. Sipping her drink on the balcony, she looks out to the view which has been such a comfort these last months. But she cannot fully relax. After three days cramped in a car, plagued with conflicting emotions, she *must* take a walk.

She clings onto the rail as she lowers herself down the high treads of the stone staircase to Woolloomooloo below. It's the same climb she navigated, in terror, the day after she arrived in Sydney. The air is still warm in the aftermath of the sunset, although a cool breeze is blowing in off the harbour. As the light fades, Harry's Café is lighting up for the evening ahead.

She criss-crosses the road just as she did on that first visit, positioning herself opposite the Bells Hotel where groups of young people are standing with glasses of beer in hand, merrily chatting on the pavement. She crosses the road to gain some perspective and, leaning against the wall for support, is pitched straight back to the scorching summer of 1958.

She sees a picture in her mind's eye. A teenage girl is lying on the mattress of an iron bed in a dark room, surrounded by beer barrels. Shafts of light spill across the bed from the barred window in the wall behind. Naked but for a loose shirt, the girl is half lying, half propped up, her long thin legs open, her blue eyes clouded as if she is blind. But this is not a new image. It has always been with her and, until this evening, she has wondered if she might have seen it in an art gallery, for it reminds her of a painting of a pubescent girl by a Swiss painter—Balthus. It is a painting she has always found offensive. But today, as the convivial buzz from the young drinkers fades from her ears, she closes her eyes and dares to look closer. There is blood between the girl's legs. And the girl? The girl is her.

She braces her hands against the wall behind her back and knows the truth behind the visions. It was Uncle Parry. Uncle Parry had wrenched her legs apart in the basement of the White Horse Hotel and raped her. *This* is what had happened.

Blood. Fire. She knows now, beyond doubt, that she had always equated the two. Crimson, consuming, painful fire. Bloody fire. The fire that Uncle Parry and Aunt Marnie had denied ever happened. The fire that had gone on burning inside her for decades. It answered the baffling question of why she was not a virgin when Charles first raped her. Her first sexual experience had been with Parry. He had broken the seal and spilled the blood. 'You haven't told anyone have you?' It was abundantly clear to her now exactly what he was afraid she might tell.

The mystery shrouding his rejection of her is no more. Parry had joined her parents in demonising her. It was the obvious course for him. And the hideous woman, the woman who thought she had just convinced her successful daughter to buy her house, had done the same. This woman had failed to protect her. Had never *intended* to protect her. Just wanted her gone.

In the days that follow this resurgence, Agnes will walk all over Sydney. She will decide to phone Jean and will meet her in the same Thai restaurant in Macleay Street where she had first dined with Jim. Jean will listen attentively to Agnes's revelations, curious for details, but strangely devoid of emotion. This juicy morsel of tittle-tattle about her father, and about Parry would, without doubt, do the rounds. But the truth is that she no longer cared who knew. The truth had to be told to *someone* in this excuse for a family.

But what will make her waver somewhat in this commitment to honesty will be Uncle Ben's voice, chuckling down the phone several days later:

*Jean tells me you told her Eric and Parry had a go at you. You were a cracking good-looking bird, Agnes. If I'd known, I would have had a go myself!*

Shocked into silence by his crudity, she will put the phone down on him. Where were the hypocritical rosary beads now? Undisguised malice in his voice, and obviously still stinging from her visit, he had thoroughly enjoyed the jibe. Well. Good old Uncle Ben would merely succeed in immortalising his gross nature for eternity.

Perhaps equally perplexing will be a call from his sweet ex-wife, Aunt Beth:

*It's me—Beth! Jean just told me! How terrible! Do you think your father died young, and Parry got that terrible illness, because of what they did to you?*

Her simpering voice and absurd notions of crime and retribution will simply die away in Agnes's ear. They will not matter. She has no further need to defend herself. Not to any of them. It is enough that she knows what happened to her beyond doubt.

To fulfil her commitment to her mother, she will go to see Madge's bank manager. It is all amazingly straightforward. Yes, her mother can borrow on her house. Yes, the inheritors will get what, if anything, is left over after payment of the bank debt. Yes, they will attend to all the paperwork on her behalf. Should they inform Mrs Keen, or will she be visiting her mother again before she departs Australia?

When Agnes alights from the taxi, she will see her mother standing like a bird of prey with a broken wing at the top of the stairs. She will stride into the lopsided house in business-like fashion to briskly inform her of the arrangement with the bank.

Her mother will seem subdued, oddly contrite, and will accept the efficient arrangement without quibble—even the news that she will have to go on living with the old purple floral carpets. She will know it is over. That Agnes is no longer anyone's slave because, naturally, she will also have been a beneficiary of the family gossip grapevine:

*I'm sorry that he did that to you, Agnes.*

*You should have protected me. Kicked him in the balls. Thrown him out of the house and changed the locks.*

Madge appears genuinely incredulous:

*But I would have had to divorce him! I couldn't possibly have done that!*

She will gaze at her mother's lined, blotched face. Her bouffant hair will look like a bird's nest, and for some bizarre reason Agnes will be reminded of the dishevelled appearance of Muammar Gaddafi and Saddam Hussein after they were captured.

*You're right. You could never have done that. Because it takes courage to leave a bad relationship. Parry too. You knowingly supported the actions of TWO criminals who should BOTH have been put in jail.*

*Parry?!*

It will be obvious from the startled tone, and the shock registering on her mother's face, that she has not been privy to this revelation. But it will make no difference. None whatsoever.

Madge will turn away from her daughter:

*Don't say anymore, please! You're getting me all churned up!*

Agnes will realise in this moment that she no longer needs to feel remorse. No longer needs to care.

A voice inside will whisper softly, 'Walk away'.

She will bid her mother goodbye.

And leave.

CHAPTER 29

## FILIAL EXTORTION AND NEW DISCOVERIES

Six months after her return to Mallorca, her mother will die peacefully in her sleep a few days before her eighty-sixth birthday. Upon receiving the news Agnes will reflect on the irony of how someone, whose chief concern in life was breaking a fingernail, was allotted such a smooth and painless end.

Her brother Bert will take control of Madge's journey to the grave. The day after their mother is found dead, he will ring Agnes to make sure she has no intention of returning for the funeral to cramp his style. Even if she wished to come, which she will not, the quick dispatch he has already organised will not give her enough time to get there.

Agnes will receive no sympathy cards or calls of condolence. Her only contact with the funeral proceedings will be to lend Jim the money to buy an air ticket to fly from Brisbane to Sydney to attend. Over the six months since parting in Sydney, she has consistently wired money into his account to pay for his dental work, and to fund urgent items on the farm. She will still live in hope that he, one day, will feel strong enough to face a bank manager looking as if he didn't desperately need a loan. Her generosity stems from love. But no love is ever returned.

Madge will elect to leave what remains of her possessions in equal shares to her three children whom she has also appointed as co-executors. After her mother's funeral, Agnes will fly to London to legally transfer her executorship to Jim at the Australian Embassy. She will hope the additional responsibility will build his self-esteem, along with the air ticket she has put in place for him to visit her in Mallorca.

Her two brothers will split their mother's possessions between them. And that will be alright because, initially, Agnes will want none of it. But the good-faith transfer of her executorship to Jim will prove to be a mistake. She will unwittingly play into his hands when, as an afterthought, she opts to receive her mother's jewellery which was intended for her as a legacy in the will. By the time she discovers Jim's betrayal, the estate will be settled, and it will be too late to do anything about it. He will also claim that the bank transfers she sent—which amounted to over $20,000—were gifts, not loans requiring repayment.

As for the air ticket, it will remain a blur in the ether—probably to be used by him and Marline to go elsewhere in Europe. Yet another blow will be Jim's collaboration in falsifying a valuation of $15,000, deducted from her share of the estate, for a sapphire ring she will never receive. She will further discover that at least half the small package of jewellery intended for her as a legacy will have been stolen from her by her own mother over the years.

But the worst betrayal will come from Bert, who will inform Agnes by phone of a letter he has found in Madge's papers—from Agnes's adopted daughter. A request received, through Sydney lawyers, for contact with her birth mother and left to fester, unacknowledged, for years. Compounding his mother's cruelty, he will fail to forward it on. But love is not hard to lose if it never existed. And where there is no love, there are only possessions.

With nothing to salvage from the ashes, Agnes will sever all further contact with her family.

\* \* \*

*From the moment I landed in Sydney, I had been gripped with a dread that I was going the wrong way. Perhaps what the Chinese say is true—we fight dragons because of the treasure they hide. My treasure has been apprehending the memory behind hidden wounds. After all, one day of liberation is worth a lifetime of struggle. I have no need for symbolic trappings. I gave my mother's pearls to Tammy—her one true and constant friend.*

*I feel now as I imagine Sleeping Beauty might feel, waking into the world. My prince's kiss is a fortified self to guide and protect me. Change is impossible to hold or touch. It happens unawares.*

*My mind geared to forgetting, could now remember. Liberated to release the past I can, at long last, truly embrace my mantra — better alone than in the wrong company.*

**THE END**

www.ingramcontent.com/pod-product-compliance
Lightning Source LLC
Chambersburg PA
CBHW030543080526
44585CB00012B/241